D1389413

SMOKE RING

SMOKE RING
The Politics of Tobacco

PETER TAYLOR

THE BODLEY HEAD
LONDON SYDNEY
TORONTO

British Library Cataloguing
in Publication Data
Taylor, Peter
Smoke ring: the politics of tobacco.
1. Tobacco industry—Political aspects
I. Title
338.4'76797.   HD9130.5.
ISBN 0-370-30513-2

© P. R. Taylor 1984
Printed in Great Britain for
The Bodley Head Ltd
9 Bow Street, London WC2E 7AL
at The Pitman Press, Bath
First published 1984

To Angela, in memory of Peter

CONTENTS

ILLUSTRATIONS

Unless otherwise stated, photographs are the property of the author

PREFACE

Smoke Ring is the result of a decade's interest in the politics of tobacco. The book is not intended to be an anti-smoking treatise but an investigation of the political questions which the growing of tobacco and the production and consumption of cigarettes pose for governments all over the world. My purpose is to consider why governments place wealth before health, and to examine the political and economic mechanisms of the power of tobacco. I am convinced by the medical evidence and the unanimous verdict of the world's leading medical authorities that cigarettes disable and kill; but I also recognise that they bring economic benefits which, in purely financial terms, outweigh the cost of human suffering. However questionable the ethics of making political decisions on the basis of such an equation, I recognise that the equation exists. I approach the subject as a journalist and not as an anti-smoking crusader. I do *not* believe that cigarettes should be banned. I recognise the right of any individual to smoke, but believe that governments have a wider responsibility in the interests of public health.

There are many I have to thank for helping to make this book possible. If I were to name them all, the list would run into several pages. I hope that all those who assisted me in Britain, the United States and the Third World will not take the omission of their names as an omission of thanks. I am deeply grateful to them all. I am also indebted to those who, because of the nature of their positions, spoke to me in confidence. I hope they feel their confidences have been respected. There are however several people I must single out for special thanks: my literary agent, Julian Friedmann, who galvanised me into writing the book and matched me with the right publisher; David Machin, the Managing Director of The Bodley Head, whose enthusiasm never flagged, even when mine did and whose critical judgment (shared

[xi]

by editor Jean Frere) vastly improved my original manuscript; his ever obliging secretary, Gaynor Johnson; Julie Scott-Bayfield, for her legal precision and concern; André Schiffrin and Wendy Goldwyn of Pantheon Books, who guided my American endeavours; the Public Affairs people at British-American Tobacco, Imperial Tobacco, Gallahers and R. J. Reynolds; David Simpson, the director of Action on Smoking and Health and his patient assistant, Patti White; Mike Daube, a senior lecturer in community medicine and former director of ASH, for sharing with me his awesome knowledge of the subject; Michael Pertschuk of the FTC and his assistant Bill Rothbard for their unflagging assistance and encouragement; Peter Bluff, for his shelter and hospitality in America; Lindsey Hilsum, for her painstaking research in Latin America; George Carey and Chris Capron of the BBC, who generously afforded me the time to write the book and bore my absence from 'Panorama' with such patience; Heather Laughton, who defiantly chain-smoked her way through the typing and retyping of the manuscript; Audrey Mitchell, who helped me move the mountain of correspondence; and Sue, Ben and Sam, without whose support, encouragement and love *Smoke Ring* would never have been possible.

INTRODUCTION: THE ORIGINS

On a winter evening in 1974, my wife and I entertained two friends to dinner: Michael Sears, a lawyer, who had just stopped smoking after a course of hypnosis and his wife, Liza, a doctor who specialised in the treatment of cancer. The meal over, we sat round the fire to have coffee. My wife, Sue, lit a cigarette. As if personally hurt, Liza turned on her and said how distressed she was to see someone so obviously intelligent smoking when she and her father before her had devoted their lives to fighting cancer. She then took me to task as a television journalist for failing to give the issue of smoking and health the in-depth and sustained coverage it deserved. She said that if any other product were shown to be responsible for the tiniest fraction of the deaths which cigarettes caused, the media would be falling over themselves to expose the scandal. She suggested we had no idea of the magnitude of the problem and the scale of human suffering which she saw daily as a doctor trying to treat cigarette smokers dying of lung cancer. In despair, she said she felt she was wasting her time when she saw Sue light up a cigarette. Her *cri de coeur* was the genesis of this book.

I had never really given the problem much thought before. I used to smoke the occasional cigarette and a few small cigars, but I had never been a serious smoker. My wife was. She had started as a student following a tour of Wills' cigarette factory in Bristol and had become addicted to twenty to thirty a day. She had tried to stop on several occasions, but never succeeded. Like ninety per cent of smokers, we both knew that cigarettes were harmful to health, but we never took the warnings very seriously. They had become part of the furniture, just like the cigarette packets themselves. Neither of us had given the fact that cigarettes killed people a second thought. Liza made us think again. I read the medical evidence, starting with the first Report of the British

Royal College of Physicians of London, 'Smoking and Health', which initially drew the world's attention to the problem in 1962.

> The most reasonable conclusions from all the evidence on the association between smoking and disease are: that cigarette smoking is the most likely cause of the recent world-wide increase in deaths from lung cancer, the death rate from which is at present higher in Britain than in any other country in the world; that it is an important predisposing cause of the development of chronic bronchitis . . .
> Cigarette smoking probably increases the risk of dying from coronary heart disease, particularly in early middle age.[1]

I read the 1964 Report of the US Surgeon-General, Dr Luther Terry, 'Smoking and Health', the first of fifteen Reports subsequently compiled by his successors (1964–82). Dr Terry's prestigious scientific advisory committee, each member of which was vetted by the tobacco industry, concluded:

> Cigarette smoking is causally related to lung cancer in men; the magnitude of the effect of cigarette smoking far outweighs all other factors . . . Cigarette smoking is much more important than occupational exposures in the causation of lung cancer in the general population . . . Cigarette smoking is the most important of the causes of chronic bronchitis in the United State, and increases the risk of dying from chronic bronchitis and emphysema . . . Although the causative role of cigarette smoking in deaths from coronary disease is not proven the Committee considers it more prudent from the public health viewpoint to assume that the established association has causative meaning than to suspend judgment until no uncertainty remains.[2]

A decade later, the message was even more alarming. In 1971, the British Royal College of Physicians of London, in their second Report, 'Smoking and Health Now', referred to the annual death toll caused by cigarette smoking as 'the present holocaust'.

The suffering and shortening of life resulting from smoking

cigarettes have become increasingly clear as the evidence accumulates. Cigarette smoking is now as important a cause of death as were the great epidemic diseases such as typhoid, cholera, and tuberculosis that affected previous generations in this country. Once the causes had been established they were gradually brought under control ... But despite all the publicity of the dangers of cigarette smoking people seem unwilling to accept the facts and many of those who do are unwilling or unable to act upon them.[3]

I talked to many doctors. They all believed that cigarettes not only caused lung cancer and respiratory disease but heart disease as well. One of them, Dr Leslie Capel of the London Chest Hospital, took me to the pathology laboratory and showed me dustbins full of diseased lungs in polythene bags. He pulled one out, slit it open and showed me the cancer. 'If he hadn't been a smoker, this lung would still have been in his chest,' he said.

Convinced by what I had read, heard and seen, I made a series of television documentaries on the subject for Independent Television and the BBC. The first, 'Dying For a Fag', was a profile of a man in his early forties called Peter who was dying from lung cancer and was prepared to talk about his fatal love affair with the cigarette, in the hope that others might avoid the same fate. Sue and I first met him over lunch. Peter said he had tried to stop smoking many times and had never succeeded: now when it was too late he had finally managed to give up. My wife never smoked again.

Peter died six months after the film was transmitted. I watched him wither away, and for the first time saw for myself the pain and suffering which Liza saw every day in her work as a doctor treating patients with lung cancer. I went to his funeral in a bleak North London cemetery, and watched his wife Angela, who had borne his illness and death with such dignity, lay him to rest. She was bitter, not against the manufacturers who made the cigarettes which the doctors said had killed her husband, but against the government for its inaction and complacency in the face of the 'holocaust' of which Peter was but one victim. Peter was not a statistic in a record book, but a man whom cigarettes had cut off at the age of forty-two. According to official government figures, he was only one of over 50,000 victims of cigarette-related diseases who died prematurely in the United Kingdom that year. I watched the medical evidence become even more conclusive. In 1975 the World Health Organisation's Expert Committee on Smoking and its Effects on Health reported:

> The evidence that cigarette smoking greatly increases the incidence of lung cancer is now irrefutable. It can therefore be forecast that, if cigarette smoking were to stop or if cigarettes free from the risk of cancer were to be produced, the world-wide epidemic of a disease that at present kills hundreds of thousands of smokers every year would be arrested and begin to recede.[4]

In 1977 in its third Report 'Smoking or Health', Britain's Royal College of Physicians of London removed any doubt expressed in earlier studies about the connection between cigarette smoking and the biggest killer of all, coronary heart disease:

> Deaths from coronary heart disease are responsible for about half of the total excess deaths among cigarette smokers and are numerically greater than the excess deaths from either lung cancer or chronic bronchitis . . . That the association between smoking and heart disease is largely one of cause and effect is supported by its strength and consistency, its independence of the other risk factors, its enhancement in those smokers who inhale, and by the progressive lessening of the risk in those who give up . . .[5]

In 1979 came the most comprehensive review of the medical evidence ever compiled—a volume two and a half inches thick and weighing over seven pounds, the Report of the US Surgeon-General, Dr Julius B. Richmond. It concluded:

> Cigarette smoking is causally related to lung cancer in both men and women . . . is a significant causative factor in cancer of the larynx . . . is a significant causal factor in the development of oral cancer . . . is a causal factor in the development of cancer of the esophagus . . . is related to cancer of the pancreas . . . is one

[xvi]

of the three major independent risk factors for heart attack . . .
and sudden cardiac death in adult men and women . . . a major
risk factor in arteriosclerotic peripheral vascular disease . . . a
cause of chronic obstructive lung disease . . . increases the risk
of fetal death through maternal complications . . . contributes
to the risk of their infants being victims of the 'sudden infant
death syndrome' [cot death].[6]

A year later the same US Surgeon-General noted in a special
Report on cigarette smoking and women:

The rise in lung cancer death rates is currently much steeper in
women than in men. It is projected that . . . the lung cancer
death rate will surpass that of breast cancer in the early 1980s
. . . The risk of spontaneous abortion, fetal death, and neonatal
death increases directly with increasing levels of maternal
smoking during pregnancy . . .[7]

By 1982, the new US Surgeon-General, Dr C. Everett Koop, had
confirmed all the findings of his predecessors in his Report
'Cancer':

Cigarette smoking . . . is the chief, single, avoidable cause of
death in our society, and the most important public health issue
of our time.[8]

By the time that statement was made, cigarette smoking
accounted for more than 300,000[9] premature deaths a year in the
United States, and nearly half a million a year in Eastern and
Western Europe.[10] Overall, the global death toll down the years
runs into tens of millions.[11] The figures are so astronomical, they
defy comprehension. What makes the scale of the problem even
more difficult to grasp is that the deaths have been caused by a
product which until comparatively recently has been so much an
accepted part of our twentieth-century society. Likewise the
companies which manufacture cigarettes have grown to become
part of our Western economic fabric.

The tobacco industry is made up of some of the richest and
most powerful multinational companies in the world. For years

they have reacted to the medical evidence by insisting, at least publicly, that the case against cigarettes was not proven: that the evidence was purely statistical; that the precise causal mechanism by which cigarettes were alleged to cause cancer had never been identified. The world's leading medical authorities dismissed their position as nonsense. Nevertheless, commercially the industry acted as if the case were proven. The cigarette companies spent millions of dollars developing low-tar cigarettes which were thought to be less hazardous and, to ensure that they were no longer totally dependent on cigarettes, broadened their economic base by diversifying into everything from food and drink to oil and insurance. But the giant tobacco multinationals, British-American Tobacco, Imperial in Britain, R. J. Reynolds and Philip Morris in the United States, and Rothmans of the South African based Rembrandt Group, remained firmly committed to cigarettes as they continued to generate the multi-million dollar profits on which their economic strength was based.

Cigarettes are not only cheap to make, they are addictive and recession proof. Although millions have heeded the medical evidence and stopped smoking (an estimated eight million in Britain and thirty million in the United States[12]), cigarettes still remain one of the world's most profitable industries with annual sales of four trillion cigarettes, worth over $40 billion.[13] Growth in consumption in the industrialised countries of the West may be limited to around one per cent, but it is one per cent of a market which remains hugely profitable. In 1980, Americans spent nearly $20 billion[14] buying 630 billion cigarettes — 135 billion more than they bought when the US Surgeon-General issued his first Report in 1964.[15] In 1981, British smokers still bought 110 billion cigarettes[16] (despite a dramatic drop in consumption that year due to heavy tax increases), as many as they had bought when the British Royal College of Physicians of London issued their first Report in 1962.[17]

Furthermore, the developing countries of the Third World, where consumption is rising by more than three per cent a year, offer the cigarette companies virtually unlimited prospects for growth. Cigarettes remain the lifeblood of the tobacco multinationals and they have no intention of letting anybody cut it off. Despite their diversified interests, they remain as addicted to cigarettes as their consumers. That is why, understandably, they will do all they can to defend the product on which their wealth and power still depend. Their protection is the Smoke Ring.

The Smoke Ring is the ring of political and economic interests which has protected the tobacco industry for the past twenty years. The main reason why governments have taken so little action against the product which has been responsible for the deaths of millions of its citizens is because governments are themselves part of the Smoke Ring. In principle, as guardians of the public health, governments ought to be the tobacco industry's fierce opponents, but in practice they are often its firm ally. Cigarettes provide governments with one of their biggest and most reliable sources of revenue: they create tens of thousands of jobs in hard economic times; they present a healthy surplus on the balance of payments; they help development in Third World countries where tobacco is grown. In purely economic terms, the political benefits of cigarettes far outweigh their social cost. (In Britain, for example, revenue from cigarettes brings the Treasury over £4 billion a year:[18] cigarette related diseases cost the National Health Service a tiny fraction of that in direct costs—£165 million a year.[19]) Politicians may invoke freedom of choice in defence of their inactivity, but their noble words do not hide the hard economic facts which have seduced governments into the Smoke Ring, and kept them steadfastly there.

The consumer is the other crucial link in the Smoke Ring. If fewer people smoke, there's less revenue, employment and trade and therefore less reason for governments remaining part of the Smoke Ring. Despite the growing social pressures which have now been added to the medical pressures to quit, most smokers stay locked in the Smoke Ring, not only because they enjoy smoking but because they are addicted to cigarettes. Nicotine is a potent drug. One drop of the pure substance extracted from tobacco and placed on a man's tongue will kill him within minutes. Nicotine does not kill the smoker because it is absorbed over a period of time and the body is capable of modifying it as it does other poisons which enter the system. It is a drug which is capable of stimulating or sedating smokers, depending on their temperament and mood. The effect is almost instantaneous. When the cigarette is lit, the nicotine which is dissolved in the moisture of the tobacco leaf evaporates and attaches itself to minute droplets less than one thousandth of a millimetre across, which are contained in cigarette smoke. These droplets are so tiny that when the smoke is inhaled they can reach the smallest passage in the depth of the lungs. The drug is absorbed by the body at remarkable speed. It reaches the brain in seven seconds and the big toe in fifteen to twenty seconds.[20] In 1982 a British clinical pharmacologist, Heather Ashton, and a research psychologist, Rob Stepney, gave their reason for people continuing to smoke:

> The inhalation of smoke is not a natural behaviour—it has to be learned, often at the cost of some initial discomfort. It is, however, an exceptionally fast and efficient way of getting a drug into the body, and in this respect is rivalled only by intravenous injection. It is therefore our view that both the unique role of tobacco, and the prevalence of inhalation, can best be accounted for by the assumption that smoking is essentially a means of nicotine self administration.[21]

Within twenty to thirty minutes of the cigarette being finished, the nicotine has left the brain and the smoker feels the need for more. Addiction, or the pharmacological need for nicotine, seems to take over once the smoker is inhaling about twenty cigarettes a day. The body's dependence on nicotine is the main reason why smokers find it so difficult to break the habit and why they may experience acute withdrawal symptoms once they try. Although around seventy per cent of existing smokers try to give it up at one time or another, nicotine ensures that only about a quarter succeed.

Nicotine is the industry's most powerful ally in keeping smokers in the Smoke Ring, but the manufacturers know that there are strong social pressures at work to try to make the users break the link. While the industry recognises that addiction will keep most of the smokers hooked, it is determined to do all it can to help: it spends $2 billion a year globally on advertising to reinforce its own myth that smoking is a socially desirable habit and to seduce new smokers, in particular those in developing countries, into joining the Ring; it spends millions sponsoring sport and the arts to get round advertising restrictions, to boost its

[xx]

own image as public benefactor and make governments further dependent upon it as a source of funds when public resources are scarce. Advertising, promotion and sponsorship are all designed to strengthen the Smoke Ring.

This Smoke Ring has successfully protected the tobacco industry in the face of overwhelming medical evidence that its product is lethal. This book is an attempt to explain why governments all over the world have taken so little action, although they accept all the medical evidence: why politicians who tried to break the Smoke Ring paid the political price; and why the tobacco industry is confident that the Smoke Ring will protect it for at least the next twenty years.

These are the politics of tobacco. But before looking at the multinational companies themselves, it is necessary to examine in detail why the Smoke Ring had to be built in the first place—because cigarettes were found to be killers.

HEALTH
Evading the Issue

For more than half a century, the world's tobacco companies were thought to be providing a great public service. In the First World War, the American General John J. Pershing cabled Washington DC: 'Tobacco is as indispensable as the daily ration; we must have thousands of tons without delay'.[1] In the Second World War, President Roosevelt made tobacco a protected crop as part of the war effort. Few suspected at the time that the product which was extolled by governments was capable of killing more people than the wars they were fighting. When the case against cigarettes was finally proven, governments refused to take appropriate action because they had become so dependent on tobacco; and the tobacco industry refused to accept it, because to have done so would have shaken the foundation of their wealth and prosperity.

When governments had faced great hazards to public health before, they had taken political action once they had identified the cause. Over 100,000 people died in the great cholera epidemic which swept the British Isles in 1848. Thirty thousand more died when cholera returned in 1853–54.[2] No one knew what caused the disease. A common factor seemed to be the social class of its victims—the poor who lived in Britain's overcrowded and insanitary cities. Within one ten-day period in September 1854, 500 people died in an area only 250 yards across, around Golden Square and the Soho district of London.[3] Florence Nightingale, then a little-known woman of thirty-three, was one of the volunteers who rushed to the neighbouring Middlesex Hospital to help. But the Soho epidemic stopped almost as suddenly as it had started, when a local doctor identified the cause. Dr John Snow, who lived in Soho Square, had suspected for some time that cholera was a disease carried in polluted drinking water. He noticed that the people around Golden Square all drew their water from the same pump in Broad Street, and suggested to the authorities that they remove the pump's handle to force the residents to seek their water elsewhere. The handle was removed and cholera disappeared from Soho almost overnight.

By the end of the nineteenth century cholera had become a rare disease in Britain, because the government took political action culminating in Disraeli's great Public Health Act of 1875, which compelled all local authorities to provide drainage, sewerage and an adequate water supply.[4] According to Dr John Snow's biographer, his action over the Broad Street pump led to:

... much sneering and jeering... The abstruse science men... wanted to discover the cause of a great natural phenomenon in some overwhelming scientific problem.[5]

The spread of lung cancer in the twentieth century, and the subsequent identification of its major cause, is very similar to the history of cholera. But when cigarettes were shown to be the agent responsible, killing thirty thousand people a year in Britain from lung cancer alone, roughly the same number as cholera had killed a hundred years earlier in the epidemic of 1853–54, no parallel political action was taken because of the commercial and political interests which cigarettes involved.

In the early part of the twentieth century cancer of the lung was rarely seen. As a student in the 1930s, Sir George Godber, Britain's Chief Medical Officer for Health in the 1960s, remembers hardly ever seeing the disease; when a case was diagnosed, students would rush to the autopsy room out of curiosity. 'No one suspected,' he said, 'there would be something so common in life as to be the cause of cancer.'

The reason why it took so long to identify cigarettes as the main cause of lung cancer, is that the disease takes twenty to thirty years to incubate, following the initial exposure of the lungs to cigarette smoke. In 1920 in England and Wales, less than 250 people died of lung cancer.[6] By 1960, the number had increased to over 10,000. There was a similar pattern in the United States, where lung cancer deaths rose from 3,000 in 1930 to 41,000 in 1962.[7] The rise in lung cancer accompanied the rise in cigarette smoking. The habit first became widespread in the First World War and accelerated rapidly in the Second World War. In Britain in 1920, men were smoking on average six cigarettes a day. By the end of the Second World War, they were smoking nearly three times as many.[8] In the United States, where people tended to smoke slightly less, Americans were smoking on average four cigarettes a day in 1930 and around ten a day by 1960.[9] (It is important to note that these are only *average* figures. Many would smoke far more than the average and would be those most likely to contract lung cancer.) As Britain's Royal College of Physicians noted in its first Report, published in 1962:

> To account for this increase it is necessary to postulate some causative agent to which human lungs have been newly and increasingly exposed during the present century. Cigarette smoke is such an agent and there is now a great deal of evidence that it is an important cause of this disease.[10]

At the time of the Royal College of Physicians' first Report in 1962 and the first Report of the American Surgeon-General in 1964, the evidence linking cigarette smoking with cancer of the lung was mainly statistical. Two dozen investigations in nine countries had surveyed groups of population, noted their smoking habits and in subsequent years ascertained the cause of death. The two most famous studies in the 1950s were those of 40,000 British doctors by Dr Richard Doll and Professor Austin Bradford Hill; and of 187,000 American smokers and non-smokers by Dr Daniel Horn and Dr Cuyler Hammond. (Dr Alton Ochsner and Dr Ernst Wynder also carried out much of the important pioneering work in America.) All these studies reached the same conclusion: that the risk of lung cancer increased with the number of cigarettes smoked and, most significantly, that the risk of contracting lung cancer decreased once a smoker had stopped smoking. These extensive surveys throughout the 1950s all confirmed that the dramatic and hitherto unexplained rise in the incidence of lung cancer in the twentieth century was the result of cigarette smoking. As early as 1950, Dr Richard Doll and Professor Austin Bradford Hill had reached the conclusion: 'Smoking is a factor and an important factor, in the production of carcinoma of the lung.'[11]

The experts have always accepted that there are other environmental and occupational causes of cancer of the lung, in particular those which result from exposure to industrial processes involving asbestos, chromium, nickel, copper and uranium.[12] In many cases, workers in some of these industries, in particular asbestos, greatly increase their risk of contracting lung cancer if they also smoke cigarettes. But such exposures only account for around ten to fifteen per cent of all lung cancer cases. The other eighty-five to ninety per cent are caused by cigarette smoking. In even the most hazardous occupations, workers are only exposed to a single or, at the most, a few chemical agents which can cause cancer. When a smoker lights a cigarette and inhales the smoke, he is exposing his body to over 2,000 chemical agents, many of which initiate and promote cancer. The cancer-initiating chemicals (carcinogens) include polycyclic hydrocarbons, nitrosamines and beta-naphthylamine. The cancer-promoting chemicals (co-carcinogens) include cresol and phenol. In addition a wide variety of irritant substances are present, the most prominent of which are acrolein, nitric oxide and nitrogen dioxide.[13] All these chemical substances are contained in what is called cigarette 'tar'—the dark brown, tarry material produced for scientific purposes in a laboratory when the particles in cigarette smoke are cooled or passed through a filter.[14] Cigarette smoke also contains a high concentration of carbon monoxide, which impairs the blood's capacity to carry oxygen and is believed to be one of the most important factors in the relationship between cigarette smoking and coronary heart disease. The activity of these carcinogens in 'tar' was confirmed in the 1950s as a result of laboratory tests on animals conducted in Scandinavia, Germany, France, Great Britain and the United States. It was repeatedly shown that when cigarette 'tar' was painted on the skins of mice, cancer was produced.

As this statistical and pathological evidence mounted throughout the 1950s, governments did nothing. The problem was most acute in Britain, where seventy-five per cent of men were smokers and the lung cancer rate had become the highest in the world.[15] One statistic illustrates that smoking and health was not a political consideration: between 1956 and 1959, less than £5,000 was spent on anti-smoking education, while the tobacco industry spent £27 million on advertising.[16] One quote shows that the British government clearly put wealth before health. Iain MacLeod, the Minister of Health in Winston Churchill's Conservative government of 1952–54, later declared:

> Smokers, mainly cigarette smokers, contribute some £1,000 million yearly to the Exchequer and no one knows better than the government that they simply cannot afford to lose that much.[17]

Throughout the 1950s the British government preferred to close its ears and count its money. At that time health ministers in Britain were guided by recommendations given to them by a body of confidential advisers, called the Central Health Services Council, which had been set up under the 1946 National Health Service Act. The Council's brief was 'to study any matter to which, in our opinion, the Minister's attention should be called'.[18] The Council had its own cancer sub-committee, which had been set up largely to develop a regional programme for the treatment of cancer by radiotherapy. In 1951 the Cancer Committee considered smoking and lung cancer for the first time and concluded that 'further investigations would be necessary before the Committee would be in a position to advise the Minister'.[19] In 1952, following Dr Richard Doll and Professor Austin Bradford Hill's famous survey of British doctors, the Committee concluded that the statistical evidence strongly suggested an association between the two, but the evidence was 'insufficient to justify propaganda'.[20] In 1953, the chief subject to occupy their attention was the possible relationship between cancer of the lung and smoking[21] and the Committee referred the matter to a special panel of medical and non-medical statisticians under the chairmanship of the Government Actuary. The panel reported back to the Cancer Committee that:

> ... in their opinion a real association between smoking and cancer of the lung was firmly established; and that there was a strong presumption, until some positive evidence to the contrary was found, that the connection was causal.[22]

In 1955, the Cancer Committee said it was time the government conducted a 'centrally directed' campaign, warning people of the dangers of cigarette smoking.[23] The Central Health Services Council, its governing body, disagreed. But, by the spring of 1956, it had changed its mind. The government, however, had not. The Minister of Health, Robert Turton, announced: 'I do not consider that the present state of our knowledge is such as to justify . . . undertaking a national publicity campaign.'[24]

Although doctors who had to deal with the growing lung cancer epidemic in Britain became increasingly frustrated as they saw the government do nothing, there were other problems of public health at the time which seemed politically more pressing. Smog, the result of industrial pollution and coal-burning fires, was regarded as the great killer in Britain's cities. The smog of 1952 killed 2,484 people in London alone.[25] As in the case of cholera, once the cause was identified—and with smog it was not difficult—the government acted. The Clean Air Act of 1956 was introduced and smog disappeared and with it many of the bronchial problems which it had created.

In the late 1950s, a medical officer from the Ministry of Health visited Dr Charles Fletcher, a chest physician at the Hammersmith Hospital in London, to see how his work was progressing on smog masks. The official was impressed by what he had achieved, but was somewhat taken aback when Dr Fletcher asked him when his Ministry was going to justify its name and do something about smoking. 'Why, do you think we ought to?' asked the surprised official. Shortly afterwards Dr Fletcher spoke with George Godber, then Deputy Chief Medical Officer at the Ministry of Health, who shared his concern over the lack of political activity, although his superiors at the Ministry of Health did not. They decided that the best hope of getting something done lay in persuading the Royal College of Physicians, the most eminent medical body in the land, to prepare a report on the issue and galvanise the government into some kind of political action. The newly elected President of the Royal College, Sir Robert Platt, agreed to their suggestion with enthusiasm. The Royal College had previously made a memorable intervention in the field of public health in 1725, when it had made representations to the House of Commons about the disastrous consequences of the rising consumption of cheap gin. Its intervention played an important part in initiating legislation which ultimately brought the abuse under control.

The Royal College of Physicians decided, on April 30th, 1959, to set up a Committee with Dr Charles Fletcher as Honorary Secretary. The Committee reported three years later and, on the basis of the medical evidence, urged the government to take 'decisive steps' to curb the rising consumption of cigarettes. Some smokers got the message. The impact of this landmark report by one of the world's most eminent medical authorities was dramatic. Cigarette sales dropped from 113 billion in 1961 to 109 billion in 1962, the year of publication. But they soon picked up again, to 115 billion in 1963.[26] Governments were still not eager to listen. Enoch Powell, who was Minister of Health at the time the Report was published, accepted the medical evidence, but remained opposed to 'a prohibition of the offering for sale of an article which it is lawful to sell'.[27] The attitude of the British government in the 1960s is probably best summed up by the advice allegedly given to Ministers: that they could say whatever they wanted about smoking and health, as long as they smoked when they said it.

In the United States, government was even less interested in taking political action. Tobacco is part of American history. It helped the early Jamestown colony to survive and financed the American Revolution by serving as collateral for the loans received from France. George Washington grew it and Thomas Jefferson had it engraved on the pillars inside the Capitol building. To attack tobacco is, in the eyes of its defenders, to attack the foundation of America itself. Tobacco is still one of America's most important cash crops, and part of the economic fabric of the country, giving employment to tens of thousands of families in eighteen tobacco-growing states mainly in the South-Eastern United States. It is not surprising that in 1962 the young President John F. Kennedy was in no hurry to face the political implications of a problem so close to home, following the publication of the Royal College of Physicians' Report on the other side of the Atlantic. Kennedy had defeated Richard Nixon in the presidential election of 1960 by the narrowest margin in seventy-six years—0.1 per cent of the popular vote. Kennedy himself admitted his victory was 'a miracle'.[28] Without the support he had received from the South, largely through his choice of the Texan Lyndon Johnson as his running mate, Kennedy would never have made it to the White House. The last thing the new President could afford to do was to attack tobacco and antagonise the powerful Southern politicians who dominated the committees in the Congress and with whom he would have to do business in the years that lay ahead. But the new President could not afford to be seen to be doing nothing. At a press conference on May 23rd, 1962, shortly after the publication of the Royal College of Physicians' Report in Britain, President Kennedy was asked:

Mr President, there is another health problem that seems to be causing growing concern here and abroad, and I think this is largely being provoked by a series of independent scientific investigations, which have concluded that cigarette smoking and certain types of cancer and heart disease have a causal connection.

I have two questions. Do you and your health advisers agree or disagree with these findings, and secondly, what if anything should or can the Federal Government do in the circumstances?

The President chose his words carefully:

That matter is sensitive enough, and the Stock Market is in sufficient difficulty without my giving you an answer which is not based on complete information, which I don't have, and, therefore, perhaps I will be glad to respond to that question in more detail next week.

[8]

Five days later the *Wall Street Journal* predicted that Dr Luther Terry, the US Surgeon-General (who had already been sent a copy of the Royal College Report by Britain's Chief Medical Officer, Sir George Godber, with the exhortation to act) would convene a committee to do what the Royal College of Physicians had done, observing that the move would serve 'the tactical purpose of gaining time' and would take 'public pressure off government officials'.[29]

Kennedy had already been under pressure from the American medical establishment and had taken steps to defuse the issue. The previous year, at the instigation of the Surgeon-General, Dr Luther Terry, the President of the American Heart Association, the Lung Association, the American Cancer Society and the Public Health Association had written a joint letter to the President, asking him to set up a special Presidential Commission. The President summoned his Surgeon-General and told him to get on with the job, with the assurance that there would be no political interference. 'Of course he knew there might be interference,' Dr Terry told me. 'There was politics written all over it.' The *Wall Street Journal* speculation was correct. Three days later the Surgeon-General announced the formation of his Committee of experts 'to study all evidence and make whatever recommendations are necessary'.[30]

From the beginning, Dr Terry consulted the tobacco industry on the formation of his Committee. He took the precaution of ensuring that the industry did not turn round and reject the Committee's findings because it did not agree with its composition. He sent the industry a list of 150 'outstanding medical scientists in the United States' and asked them to strike out any names it found unacceptable. He remembers 'three or four' names being crossed off from his original list. In the end, eleven scientists were chosen whose names were acceptable to all the parties concerned. Five of them happened to be smokers.[31] The prerequisite of membership was that none of them should have taken a public position on the issue. There was an early casualty. The scientist from the National Cancer Institute, Dr Herman Kraybill, who was named as the Committee's Executive Director, was forced to step down when he told a reporter back home that he believed the evidence 'definitely suggests that tobacco is a health hazard'.[32] The tobacco industry was not to be allowed to blame the messenger when the news arrived. The Surgeon-General's Advisory Committee was given a whole block in the sub-basement of the new National Library of Medicine in Bethesda, Maryland, in which to carry out its work. 'We knew there were going to be attempts by the press and the tobacco industry to break our wall of confidentiality and get advance information, but there wasn't a leak,' Dr Terry told me. 'I still don't know how we did it. When the report was at the government printers, it was given the same security classification as military and state secrets.' The Committee sat for over a year, analysing the now vast corpus of information on smoking and health, running to some 6,000 articles in 1,200 publications. 'The industry did submit their view,' said Dr Terry, 'but it didn't convince the Committee that they were right and others were wrong.' Security was maintained to the last. Even senior government officials, who wanted to know what lay in store so they could prepare themselves for when the Report was published, were told they would have to wait like everyone else. The Report was launched on a Saturday for maximum impact, although the more cynical said it was because the Stock Exchange was closed. The State Department auditorium was borrowed as neutral and prestigious ground on which to hold a press conference. At nine a.m. journalists were given their first sight of the historic Report and an hour in which to digest it before questioning the Committee. The press conference over, they rushed to the telephones. 'It was like flushing ducks off a pond,' remembers Dr Terry. The Report confirmed the tobacco industry's worst fears. It said that cigarette smoking was causally related to lung cancer; was the most important cause of chronic bronchitis and increased the risk of dying from the disease and emphysema as well; and that it was prudent to assume from the public health viewpoint that cigarette smoking caused coronary disease. It summed up its judgment in a brief sentence: Cigarette smoking is a health hazard of sufficient importance in the United States to warrant appropriate remedial action.[33]

In America the Surgeon-General's Report had the same immediate impact on sales as the Royal College of Physicians' Report had done in Britain, two years earlier. In 1963, the year before publication, 510 billion cigarettes were sold in America. In the year of publication they fell to 495 billion.[34] The year after, again following the British pattern, they picked up again, and more than made up for the loss by soaring to 518 billion. However short smokers' memories, or however unshakeable their addiction, the tobacco industry knew it was in trouble. Looking back on the period, one of their scientists told me, 'We were far more concerned about the Surgeon-General's Report. We'd vetted the names on the Committee. We agreed before it started work that it was sound and had given the Surgeon-General our commitment that we were happy with its composition. We couldn't turn round and say "These people aren't experts".'

If the industry feared that these Reports from the US Surgeon-General and the British Royal College of Physicians in the early 1960s would change the political perspective on tobacco and drive governments out of the Smoke Ring, there was little to worry about. The worst 'blows' the industry suffered were having cigarette advertisements banned from television in Britain in 1965, and in America in 1970 (the companies simply replied by switching the millions they saved into other media); and being forced to put health warnings on packets in 1965 in America ('Caution: Cigarette smoking may be hazardous to your health') but not until 1971 in Britain ('Warning By HM Government: Smoking Can Damage Your Health'). These health warnings were even privately welcomed in some quarters of the industry on the grounds that if consumers, particularly in America, were to sue for damages, they could not claim ignorance. (Consumers did sue. By the end of the 1970s these 'product liability' claims totalled over $40 million.[35] To date no suit has been successful.) These measures enabled politicians to satisfy the public's desire for action without seriously damaging the industry's wealth and the economic benefits which government derived from it.

The industry's main concern in response to the medical evidence was to make sure that consumers carried on smoking. It had already met their growing awareness of the medical problem in the 1950s by introducing filter cigarettes, although the original reason for their design was vanity, not health; filters were meant to attract female smokers by offering them a cigarette whose end didn't go soggy. The tobacco companies had also taken steps to protect themselves by starting to diversify in case governments and consumers did desert the Smoke Ring once the case against cigarettes was proven. The industry's main problem was to *reassure* smokers. This it sought to do by publicly refusing to accept the medical evidence, while commercially developing cigarettes which were lower in 'tar' and therefore less hazardous. The industry met the obvious contradiction by insisting that they were developing 'low tar' cigarettes in response to consumer demand, not because they accepted the medical evidence. For tobacco companies to have admitted that cigarettes were harmful would not only have laid them open to economic ruin in an avalanche of successful product liability suits, but might have triggered mass defections amongst smokers which would have had the same economic effect. To admit responsibility would risk destroying the Smoke Ring. The industry had no intention of committing suicide. Guided by the advice of its scientists and public relations experts, it constructed a defence in the 1960s to which it has clung ever since. The commercial defence was that the tobacco companies were selling a legal product; they were not doctors and if governments believed what their medical experts told them, it was up to them to act and not expect the industry to cut its own throat. The medical defence was that the case against cigarettes was not proven; the evidence was purely statistical; the precise causal mechanism by which cigarettes were alleged to produce cancer had never been identified; that no one knows the root cause of cancer and only unbiased scientific inquiry will provide the answers. This defence became known within the industry as the 'tightrope' policy and was most widely propagated by the Tobacco Institute in Washington DC, the industry-financed propaganda organisation which lobbied on its behalf. The Tobacco Institute insisted: 'Years of scientific research have failed to provide conclusive evidence that smoking causes disease.'[36]

This was not a view with which the industry's own scientists necessarily agreed, having done years of research themselves. In the late 1950s and early 1960s when the industry first realised it had what it referred to as a 'problem', many of these scientists left their jobs in the research departments of other industries, such as food, pharmaceuticals, atomic energy and textiles, to join the tobacco industry's growing research teams. Many were attracted by the scientific challenge of either disproving the evidence or, if that proved impossible, of developing less hazardous cigarettes. Some who joined in the early days found that code names were used instead of the word 'cancer': that medical journals like *The Lancet* which contained learned papers on the disease were sent round in locked correspondence boxes for the eyes of senior executives only; that rumours abounded such as the one about the director of one tobacco company who suggested closing down and giving the shareholders their money back if the case were ever proven. 'They'd never met anything like this,' one scientist told me. 'They didn't know how to handle it. I remember saying to them, "Look, you have a problem which would shake a pharmaceutical company to its foundations and yet you've no background in research. There isn't anybody on the board who's even got a good working knowledge in chemistry." '

One of the new research recruits told his employer that if he had £100 million to spend on the problem, he would spend £80 million diversifying and most of what was left on public relations: he believed that any organic material which was burned was bound to produce carcinogens and was not prepared to put his money on a research solution.

The industry spent millions on research. It set up its own laboratories to examine the chemical constituents of cigarette smoke and its biological activity. Less hazardous cigarettes could only be developed once the existing hazards in 'tar' were identified and modified. To do this required technical analysis and animal experiments on a huge scale. Much of this pioneering work was done in Britain in the 1960s. The industry opened its own laboratories in Harrogate, with a staff of 120 and an annual budget of £2 million. As far as the scientists were concerned, the animal experiments which had been conducted in the 1950s were perfectly valid but lacked any statistical significance because there were not enough of them. At the Harrogate laboratories experiments were conducted on over 100,000 mice. The researchers took the fact that cigarettes caused cancer as a working hypothesis. 'If they don't,' one of them told me, 'we don't have a problem. If they do, we'll solve it.' Most of the work consisted of 'lump counting', analysing the tumours which appeared on the skin of mice when painted with cigarette 'tar'. 'We confirmed with our massive experiments all that smaller experiments had claimed before: that cigarette tar caused skin cancer on mice and that there was a dose–response relationship [the cancer produced was related to the tar painted on the skin]', said one of the scientists closely associated with the work at the Harrogate laboratories. 'There's absolutely no doubt, and there's no one in the world who knows anything about it could say differently, that cigarette tar is carcinogenic.' The work at Harrogate continued for ten years and provided much of the scientific basis for the development of low-tar cigarettes. When the work was finished, which confirmed the scientists' working hypothesis that cigarettes caused cancer, the laboratories were closed down and sold to an American company for over £1 million.

Despite the fact that many of their own researches confirmed the scientific evidence, the industry maintained its 'tightrope' policy on the health issue. Tobacco company spokesmen, when asked questions on smoking and health, retreated behind the slogan, 'We are not doctors'. One scientist told me he couldn't understand 'why somebody never said, "Well get some bloody doctors" '. Impatience grew. In the early 1970s, the industry was told by one of its scientists:

> I believe it will not be possible to maintain indefinitely the rather hollow 'we are not doctors' stance. In due course we shall have to come up in public with a rather more positive approach to cigarette safety. In my view it would be best to be in a position to say in public what we believe in private.[37]

The advice went unheeded. The industry stuck to its view that the case against cigarettes was not proven, because the precise causal mechanism by which cigarettes 'are alleged' to cause lung cancer had never been demonstrated. The British Royal College of Physicians had answered this charge in 1962 when it noted that political action in the face of the great cholera epidemics of the nineteenth century had not been dependent upon the identification of the precise mechanism by which the disease was caused:

. . . the great sanitary movement in the mid nineteenth century began to bring infective diseases such as cholera and typhoid under control long before the germs that caused these diseases were discovered. The movement was based on observations such as that drinking polluted water was associated with the disease. If the provision of clean water had had to await the discovery of bacteria, preventable deaths, numbered in thousands, would have continued to occur for many years.[38]

At least one industry scientist dismissed the insistence on the identification of the causal mechanism as 'rubbish'. He believed that in demanding the 'billiard ball' proof of cause and effect, the industry was applying the mechanistic principles of the nineteenth century to twentieth-century science when they were no longer applicable. 'In my view,' he said, 'the case that cigarettes cause lung cancer is proven. The fact that lower smoke deliveries [lower tar cigarettes] produce lower risk is a clincher for causality. If people stop smoking or smoke less, then lung cancer in the population is reduced.' At one stage he informed the industry that as long as it stood by this nineteenth-century definition of 'proof', its position would be impregnable as there was no way the standard could be met: but he also pointed out that no twentieth-century scientist would ever seek to apply it and, although it might be convenient, it was irrelevant. 'There is no controversy on smoking and health,' he concluded, 'it's an invention of the tobacco industry.'

This creation of the illusion of controversy is a vital part of the industry's strategy to keep smokers on its side. The Tobacco Institute is their champion:

The 'war against cancer' . . . degenerated into a war against cigarettes . . . Now it has further degenerated into a war against smokers, waged through vilification, banishment from public places, denial of employment and repressive taxation. No one really knows whether this personalised warfare against tens of millions of Americans will prevent a single case of lung cancer or heart disease . . .
Many people do look for a 'scapegoat' when they feel threatened. In this case it is smoking. We are on the brink of

paranoia . . . In the meantime, the quest for knowledge about disease is prejudiced . . . The smoking controversy must be resolved by scientific research.[39]

The industry has made a great contribution to that research. Although the tobacco companies do not carry out medical research themselves, they have made over $70 million available over the years[40] to enable other bodies to do so. This research which they have sponsored has not undermined the medical evidence. The longest, most detailed and most expensive programme the industry financed only confirmed what the US Surgeon-General had said in 1964. The study 'Tobacco and Health' was carried out by the American Medical Association, took nearly fifteen years to complete, and was financed by the tobacco industry to the tune of $10 million. The AMA announced the proposed study and the industry's financial commitment to it in January 1964, the month the US Surgeon-General issued his Report. The study was published fourteen years later in 1978. The Committee's brief was to commission *new* research in the field of smoking and health, as the Reports of the US Surgeon-General and the British Royal College of Physicians had been based on *existing* scientific evidence. The purpose was to examine:

Human ailments that may be caused or aggravated by smoking, the particular element or elements that may be the causal or aggravating agents and the mechanisms of their action.[41]

A massive amount of research was commissioned. Eight hundred and forty-four research scientists from America and overseas produced 795 new papers on tobacco and health.[42] In a progress report, five years into the study, the AMA announced that it 'had not altered the conclusions of the . . . report of the Surgeon-General'. When 'Tobacco and Health' was finally published a decade later, it concluded:

The Committee believes that the bulk of research sponsored by this project supports the contention that cigarette smoking plays an important role in the development of chronic obstructive pulmonary diseases and constitutes a grave danger to individuals with pre-existing diseases of the coronary arteries.

The A M A was not ungrateful for the tobacco industry's support. Throughout this time, it kept $1.4 million[43] worth of shares* in the R. J. Reynolds and Philip Morris companies in its pension fund and continued to give political support to the federal government's annual subsidy of $50 million to America's 500,000 farm families who grow tobacco.[44]

There was certainly no shortage of the research which the industry kept insisting was the only solution to the problem. But scientists involved in tobacco-funded research did not always find that it was free from political considerations, especially when carried out in the heart of tobacco country or in the industry's own laboratories. In 1970 the state of Kentucky, America's second biggest tobacco producer, established its own Tobacco and Health Research Institute, which was financed by a half cent-tax placed on every packet of cigarettes sold in the state.[45] In twelve years the Institute cost Kentucky smokers nearly $35 million. The purpose was to 'prove or disprove' the health hazards of cigarette smoking and to 'preserve and strengthen' Kentucky's tobacco industry. The Chairman of the Institute's advisory board, Tom Harris, a Kentucky tobacco farmer, declared:

It is incumbent on us to find if there is something wrong health-wise with tobacco. If it's so, alright, let's find out what it is and take it out. If it isn't so, let's prove them to be liars and get them off our backs.[46]

The Institute was plagued with internal problems, mainly the result of the inevitable political conflict between tobacco and health in a state where tobacco is worth over $600 million a year, employs nearly 120,000 people, and raises nearly $10 billion in state and local taxes.[47] In its twelve years the Institute went

* The A M A finally disposed of these shares following pressure from some of its members, in 1981.

through six directors. One who left after sixteen months said:

> The programme was created by politicians for political reasons. As such, scientific objectives were secondary. The tobacco industry needed . . . an Institute as a symbol to their commitment to tobacco and health research. Some in this state even have indicated that it did not matter that the research was not good, as long as there was visible image of research on tobacco and health.[48]

I contacted one of the scientists who had worked at the Institute. He said some good work had been done, but 'they were very reluctant to face the issue of lung cancer': when he wrote a grant application he had to be circumspect, wording it so as not to appear that he was really looking at cancer. 'Kentucky is very economically dependent on the tobacco industry,' he said, 'the state legislature did the funding of research. They had to approve it. If people came down hard on the problem of lung cancer, the state legislature would say, "Why are we spending money to kill our main industry?" You can see why people were circumspect.' I asked him if he thought cigarettes caused lung cancer. He said of course he did.

Scientists working in the tobacco industry's world-famous research laboratories in Hamburg, West Germany, also encountered political problems. The work of its team of scientists under the Institute's director, Professor W. Dontenwill, was internationally renowned and featured prominently in all the world's major reports on smoking and health. Hamburg carried on the experiments with animals where Harrogate left off, improving inhalation techniques to study the effect of cigarette smoke on the respiratory system. Using Syrian Golden Hamsters, they produced for the first time cancer in the larynx of an animal. The 1982 US Surgeon-General's Report, 'Cancer', pointed out that carefully controlled animal experiments such as these were sufficient to allow 'clear experimental demonstration of causality', adding:

> The application of these rigid laboratory techniques for

establishing causality to the study of cancer in humans is clearly impossible. The idea of exposing human subjects to potentially cancer-producing agents in order to establish causality is morally and ethically unacceptable.[49]

Having succeeded in inducing cancers in the larynx of Golden Hamsters, the team then began experiments with pigs, whose respiratory system and arterial linings are most akin to those of a human being. These experiments, which opened up a completely new field in smoking and health research, were designed to examine changes in the vascular tissues which lead to coronary disease and to arteriosclerosis (hardening of the arteries) in particular. One member of the team told me that their preliminary experiments showed that there appeared to be a connection between the inhalation of carbon monoxide, the injection of nicotine and arteriosclerosis. Given time, the team thought they could prove the connection between smoking and arterial disease. (Diseases of the heart and arteries claim far more victims than lung cancer.) But it never got the chance. Suddenly, in 1976, the Institute was closed down. An official statement was issued which said that the Institute did not have the resources for new research and the director, Professor Dontenwill was ill. The scientist I spoke to said the news came 'like a flash of lightning out of the sky'.[50] I asked him if the Professor was ill. He said he was not and had joked about how 'ill' he felt when they had talked about the official announcement. What did he and his colleagues think had happened? 'We suppose that the Institute was closed down because of the results we were getting from our experiments into arteriosclerosis,' he said. 'If a connection between smoking and vascular disease was established, the cigarette industry would be pushed even more into the firing line.' The industry closed down its laboratories and rented them to the Hamburg health authorities for twenty years at a nominal charge of one Deutschmark a year. Redundancy payments were generous. Professor Dontenwill received nearly half a million pounds (1·6 million Deutschmarks) to cover his salary until he was sixty. When I contacted the Professor and asked him about his research, he said he was no longer involved, had forgotten it, and had no wish to give an interview on smoking and health.[51]

[19]

Above all, the industry needs to convince its own employees of its case. Attracting and keeping high-quality recruits is not easy. One former employee of an American cigarette company told me of his experience. He had stopped smoking some time before he applied for the job. At the interview, a packet of the company's latest brand was pushed across the table for him to try. He did not refuse because he wanted the job. When he went for the company physical examination to an outside doctor whom the company retained, he was asked if he smoked. He said he had just stopped. The doctor told him not to start again. He pointed out that he was going to work for a tobacco company. 'It doesn't matter,' the doctor said, 'you still shouldn't smoke.' But once inside the company, the social pressure was stronger than the doctor's advice. 'They say there are lots of people in the industry who don't smoke,' he said. 'I never found any of them.' The only advice on smoking he was given was by a more experienced colleague who warned that if he smoked a competitor's brand, he should make sure he put it in one of his own company's packets. As part of his apprenticeship, he was enrolled as a student in the tobacco industry's 'college of knowledge', a seat of learning in a Washington hotel which the industry used to hire for a week of indoctrination. There were lectures by doctors who said that cigarettes were good because they helped you relax and who assured their audience that the case against cigarettes was not proven. I asked whether anyone in his class ever raised questions about the years of research. He said they didn't. 'We were all pre-selected and in the company's judgment ready, willing and able to go out and tell the story. It was preaching to the choir.' Graduation day came at the end of the week, when students were presented with scrolls to certify that they were now graduates of the 'tobacco college of knowledge'. But the reluctant cigarette executive found it increasingly difficult to remain one of the true believers. 'One has to have some moral compass to even feel the pressure in the first place,' he said. 'It becomes pretty intense after a time. If others had moral compasses, they shut them off. I sometimes sat down over dinner with friends and talked of how ludicrous it was to be fighting a battle which was essentially wrong. Some of my colleagues felt the same. It was tough. You either suffer or you leave.' In the end he left and paid out $300 for a SmokeEnders (sic) course to help him stop smoking all over again.

The only person out of step on the issue of smoking and health is the tobacco industry itself, which stands like King Canute, denying the rising tide of medical evidence. Even many of its staunchest political allies, the politicians in Washington D C who represent the great tobacco growing states of America, accept the medical evidence. The senior aide to a North Carolina congress-man assured me that tobacco politicians would have no credibility on Capitol Hill if they took the industry line on the health issue. He explained that their defence of tobacco was purely economic. 'Our Congressman thinks that cigarettes can kill you,' he said. 'Most of the tobacco state guys do. Sure, cigarettes cause cancer, but so do lots of other things. You've got the tobacco industry out there saying, "There isn't any proof. There's no causal relationship." You can't carry that line through Congress. You're not productive or effective doing that. You can't kid our guys. They're brighter than that.' I asked him how he thought senior executives he knew in the tobacco industry really felt about the health issue. He said they were concerned about corporate profits, not the health of America: that was the government's job. In Britain a blunter view of the industry's position is taken by Sir George Godber who, as Chief Medical Officer for Health from 1960 to 1972, was one of the industry's most bitter opponents. 'I just don't believe that anybody could be unconvinced who's really taken the trouble to look at the evidence,' he told me. 'They know they're selling death now. They're not stupid. They just don't choose to admit it. I think they're an enormous, wealthy industry in which the major decision-makers can distance themselves sufficiently far from the outcome of the use of their product to ignore it.'

2

WEALTH
The Tobacco Giants

The Smoke Ring protects six giant multinational companies which manufacture the billions of cigarettes that cause the diseases which can disable and kill. They are Philip Morris Incorporated, R. J. Reynolds Industries Inc. and American Brands Inc. in the United States; British-American Tobacco Industries and the Imperial Group in Britain; and the Rembrandt Group in South Africa. Although they publicly refuse to accept the medical evidence, and have all diversified largely because of it (note the general absence of the word 'tobacco' from their corporate titles), they have no intention of giving up the product which continues to generate profits of $3,000 million a year. The tobacco multinationals are addicted to cigarettes just like governments and smokers. They close ranks when their interests are threatened, but remain bitter rivals in the marketplace. Their strategy is to sell as many cigarettes as possible, while presenting to the world a corporate image which belies the harmful nature of their product.

The tobacco multinationals of today are largely the offspring of the tobacco empire created a hundred years ago by one man—the American, James 'Buck' Duke. When 'Buck' Duke's father, Washington Duke, returned home at the end of the American Civil War in 1865, he had, according to the mythology, fifty cents in his pocket.[1] He found his 300 acre farm near Raleigh,

North Carolina, devastated by the war. All that was left was some flour and a few tobacco leaves. He sold the land to raise working capital and then rented some of it back to make a living. With the aid of his three sons, Brodie, Ben and Buck, he processed the little tobacco he had, packed it in muslin bags and stuck on the brand name 'Pro bono publico'. In a wagon drawn by two blind mules, so the story goes, the Duke family travelled to the nearest big town, Raleigh, on their first ever sales trip. They had no difficulty selling their tobacco and used the proceeds to buy bacon for the family. 'Pro bono publico' with its pack showing an Indian puffing a pipe and the exhortation 'Do this', soon caught on. Previously, most tobacco in America had been chewed in 'plugs', taken as snuff, or smoked in pipes, in the manner of the Indians the frontiersmen encountered. The American Civil War created the great national demand for smoking tobacco. While 80,000 Confederate and Union troops were awaiting the outcome of peace negotiations near Durham, North Carolina, they tried smoking the local tobacco, for want of anything better to do. They liked the new experience and wanted more of North Carolina's tobacco when they went home at the end of the war. Buck Duke was ready to meet the demand. He outsmarted his rivals by leasing the world's first cigarette-making machine, which they had rejected on the grounds that their customers wanted their cigarettes hand-rolled, not machine-made. This machine, the brainchild of a Virginian called James Bonsack, generated the twentieth-century cigarette revolution. When Duke took it over, it produced 120,000 cigarettes a day, the equivalent of what it would have taken forty workers to roll out by hand. (A hundred years later, cigarette machines were turning out over six million a day.) These economies of scale enabled Duke to undercut his rivals, who were selling their cigarettes at ten cents for twenty. He was selling his at half the price.

Within a few years Duke had bought out his rivals, including Richard Joshua Reynolds (the founder of the R. J. Reynolds Tobacco Company), who sold Duke two-thirds of his stock to raise capital for his own business, manufacturing chewing tobacco,[2] which was still far more popular than cigarettes. Reynolds disliked cigarettes and did not start making them until the turn of the century. In 1890 Duke formed the American

Tobacco Company, with a capitalisation of $25 million, and laid the foundation for the biggest tobacco enterprise the world has ever seen.

Duke was not satisfied with his American acquisitions, and looked across the Atlantic to the lucrative British market, where cigarettes were rapidly growing in popularity.[3] By 1890, Wills of Bristol, the biggest of the UK's thirteen family tobacco businesses which had grown up over the years through importing leaf, had eleven Bonsack machines turning out 85,000 cigarettes a day.[4] Wills' main rivals in Britain were Lambert & Butler of London, Stephen Mitchell & Son of Glasgow, and John Player & Sons of Nottingham. All knew that Buck Duke had his eye on them. During the preliminary foray to England, Duke is reputed to have burst in on the Player brothers and announced, 'Hello boys: I'm Duke from New York, come to take over your business.'[5] He was shown the door, but the British companies knew that he would be back. Determined that they should not fall prey to the American invader, the thirteen British companies joined forces in 1901 under the banner of the Imperial Tobacco Company with Wills of Bristol at its head. On the theory that the best form of defence was attack, Imperial challenged Duke on his own ground, with plans to set up business in America. A truce was declared. Both sides decided it was better to do business together and market each other's brands than to fight. In 1902, Imperial and American Tobacco formed the British-American Tobacco Company (BAT). American Tobacco owned two-thirds of the stock and Imperial the rest.

Buck Duke became BAT's first Chairman.[6] The role of the new company, which was based in Britain, was to handle all the overseas business of the two companies which had formed it. But within a decade, the political climate had changed. The US government held that monopolies such as Duke's American Tobacco Company, and Rockefeller's Standard Oil were injurious to the principle of free trade and against the public interest. In 1911, the US Supreme Court ordered Duke to break up the monolith he had created. The American Tobacco Company was dismembered. The companies which Duke had swallowed— among them R. J. Reynolds, Lorillard and Liggett & Myers— were set free again to compete with a much slimmer American

Tobacco Company.[7] American Tobacco also sold off its majority shareholding in BAT mainly to British investors, although Buck Duke agreed to stay on as Chairman, promising to develop and expand its overseas operations.[8] The companies which had formed Imperial Tobacco, in particular Wills and John Player, stayed together as friendly rivals, now free from any American threat. They were safe for half a century, until 1968, when American Tobacco, which by that time had become a diversified multinational called American Brands, returned to Britain and bought Imperial's biggest rival, Gallaher's, the tobacco company which had started in Northern Ireland at the end of the nineteenth century.[9]

Philip Morris and the Rembrandt Group have no direct historical link with Buck Duke's tobacco empire. Philip Morris has its origins in a London company, which made hand-rolled Turkish cigarettes in the nineteenth century and which Americans took back to New York to show their friends.[10] In 1902, Philip Morris set up a corporation in New York to sell its brands under Buck Duke's nose.[11] The company grew from there. One of its principal assets listed when the first Philip Morris Corporation was formed in the USA was a brand sold in London, called Marlboro. Seventy years later, Marlboro had become the world's best-selling brand and had generated billions of dollars for Philip Morris, making it one of the most powerful and successful of all the tobacco giants. The Rembrandt Group, the youngest of the multinationals, was created after the Second World War by the South African financier, Dr Anton Rupert.[12] The Group became South Africa's third largest corporation, with interests in mining, textiles and brewing, as well as tobacco. It widened its tobacco interests in the 1950s by buying into the British companies Carreras and Rothmans[13] and expanded them still further in the early 1970s with the creation of Rothmans International, a merger of the Group's British, West German, Belgian and Dutch tobacco operations. The Rembrandt Group's subsidiary, Rothmans International, became the world's fifth largest tobacco company, making one out of every twelve cigarettes sold in the world.[14]

Together these six giant multinational tobacco companies produce around forty per cent of the world's cigarettes. The rest are produced by the centrally planned economies of the Soviet Union, China and Eastern Europe, and by state monopolies such as France, Japan and Italy, which have traditionally wished to keep the lucrative business of cigarettes firmly in their own hands.[15] But many of these hitherto closed markets are now open to the multinationals' penetration through brand licensing and local manufacturing agreements.[16] Philip Morris now sells in the Soviet Union and Eastern Europe. R. J. Reynolds now manufactures in China, the world's biggest cigarette market, where 700 billion cigarettes are sold every year—100 billion more than in the USA.[17] The tobacco giants are slowly taking over the world. In the process, they use all the vast resources and marketing skills they have acquired over the century to convince governments and their people that they are the benefactors of mankind.

British-American Tobacco Industries

British-American Tobacco Industries is the world's biggest tobacco multinational, employing a quarter of a million people, and selling $10 billion worth of cigarettes a year in seventy-eight countries on six continents.[18] Most of the British-American Tobacco Company's (BAT) markets are in the developing countries of the Third World, in Africa, Asia and Latin America, where the company has had its base since the days of Buck Duke's tobacco empire at the beginning of the century. But BAT also has powerful subsidiary companies in the West: in the United States, its subsidiary, Brown & Williamson is America's third biggest cigarette company (manufacturing Kool, Barclay and Viceroy); in West Germany, its subsidiary, BAT Cigaretten-Fabriken, manufactures HB, which for years has been the country's best-selling cigarette. Since 1978 BAT has been permitted to sell its brands in Britain—most notably State Express 555 and du Maurier—having been prevented from doing so since 1902 as a result of the agreement whereby Imperial kept out of America, American Tobacco kept out of Britain, and BAT kept to the rest of the world.

In the 1960s and 1970s, BAT diversified for the same reasons that most of the tobacco companies did: the opportunities for further expansion in the tobacco business seemed limited (largely because the medical evidence on smoking and health was generally accepted by the public), and other ways had to be found of reinvesting the huge profits which cigarettes continued to produce. BAT diversied into retailing, paper and packaging, and cosmetics. The company now owns the department stores Gimbels and Saks, Fifth Avenue, in America, as well as the Kohl mid-Western supermarket chain; International Stores and Argos discount shops in Britain; Wiggins Teape Paper and Mardon Packaging; and Yardley, Lentheric, Mornay and Cyclax beauty products. But sixty-five per cent of BAT's profits still come from cigarettes. Its tobacco profits of £469 million in 1981 were made up of £168 million from its US subsidiary, Brown & Williamson; £127 million from Latin America (most of it from Brazil); £56 million from Asia; £45 million from Europe (most from HB in West Germany); £38 million from the UK; £33 million from Africa (mainly Kenya, Nigeria and South Africa); and £2 million from Australia and New Zealand. Profits from tobacco far exceed those from BAT's other divisions: retailing £72 million; paper £47 million; packaging £20 million; cosmetics and other activities £26 million.[19] BAT has £469 million worth of reasons for not letting the health issue destroy its most profitable business. The Company does not accept that cigarettes cause cancer.

In 1981, its new Director of Research and Development, Dr Lionel Blackman (a scientist), declared:

> Despite a never-ending stream of research on the possible health hazards of smoking, there is no proof of a cause-and-effect relationship between cigarette smoking and various alleged smoking diseases.[20]

BAT is very sensitive about its image, especially as far as its Third World operations are concerned. It presents itself as 'a resource of considerable value to governments', and as a company which helps 'certain nations to overcome some of the difficult problems of development', and one which plays 'a valuable role in the world'.[21] The cover of a mid-1970s glossy publicity brochure extolling its work in developing countries shows a group of smiling black children sitting on top of a pile of freshly picked tobacco leaves: above them is a quote from *Gulliver's Travels*:

And he gave it for his opinion that whoever made two ears of corn or two blades of grass to grow upon a spot of ground where only one grew before would deserve better of mankind, and do more essential service to his country than the whole race of politicians put together.

BAT have millions of pounds as well as Jonathan Swift to help them get their message across and convey the right company image. Sponsorship is an ideal vehicle especially when it is associated with art and music.

In 1981 BAT announced its two-year, £600,000 sponsorship of the du Maurier-Philharmonia orchestral concerts. No setting and no occasion could have been better designed to improve BAT's position and prestige than the du Maurier Leeds Castle concert—as well as helping it to sell cigarettes. On a warm English summer's evening in July 1982, a column of people armed with picnic chairs, hampers and bottles of chilled white wine, threaded its way across the green lawns of Leeds Castle in Kent. They made their way past the moat ringed with bull-rushes towards a red awning set in the fold of a natural amphitheatre, where the Philharmonia Orchestra was to present one of its series of du Maurier classical concerts. (Sir Gerald du Maurier was a famous actor of the 1920s, noted for his 'style and success'.[22] He gave his name to a brand of cigarettes, thereby, presumably, endowing them with the same qualities.) After an evening of Dvořák, Tchaikovsky, Schubert and Rossini, fireworks lit up the night sky in the grand finale of Elgar's Pomp and Circumstance. The concert may not have sold that many cigarettes, but it breathed class and respectability all over its sponsor. For three hours, in a perfect English setting, 15,000 people (most of them non-smokers) may have associated a tobacco company with Elgar and Tchaikovsky, instead of cancer and bronchitis. Perhaps few noticed the irony that the purpose of the charitable trust which now administers Leeds Castle, is to promote 'outstanding achievement in medical science'.

Philip Morris Incorporated

Philip Morris is the most dynamic, aggressive and successful of all the tobacco giants. Over the decade of the 1970s, its worldwide cigarette business enjoyed spectacular growth: on an annually compounded basis, worldwide cigarette unit sales grew ten per cent from 1970 to 1979, revenues were up eighteen per cent and operating income increased twenty-one per cent. *Fortune* business magazine called Philip Morris 'one of the ten most impressive business triumphs of the decade'. A rival executive said of the company, perhaps with some envy: 'Philip Morris is like the British Empire in colonial days. They think they're better, smarter and more sophisticated and, by God, they're going to have what they want.'[23]

The foundation of its success is Marlboro, the brand now synonymous with the cowboy image and the slogan 'Come to where the flavour is. Come to Marlboro country', which for more than a decade has been the world's best-selling cigarette. For many years the brand, which had been in Philip Morris' stable since 1902, was marketed as a lady's cigarette, with a red tip to hide her lipstick marks. 'Women,' ran the advertisements, 'quickly develop discerning taste. That is why Marlboros now ride in so many limousines, attend so many bridge parties, and repose in so many handbags.' In 1954 an advertising genius from Chicago, called Leo Burnett, took Marlboro out of the handbag and put it on a horse. The Marlboro cowboy rode out and became the most successful campaign in cigarette advertising history. 'We chose the cowboy because he's close to the earth,' said the company's Chairman George Weissman, 'he's an authentic American hero. Probably the only one. And it worked.'[24] The Marlboro cowboys, with their rugged good looks and weather-beaten faces, rounding up cattle and horses as they rode across Marlboro country, captured the imagination of smokers the world over. By 1980 over 100 billion Marlboro cigarettes were being sold every year in the United States and 70 billion around the rest of the world.[25] The Marlboro cowboys became a symbol that cigarettes made you virile, not sick. They trampled the health warnings into the dust. Marlboro has made Philip Morris tens of billions of dollars. By 1982, the 'big red machine' (so-called because of the colour of the packet) was generating nearly $4 billion a year—thirty-five per cent of the company's total annual revenue of $11 billion.[26] Besides Marlboro, Philip Morris also

manufactures Merit, Virginia Slims, Parliament and Benson &
Hedges (which is no relation to the British cigarette of the same
name), as well as over 160 other brands in more than 170
countries.[27] Cigarettes in general, and Marlboro in particular,
provided Philip Morris with the cash to diversify into beer, soft
drinks, property development and paper and packaging. The
Company has diversified more successfully than most of its rivals,
because it has concentrated on products it knew how to handle:
high-volume, low-cost consumer items, like beer and soft drinks
which, like cigarettes, tend to be recession-proof and responsive
to the brilliant marketing techniques which Philip Morris had
developed in making the world 'Marlboro Country'. Miller Beer
has become a success story like Marlboro. The ailing brewery
which Philip Morris took over in 1970 now produces revenues of
$2 billion a year and presses the market leader, Budweiser (made
by Anheuser-Busch) for the Number One spot. The same success
story has still to be repeated with Seven-Up, the soft drinks
company acquired in 1978 at a cost of $518 million, largely
because the market is dominated by Coca-Cola and Pepsi Cola
who are Philip Morris' equal masters in marketing.

At Philip Morris, success breeds success. The company's
corporate image has been polished until it dazzles. Its new
international headquarters (designed by Ulrich Franzen) opposite
New York's Grand Central station, contains a branch of the
Whitney Art Museum for which Philip Morris assumes full
financial responsibility. A street-level pedestrian plaza contains a
specially designed 5,000 square-foot sculpture court (with
newly-commissioned works by John Chamberlain, Mark di
Suvero and George Segal) and a 1,000 square-foot gallery which
presents six changing exhibitions every year. Works by
Bourgeois, Calder, Graham, Hunt, Lichtenstein, Oldenburg and
Saret stand in the huge forty-two foot high covered garden. The
company proudly proclaims it has been a patron of the arts for a
quarter of a century—almost as long as the Marlboro cowboy
has been riding his horse. In addition to acquiring works of art to
adorn its premises throughout the world, it also sponsors
everything from the British Museum's Michelangelo exhibition in
New York and the US tour of the La Scala opera of Milan, to
exhibitions of black American art and Andy Warhol. Of all the

tobacco multinationals, Philip Morris is the most conscious of the way that others perceive it. 'Good people do good things', declares the headline above one of its corporate advertisements. Below are fifteen colour photographs of 'people within our Philip Morris family in our home towns around the world'. They are life-savers, fund-raisers, helpers of the handicapped, animal protectors and church workers. 'Good people do good things' concludes with a pat on the back for the reader: 'And you wouldn't have read this far if you weren't a pretty good person yourself.' Philip Morris declares that it is devoted to the public good:

> Good corporate citizenship is not an afterthought but an active concern in everything we do . . . Our social activities are not pursued solely for the sake of profit. They are mounted simply because that is the kind of company Philip Morris is.[28]

Besides being the most sophisticated and successful of all the tobacco multinationals, Philip Morris is also the company which is perhaps the most critical of the medical evidence against the product to which it owes that success. The company greeted the massive US Surgeon-General's Report of 1979 — the 1,100 page document which concluded that cigarettes were far more dangerous than was ever supposed in 1964 — with the observation:

> Fifteen years elapsed between the first Report by the US Surgeon-General in 1964 and the Surgeon-General's Report in 1979. During those years millions and millions of dollars of government and private funds have been spent on health research. Although much of the research was concentrated on finding evidence that smoking causes diseases, no conclusive medical or clinical proof has been discovered . . . The tobacco industry continues to maintain the controversy can be resolved only by medical and scientific knowledge.[29]

Philip Morris remains confident that its future lies in cigarettes. Looking ahead to the mid-1980s, and perhaps beyond, the

President of the company's US Cigarette Division, Shepard Pollock, said:

> We as a corporation, as Philip Morris (Inc), will still make most of our money in tobacco. We'll still be mostly a cigarette company, and we'll still be damn proud of it.[30]

On the front of the Marlboro pack is the company's coat of arms, with the inscription '*Veni Vidi Vici*'—'I came. I saw. I conquered'. Philip Morris shares its motto with Julius Caesar. Like Caesar, it has no intention of letting anything stand in the way of its progress.

R. J. Reynolds Industries

R. J. Reynolds is the most multinational of all the tobacco giants. According to its Chairman, J. Paul Sticht:

> On any given day, R. J. R. is growing pineapples in Costa Rica for the US and Europe, bananas in the Philippines for Japan; making cigarettes in Germany for France, in Puerto Rico for the Bahamas; carrying goods from Hong Kong to California; extracting gas from under the North Sea for the Dutch and punching holes in the Gulf of Mexico and the Appalachians to find more oil and gas for the US.[31]

Reynolds started by following the traditional path of diversification, into food, beverages and packaging, before spreading its wings across the world. In 1969 it bought Sea-Land, the world's largest containerised freight operation; in 1970 it acquired the American Independent Oil Company (Aminoil) with its refineries in the Middle East; and in 1979 it took over Del Monte, the worldwide fresh fruit business. But, despite this ambitious diversification, Reynolds depends on cigarettes even more than BAT and Philip Morris. In 1980 tobacco accounted for seventy-three per cent of its total operational earnings of $1.72 billion: energy accounted for fourteen per cent; transportation thirteen per cent; foods and beverages seven per cent; and packaging one per cent.[32] The company has no inhibitions about its continued reliance upon cigarettes. In November 1981, the Chairman told the gathering of Stock Exchange investment analysts in California:

> The tobacco business is alive and well, not only in the United States, but around the world as well . . . R. J. Reynolds will continue to actively and aggressively participate both in the US and the rest of the world. R. J. R. has been the US industry leader for 23 years. We plan to continue that leadership. In the past five years, our international tobacco operations have grown handsomely and we plan to pursue this growth with all possible vigor.[33]

Nor, the Chairman assured his audience, was his company worried by the medical evidence: 'We believe the campaign against tobacco is based on statistical inferences unsupported by clinical findings.'[34] On another occasion, Mr Sticht declared: 'Despite the fact that millions of dollars have been spent on research, no element as found in cigarette smoke has been shown to be the cause of any human disease.'[35]

The reason for the Chairman's presentation to fifty of America's leading investment analysts was to assure them that R. J. Reynolds Industries was still a good place for their clients to invest their money. The fact that such reassurance was necessary is a measure of the problems which have beset the Company. While Philip Morris breathed success all over Wall Street, Reynolds' stock was being sold at a twenty per cent discount, not just because diversification had presented its problems, but because its position as leader in the US cigarette market which it had held for a quarter of a century was under severe attack. For ten years Reynolds watched its own market share remain static at thirty-three per cent, while its rival, Philip Morris, galloped up fast from behind. In 1971 Philip Morris had eighteen per cent of the American cigarette market, twenty-five per cent in 1976, thirty per cent in 1980,[36] and thirty-three per cent in 1982,[37] only a fraction of a percentage point behind Reynolds. But Reynolds fought back, revamping the image of its five main brands, Winston (which had held the Number One spot for most of the 1970s, until Marlboro took over), Salem, Camel, Vantage and

More. It even took the fight to Marlboro Country by relaunching Camel as the cigarette of the great American outdoors. (Camel had done for Reynolds in the 1920s, with its slogan 'I'd walk a mile for a Camel', what Marlboro Country had done for Philip Morris in the 1970s.) The images and the settings were the same: a rugged man alone in the wilds, with a back pack instead of a Stetson, lighting his Camel by a campfire. Camel became a growth industry. Thomas Cook organised Camel expeditions to wild, romantic places and advertised them in travel brochures which carried the Government Health Warning: for $2,000, urban adventurers could spend five nights in a tent in the jungles of Ecuador where 'at night the eyes of alligators will gleam at you from the shore'. The strategy of making Camel a macho cigarette like Marlboro was successful. In 1982, Camel had become America's fifth best-selling brand, having increased its sales by five billion cigarettes in two years. Reynolds was playing Philip Morris at its own game and, as the company proudly admitted, winning more young smokers in the process:

> In the past some observers have criticised us because they viewed our brands as appealing primarily to older smokers, while younger adult smokers turned to our competitors ... During the first half of 1981, our research shows that we exhibited far more growth among young adult smokers [eighteen to twenty-four years old] than any other company.[38]

Reynolds, like its rivals, knows that the potential for growth in its domestic market is limited, because although smokers may be smoking more, which mainly accounts for the one per cent annual growth in the market, the number of smokers is declining overall. (In 1964 at the time of publication of the first US Surgeon-General's Report, there were nearly 70 million cigarette smokers in America. By 1982, the number had fallen to 53 million.) For Reynolds in particular, the real opportunities for expansion lie overseas where it has just over two per cent of the market and ninety-eight per cent in which to grow. That two per cent of the world market brought Reynolds revenues of $2 billion a year: the rewards on offer were enormous. Reynolds' problem was to find a way of elbowing its way in. In 1981, its Chairman, J. Paul Sticht, found a way of doing it, hopefully by arranging a marriage with Rothmans International, the cigarette subsidiary of Dr Anton Rupert's Rembrandt Group. Such a union would give Reynolds combined world sales of 435 billion cigarettes and bring it within striking distance of Philip Morris' 440 billion. It perhaps might even make BAT nervous, with its lead of 475 billion.[39]

But the marriage was not to be. Philip Morris snatched the bride with a dowry of $350 million. Reynolds was left standing at the altar.

The Rembrandt Group

Rothmans International is part of Dr Anton Rupert's $4.5 billion empire, the Rembrandt Group. Dr Rupert, a chemist by training, once sold Rothmans cigarettes in South Africa. He bought local manufacturing rights for the brand and built up his empire from there, and with it his reputation as one of the toughest and most secret of negotiators on the international scene.[40] Rothmans International was an attractive proposition for any suitor. In 1982 it announced profits of £105 million. The company sells more than sixty per cent of its cigarettes in Europe, in particular its international brands, Rothmans, Dunhill and Peter Stuyvesant. It has fifty-one per cent of the market in Ireland, forty-seven per cent in Holland, forty-two per cent in Belgium, thirty per cent in Switzerland, eighteen per cent in West Germany and thirteen per cent in the United Kingdom. These European sales amount to nearly 70 billion cigarettes a year.[41] In addition, Rothmans has seventy-five per cent of the market in New Zealand, thirty-six per cent in Australia and twenty-six per cent in Canada — additional cigarette sales of nearly 25 billion.[42]

Rothmans publicly deals with the health issue by declining to say anything: the company 'never comments on opinions expressed by members of the medical profession'.[43] Rothman's Chairman, Sir David Nicolson, speaking as a Member of the European Parliament, had been more specific. In February 1980 he said:

Now there is no doubt that excessive smoking like anything else taken in excess is bad for you. However I would emphasise that there is no medical evidence to prove that a few cigarettes, say 10 or 15 a day, are bad for you. And the key, as you all know perfectly well in both smoking and alcohol, is moderation.[44]

Rothman's strength in the lucrative West German market, where its Lord brand was Number Three and where smokers bought nearly 130 billion cigarettes in 1981 (20 billion more than in Britain), was particularly attractive to Reynolds, whose Camel brand was Number Four. In 1981, Reynolds' Chairman, J. Paul Sticht, began negotiations with Anton Rupert. Dr Rupert controlled Rothmans International through a complicated network of companies with interlocking shareholdings: the Rupert Foundation, based in Luxembourg, controlled Rothmans Tobacco Holdings, which owned forty-four per cent of the equity of Rothmans International, fifty per cent of its votes and most of its convertible stock. Sticht negotiated to buy half of Dr Rupert's forty-four per cent holding with Rothmans International, but that was only to be the first step. The real aim, as the Chairman told Dr Rupert in a confidential telex, was to gain ' . . . ultimate control at some point in the future when you and others with whom we have friendly relationships have left the scene'.[45]

If Reynolds found Rothmans desirable, Philip Morris found the company irresistible. It not only offered an even greater advantage in the West German market where Marlboro was Number Two (behind BAT's HB), but would give its UK operations a much-needed boost, as Marlboro had only succeeded in gaining two per cent of the British market. Furthermore, it would deny Reynolds the wider access it sought to the international markets. But Philip Morris snatched the prize. Reynolds was stunned. 'We thought we had a gentlemen's agreement with Anton Rupert,' lamented Reynolds.[46] But it was too late. Philip Morris, true to its motto, came and saw and conquered.

American Brands Inc.

American Brands is the direct descendant of Buck Duke's American Tobacco Company. Between 1965 and 1980, the company spent $1.8 billion on diversification[47] and watched its dividend grow at twice the rate of the Dow Jones Industrial Index. It had to change its name in order to do so, as its founder had expressly forbidden the company to engage in any business other than tobacco. It bought Jim Beam Bourbon (liquor sales were rising at seven per cent a year); Sunshine Biscuits (snack and candy sales were growing at four per cent); and Jergens soap and shampoos. It took over companies making locks, golf clubs, staplers, knives, scissors and selling life insurance.[48] Like all tobacco companies, American had the money to diversify (its huge tobacco stocks were ample collateral for the loans), but had additional reasons for doing so as it watched its traditional leadership of the American cigarette market slip from its hands.

Until after the Second World War, cigarettes had been synonymous with its brand, Lucky Strike, which had been the market leader for much of the 1920s, 1930s and 1940s. In 1955, American Tobacco still led the field with thirty-three per cent of the market.[49] But its filter brand, Pall Mall, failed to hold off the challenge from R. J. Reynolds' Winston and Philip Morris' Marlboro. By 1970 American's market share had fallen to nineteen per cent,[50] and by 1980, to eleven per cent.[51] But American skilfully rebuilt its tobacco business by buying the British tobacco company, Gallahers, and in the United States by concentrating on the increasing popularity of low tar cigarettes, which it satisfied with its brand, Carlton. In 1981, tobacco still brought American Brands £438 million—fifty-six per cent of its total operating income.[52] Gallahers' UK operations accounted for nearly one-third of the tobacco total.

After a fierce battle with Philip Morris, which was also anxious to get a foothold in Britain, American Brands bought its way into Gallahers in 1968, and took full control of the company in 1975. Gallahers is Britain's most successful tobacco company, although it is dwarfed in size by Imperial. Gallahers' success is based on two brands: its king size filter, Benson & Hedges, and its low tar cigarette, Silk Cut. Gallahers displayed all the marketing skills which had once made its parent the greatest tobacco company in the world. Duke was first to realise that advertising was the key to a cigarette success. He ploughed back as much as twenty per cent of his gross receipts into advertising his brands in newspapers, magazines, on billboards and on the cigarette cards he introduced in the packets. Duke tramped the sidewalks of New York City, picking up cigarette packets to check that more people were buying his cigarettes than anyone else's.

George Washington Hill, who became the President of American Tobacco in 1925, was a salesman in Buck Duke's mould. By using the new medium of radio and memorable slogans like 'reach for a Lucky instead of a Sweet', Hill trebled the sales of Lucky Strike from 14 billion in 1925 to 43 billion in 1930. Lucky Strike stayed at the top for most of the next twenty years.[53] In those years smokers were largely unaware that cigarettes were dangerous, perhaps not surprisingly when some even had the imprimatur of the medical profession. One advertisement even boasted, 'More doctors smoke Camels'.[54]

In the 1960s and 1970s, a cigarette's image became more important than ever, not only because it was meant to confer its qualities on the smoker, but because it was designed to blind consumers to the true nature of what they were buying. In Britain no cigarette was more skilfully marketed than Gallahers' Benson & Hedges. Its shiny gold pack, complete with royal coat of arms and seal of approval 'By Appointment to Her Majesty the Queen', was the feature of a brilliant ten-year advertising campaign, which helped make Benson & Hedges Britain's best selling cigarette. The following story illustrates how vulnerable the image was.

The campaign, which won an armful of advertising awards, was based on the idea of 'gold', and depicted the pack in a series of surrealistic settings: it became the substitute for the bird in the gilded cage; for the picture hanging in the art gallery; for one of the pyramids; and for a fossil encrusted in a rock at the bottom of the sea. The Benson & Hedges posters became a cult and were sold as limited editions. Tony May, a British feeelance photographer, had worked on the campaign in the early 1970s. He had photographed 'Turn Again Whittington'—a golden packet and the sign 'London—33 miles'; 'Panning for Gold'—an ancient map, a prospector's pan and hammer, and a packet of Benson & Hedges; and many others. In May 1978 May, a non-smoker, turned the image on itself. He was asked to work on an anti-smoking campaign for the government-financed Scottish Health Education Unit. A set of a graveyard was built in a London studio and May photographed a golden cigarette packet with the health warning on the side, being lowered into the ground. The original caption was meant to be, 'Some people have been known to die in the search for gold'. But the poster was buried as well as the packet. The campaign was a closely guarded secret, but there was a leak and Gallahers found out before the posters were published. The company complained to the Advertising Standards Authority, the regulatory authority charged with ensuring that all advertisements in Britain are 'legal, decent, honest and truthful'. The Authority said the poster could not be allowed as it was a pastiche of Benson & Hedges. The then Director of the Scottish Health Education Unit, Dr David Player (and the Director of the anti-smoking group Action on Smoking and Health, Mike Daube) argued with straight faces that it was sheer accident and pointed out that many cigarette packets were gold. The Authority was not convinced. After much haggling a compromise was reached. A coffin in grained pine was substituted for the one in gold; the original posters were shredded. Benson & Hedges remained untarnished, and became Britain's best-selling brand for four years running. Gallahers knocked Imperial into second place.

Imperial Group Limited

For seventy-five years, since its foundation in 1901, Imperial Tobacco ruled without rival. Down the century its brands, Woodbines, Navy Cut, Capstan, Gold Leaf, No. 6, Embassy and John Player Special, became household names in Britain. Its headquarters in Bristol, with its polished brass plate on the door and grandfather clock ticking slowly in the lobby, still breathes respectability and tradition. On the wall, standing on black pillars, is a great slab of white marble with 300 names and the inscription 'In ever grateful memory of the men who went out from the factories and offices of Imperial Tobacco and gave their lives for their country. 1914–19.' On the wall opposite is another slab, with another 300 names, the victims of the Second World War.

The members of the Wills family, who were the driving force behind the foundation of Imperial Tobacco, were great public benefactors. Unlike many of their successful contemporaries, they kept their money in the city where they had made it: they founded Bristol University and donated its main buildings; they gave the city one of its most famous beauty spots, Nightingale Valley; they presented the premises for an art gallery and museum; they founded a hospital and a convalescent home. The company made its position clear on the smoking and health issue in a letter to me in June 1982. It said it was not its function to make judgements on medical matters: its policy was to behave responsibly in the light of opinions expressed by the medical authorities and to take account of their conclusions in deciding what to do.

The public is encouraged to think of Imperial in its role as public benefactor: the provider of revenue and jobs, the patron of sports and the arts, and the creator of wealth. 'Imperial — part of the country's foundations', proclaimed an advertisement in the British press in 1980, depicting the country standing on stone pillars spelling out the word IMPERIAL. By then, Imperial had dropped the word 'Tobacco' from its title (Imperial Tobacco became a division) and had been transformed into a diversified company, selling Ross frozen foods, Buxted chickens, Golden Wonder crisps, Smedley and HP foods, Young's sea foods, and Courage and John Smith beers. That same year it also crossed the Atlantic and bought the Howard Johnson US chain of hotels and restaurants for $640 million. The advertisement did not reveal that Imperial's own foundations had begun to crumble.

Normally when tobacco companies diversified, they always reckoned they had tobacco to fall back on if their other interests ran into difficulties. Imperial found itself in trouble on both fronts. In the five-year period, 1976–81, the group's pre-interest profits only rose from £168 million to £172 million.[55] Growth in its 'star' brewery division lagged behind its competitors;[56] profit margins in the food division fell to one per cent;[57] and there were disastrous returns on poultry and eggs, which had been losing £8 million a year on sales of £382 million.[58] Over the same period, Imperial saw its share of the cigarette market, which it had dominated for three-quarters of a century, collapse from sixty-six per cent in 1976 to fifty-two per cent in 1981.[59] The reason for the crash was partly of Imperial's own making. The company had failed to develop a king size brand to cash in on the market change which followed the switch in the way tobacco was taxed in 1976. Traditionally, duty on the British cigarette had been charged on the amount of tobacco it contained. This meant that king size cigarettes were more expensive. Under new European Community rules part of the duty was to be levied on each individual cigarette, thereby eroding the price differential which had long made king size cigarettes a luxury. The king size filter became Everyman's cigarette. Imperial lost out and Gallahers cashed in with Benson & Hedges. In desperation, Imperial fought back to retrieve its lost market and spent around £13 million relaunching John Player Special—a king size cigarette in a shiny black pack with golden JPS insignia. Britain was wallpapered with its advertisements. The John Player Special Formula One racing car was wheeled out again to promote the brand on the race tracks of Britain and the world. But the cost of promotion and the heavy price discounting which was a sign of the intense brand competition at the time made Imperial's balance sheet look even worse.

The other factor which affected Imperial's tobacco performance was not of its own making. The British cigarette market had been in decline for most of the 1970s, encouraged by systematic government tax increases designed to increase the revenue and discourage smoking (although not too much) in the process. The market reached its peak in 1973, when over 137 billion cigarettes were sold.[60] By 1980, sales had fallen to 120 billion.[61] In 1981, the British government increased the tax on a packet of cigarettes twice, and sent the price through the psychological barrier of £1. Sales dropped by 10 billion. All the companies were hurt, but Imperial was hurt the most. The group's Chairman, Malcolm Anson, resigned. He was replaced by Geoffrey Kent, the former advertising director of John Player, who rationalised the company's structure, sold off its loss-making operations, cut its workforce and office staff, and reassured anxious shareholders that Imperial would retain cigarette market leadership:[62]

> Despite fiscal measures and social attacks, the UK tobacco market is still capable of producing good profits . . . There is good reason to be confident that tobacco still has a vital part to play in our future.[63]

[41]

The Imperial group reaffirmed its faith in the product on which its fortune had been built.

The opponents of these six fabulously wealthy multinational companies vary in size and resources. Government Health Departments provide the main opposition, although their effectiveness depends on the commitment of the politicians in charge and, more importantly, on the backing they receive from their Cabinet colleagues. These Health Departments also have their own sub-organisations, like America's Office on Smoking and Health and Britain's Health Education Council whose Director, Dr David Player, has a budget of £2 million (1983) to spend on anti-smoking campaigns. (The Health Education Council has a total budget of £8.5 million to spend on every aspect of health education: in fact it spends more than its allocated £2 million on smoking and health.) The biggest and best financed of the voluntary bodies are the large American health agencies such as the American Cancer Society, the American Lung Association and the American Heart Association. They are mini corporations in their own right, and are seen as part of the American medical establishment. Because of their size and membership, they tend to favour conventional and often more conservative tactics. Their budgets run into millions of dollars, but much is spent on research and smoking is only one of the issues they cover. The American Cancer Society and the American Lung Association spend around $7 million a year on smoking and health. They point out that the tobacco industry spends over $1 billion a year promoting cigarettes. Traditionally their anti-smoking activities have been largely educational although by the early 1980s they were becoming increasingly involved in political lobbying.

In contrast, the groups which have spearheaded the attack on tobacco are grass roots organisations forced to rely entirely on the dedication and skill of their officers and volunteers, in the absence of substantial resources. These play David to tobacco's Goliaths. In America, Action on Smoking and Health (ASH) is financed entirely by voluntary contributions: its founder, John F. Banzhaf III, was instrumental in getting cigarette advertisements banned from television in 1970, and was the pioneer of the legal battles for non-smokers' rights. Other similar groups in America like GASP ('Group Against Smokers' Pollution') and Californians for Nonsmokers' Rights, who have also been in the forefront of the battle, rely too on the generosity and enthusiasm of their supporters. In Britain the battle has been waged almost single-handedly by Action on Smoking and Health (which is no relation to its American counterpart). ASH was established in 1971 by the British Royal College of Physicians, following the publication of their second Report, 'Smoking and Health Now', with the purpose of mobilising and co-ordinating voluntary action against smoking. It depends on the government for ninety-five per cent of its income, in the form of an annual grant from the Department of Health and Social Security (£115,000 in 1982). ASH, whose London headquarters is staffed by eight full-time workers, makes up in energy what it lacks in resources. Although it started as a smoking education pressure group, under the determined leadership of its Directors, Mike Daube, 1973–1979, and its current Director, David Simpson, it has become an effective political lobby as well as the industry's most persistent critic (ASH also has several staff outside London funded by the Scottish Home and Health Department, the Ulster Cancer Foundation and various Regional Health Authorities). But ASH knows that it survives by grace of its government grant and is sensitive to the risk it runs (especially in difficult political times) if it bites too hard at the hand that feeds it.

But these opponents cannot match the tobacco companies in either wealth or political influence. To the industry they are mainly an irritant, not feared enemies who threaten the Smoke Ring's existence. The tobacco giants have grown rich while challenging the verdict which the world's medical authorities have repeatedly passed on their product. The Smoke Ring has enabled them to do so with impunity.

3

The Media Gets
the Message

Advertising is a vital link in the Smoke Ring, because advertising conditions the way cigarettes are perceived. Every year the tobacco industry spends around $2 billion[1] globally to ensure that cigarettes are associated with glamour, success and sophistication, instead of lung cancer, bronchitis and heart disease. The industry needs to make this huge and ever-increasing investment to perpetuate this false image in order to counter the evidence that cigarettes are not desirable but dangerous. After addiction, advertising is the industry's most powerful ally in its battle for the hearts and minds of the smoker and in its drive to seduce more recruits into the Smoke Ring. That is why, when the link is attacked, the industry will do all in its power to defend it, especially when the attack comes from the media which normally carries its message.

Many newspapers and magazines are heavily dependent on cigarette advertising which they are loath to jeopardise, particularly in times of economic recession. Cigarettes are the most heavily advertised product in America, where the industry spends half its $2 billion on advertising a year.[2] In 1979, the largest single advertiser in magazines was R. J. Reynolds, which spent $25 million on Winston alone. Philip Morris spent over $60 million overall on magazine advertising. In newspapers the most advertised brand in 1979 was Lorillard's Kent ($30 million) followed by Philip Morris' low tar Merit ($26 million).[3] An article in the *Columbia Journalism Revue*, examining coverage which leading national magazines had given to cigarettes and cancer in the 1970s, concluded it was:

> ... unable to find a single article in 7 years of publication that would have given readers any clear notion of the nature and extent of the medical and social havoc being wreaked by the cigarette-smoking habit . . . one must conclude that advertising revenue can indeed silence the editors of American magazines.[4]

Several American publications, most notably the *Readers Digest*, *Good Housekeeping*, the *New Yorker* and *Washington Monthly*, do not accept cigarette advertising on principle. In 1982, the American Council on Science and Health conducted a survey of the coverage which eighteen popular American magazines had given to smoking and health from 1965 to 1981 and detailed the amount of cigarette advertising each publication received.[5] The *Readers Digest* (whose long crusade on the issue is second to none) and *Good Housekeeping* came out on top. Some of the women's magazines came at the bottom of the list. *Cosmopolitan*, which receives $5.5 million a year in cigarette advertising (nearly ten per cent of its total revenue), devoted only 2.3 per cent of its total health coverage to smoking ('although smoking was noted as a risk factor in heart disease, it was never mentioned in preventive health articles or in reference to lung cancer'). *Mademoiselle*, which receives $1 million in cigarette advertising (seven per cent of its total revenue), devoted less than two per cent of its health coverage to smoking ('unreliable source of information about the hazards of smoking. Used editorial ploys to de-emphasise smoking, gave misinformation, and excluded smoking from mention on relevant health topics altogether. One of the worst'). *Ms*, which receives $500,000 in cigarette advertising (nearly fifteen per cent of its total revenue), ran no articles at all on the issue ('the complete absence of articles on the hazards of smoking is particularly striking in this magazine, which covers many other important issues in women's health'). *Red Book*, which receives $7.5 million in cigarette advertising (sixteen per cent of its total revenue), ran eighty health-related articles but not one of them on smoking ('not a single mention of smoking between 1970 and 1981. Other health topics, like breast cancer, VD, ... hysterectomies ..., drugs, alcohol ... were discussed'). *Red Book*, however, hit back and accused the Council of 'sloppy' research, saying it had indeed devoted coverage to the issue. *Parade* received $35 million from cigarette advertising (twenty-five per cent of its total revenue), more than any other magazine except *Time* ('articles on smoking were few and, when present, almost encouraged the smoking habit').

Elizabeth M.Whelan, the Executive Director of the American Council on Science and Health, had personal experience of the cigarette advertising pressure which may affect a magazine. In the late 1970s she was asked by *Harper's Bazaar* to write an article called 'Protect Your Man From Cancer'. The Council reported what happened to the article:

> The author was paid in full for the piece, but the article never ran because, in the words of the editor, 'it focussed too much on tobacco' and 'the magazine is running three full page, color ads [for tobacco] this month'.[6]

Smaller publications are also sensitive about cigarette advertising. In April 1982, Paul Fishman Maccabee, the music critic of a mid-Western alternative weekly called the *Twin Cities Reader*, came unstuck when he penned a satirical piece about Kool's sponsorship of a local jazz festival. The article was headed 'Kool Jazz and Burning Ashes'. Maccabee wrote:

> ...Kool's manufacturer, Brown & Williamson of Kentucky (a subsidiary of England's $500 million BAT Corp. which owns Yardley Cosmetics and Saks Fifth Avenue), can certainly afford to subsidise public good-will for tobacco. Brown & Williamson sell 55 million Kool cigarettes a year.
>
> But the American public's curious aversion to lung cancer has been crippling tobacco sales lately, as evidence mounts to support links between smoking and cancer, heart disease and Buerger's Disease. Buerger's is a degenerative nicotine-linked condition which leads doctors to amputate toes and feet one-at-a-time, like snipping grapes off a vine.
>
> Definitely not sexy. Definitely un-Kool.

He concluded:

> Strange bedfellows, cigarettes and jazz. Duke Ellington died of
> lung cancer in 1974.

Mr Maccabee was not aware that his publication had an
understanding, as is usual in such cases, with the cigarette
advertisers that they be advised in advance of any forthcoming
anti-smoking articles. Mr Maccabee was promptly fired by his
publisher. The editor resigned shortly afterwards.[7] Maccabee was
not fired because Brown & Williamson complained—in fact they
did not—but because the publisher, Mark Hopp, was fearful of
losing future cigarette advertisements which totalled four to five
pages a week at about $1,750 a page. When I spoke to Mr Hopp,
he told me he had twelve pages of cigarette advertisements a year
from Brown & Williamson and fifty jobs to protect. He also
confirmed his previous remark that if he had to fly to Brown &
Williamson's headquarters in Louisville, Kentucky, and go down
on bended knees to beg Kool not to take its advertisements out of
his magazine, he would do it. But Mr Maccabee was not out of
work for long: he was snapped up by a St Paul advertising agency,
which was so impressed by his chutzpah, that it made him
Director of Public Relations.

Such sensitivities are not confined to magazines or to America.
In 1979 the *Ottawa Citizen* reported under the headline,
'Tobacco firm pulls ads for July':

> Imperial Tobacco Limited has pulled the balance of its June and
> July advertising from the *Citizen* in the wake of an intensive
> Stop Smoking campaign launched by the newspaper June 9 . . .
> Imperial marketing vice president Anthony Kalhok . . . said he
> was 'surprised' the *Citizen*'s sales department hadn't called his
> department to 'let us know you were running this type of
> campaign and ask us in advance if we wanted to run our ads
> during that time . . .' Kalhok refused to explain the company's
> reasoning behind the decision.
>
> 'We don't ask you to explain or justify your editorial
> comment, so I don't see why we have to answer any ques-
> tions . . .'

Kalhok emphasised that Imperial were selling a 'legal product and millions of people are buying it'.[8]

In Australia, where the industry spends nearly $40 million[9] on advertising and promotion (around twenty per cent of it on sports sponsorship), in 1982 newspapers, magazines and sporting bodies were alarmed by the progress of a Bill through the Western Australian Parliament which would ban all forms of cigarette advertising and promotion. The Bill was sponsored by a general practitioner and Member of Parliament, Dr Thomas Dadour, who was backed by 500 doctors in the state.[10] If the Bill had become law, one of the most immediate casualties would have been the advertising at the England versus Australia Test Match, which was sponsored by Benson & Hedges (who have been the Australian Cricket Board's main sponsor for ten years, with an outlay of nearly $6 million).[11] There was intensive lobbying to make sure the Bill never reached the statute book. Newspapers played their part. *The Sunday Times* (of Australia) contacted a local paper, the *South Perth Times*, and asked it to try to get its local MP to vote against the Bill. The pressure did not work. The *South Perth Times* wrote:

This newspaper was asked by the *Sunday Times* yesterday afternoon to try to influence the Member for South Perth, Mr Bill Grayden, not to support Dr Tom Dadour's Bill to ban cigarette advertising. The *Sunday Times* is concerned about the loss of revenue that would result if this Bill was passed, and it felt that Mr Grayden's vote might be crucial in a tight contest on the floor of the House. We told the *Sunday Times* that . . . he had a mind of his own and we had no intention of trying to influence him on this or on any other matter.[12]

Dr Dadour's Bill was narrowly defeated, and the Benson & Hedges Test Match went ahead, thereby advertising its brand not just to Australia, but via satellite to Britain as well.(The following year a further attempt was made to pass similar legislation banning all cigarette advertising and promotion in Western Australia which had now become the Maginot Line on the issue. Following the election of a new Labor Premier, Brian Burke, in

February 1983, the state government sponsored a Bill similar to Dr Dadour's. On October 27th, 1983, the Bill met the same fate after intensive lobbying by the tobacco industry and its supporters, in particular those connected with the cigarette-sponsored sports under threat. Again, it was defeated by the narrowest of margins—by 17 votes to 15 in the Upper House of Parliament. Sport and cigarette advertising remained safe in Western Australia—at least for the time being.)

But the mechanisms by which the pressure is exercised are usually far more subtle. Velvet gloves suit the tobacco industry far more than mailed fists where matters of such delicacy are concerned. The last thing a cigarette company wants is a front page story that it has tried to influence a client. In the United Kingdom, the Sunday and weekend colour supplements are the second biggest recipients of tobacco advertising—£7.2 million in 1981.[13] (The 'popular' daily papers are first with £9.6 million.) Each supplement may receive up to a million pounds a year in cigarette advertising revenue. They offer the perfect showcase, glossy and widely read.

The financial year 1980–81 was not a good one for Britain's largest tobacco company, Imperial, as it watched overall sales in the British market plummet by over 10 billion cigarettes, as a result of a series of heavy tax increases.[14] The Chairman had warned of 'fiscal pressures and social attacks'.[15] The last thing Imperial wanted was what it saw as a concerted anti-smoking campaign by one of Britain's most prestigious Sunday newspapers, *The Sunday Times*. At the time, *The Sunday Times* magazine was taking nearly three-quarters of a million pounds worth of cigarette advertising. A full page advertisement cost around £7,000. Imperial were buying about fifty pages a year, and Rothmans and Gallahers about thirty each. *The Sunday Times* magazine for October 19th, 1980, contained a double page advertisement for Benson & Hedges; a Rothmans advertisement for Dunhill; and two Imperial advertisements—one for Lambert & Butler and the other for Embassy. The edition won an award for its journalism and caused a fierce backstage row with Imperial. Most of the magazine was devoted to a feature by *The Sunday Times* medical correspondent, Oliver Gillie, on a heart transplant operation at Harefield hospital.[16] In the course of the

article, he profiled seven men who had undergone the operation.
Six of them had been heavy cigarette smokers. Gillie believed that
cigarettes had contributed to their heart disease, and not only said
so in the piece but also named the brands they had smoked. He
took the view that had it been a drug involved, he would have
given its name, so why not name the brand of cigarette?

James Burkhill . . . smoked 80 Capstan Full Strength a day . . .
This heavy smoking probably caused his first heart attack when
he was 44.

Ernest Field (50) . . . got through 40 a day. His favourite brands
were Players No.6 and Piccadilly—they were a major factor in
his illness.

Joe Burnside (50) . . . smoked 25 a day since he was a teenager,
first plain and then filter tips. They had damaged his heart.

James Kelly (46) . . . smoking 40 cigarettes a day, mostly
tipped. Smoking was probably a major cause of his arteries
silting up.

John Gardiner (44) . . . whose heart was permanently damaged
by smoking 60 cigarettes a day—Benson & Hedges were his
favourite brand.

Ken Davis (51) . . . smoked 60 cigarettes a day, at first Senior
Service and then Embassy King Size, and they were helping to
kill him.

It was significant that the brands which Joe Burnside and James
Kelly smoked were not mentioned by name. Both had smoked
Embassy as Gillie had noted in his original draft. The brand
names had been omitted just in time. On the page immediately
opposite their story was an advertisement for Embassy. Imperial's
other advertisement for that week, Lambert & Butler, was also
sandwiched in the feature. Nick Hill, *The Sunday Times*
Advertising Director at the time, knew there was trouble coming.
Just before the magazine went to press, he received a telephone
call from its editor, saying that brand names were being
mentioned. Normally in the event of such a conflict between

editorial and advertising content, the advertiser would be forewarned and given the option of pulling out and going in another week. Somehow, in this instance, the system had broken down. Hill says that at that stage it was too late to pull back completely. 'It would have cost us £25,000 to make a new set of plates so we just went ahead, published the damned thing and kept our heads down.' He did, however, ring Masius, the agency which had placed the advertisements, and apologised for the 'cock up'. 'We waited and waited for a few weeks for the shit to hit the fan,' he said, 'and of course when the magazine was published, it did. We buttoned down our tin hats for Monday morning.' Monday morning came, and with it the flak. Hill met with Masius, full of profuse apologies. 'We did our breast-punching bit. *Mea culpa. Mea maxima culpa.* Admin error. Problem. Problem.' Oil was duly poured over the water and Imperial was given a couple of free spots by way of compensation.

Shortly afterwards, the wound was opened again when *The Sunday Times* sports section ran a series on 'How I gave up smoking and became fit' (the section had long been a vociferous opponent of cigarette sponsorship of sporting events). The beleaguered Nick Hill received further representations to the effect, 'Look, you've screwed us in the magazine. What's all this in the sports pages?' The Advertising Director of Times Newspapers, Donald Barrett, then received a telephone call from Imperial's Manager for External Affairs, Trevor King. They had known each other for several years. King suggested they had a meeting at *The Times*. He asked Hill and Barrett *The Sunday Times'* view of cigarette advertising and whether it intended to take a consistently anti-tobacco line, which was the impression he had received from recent articles. King suggested it might be better if *The Sunday Times* took a more 'balanced' view, as there were also good things to be said about tobacco. *The Sunday Times* executives denied there was any absence of 'balance'. At no stage did King ever threaten or hint that Imperial might withdraw its advertising if *The Sunday Times* did not come into line. 'He wasn't in the least bit punchy,' recalls Hill. However, King did suggest that *The Sunday Times* might like to restate its policy on the issue. 'With a company like Imps,' says Hill, 'you're walking on eggs. No way were they going to make threats. Oliver [Gillie] would have been up that drainpipe in a flash.' The ball was back in *The Sunday Times'* court. The issue was taken up at Board level. Harold Evans, then *The Sunday Times* editor, defended his right to editorial freedom. It was not the first time he had sailed in such waters. In the 1970s he had fought a famous campaign against Distillers, the manufacturers of the drug Thalidomide. His campaigning journalism won awards but lost his paper around £5 million worth of advertising. Distillers, as well as making Thalidomide, also made Johnny Walker, Haig and Dewar's whisky, as well as Gordon's Dry Gin. After the Board meeting, Evans called in his medical correspondent, Oliver Gillie, and sports editor, John Lovesey. He informed them that there had been a vigorous discussion: the Advertising Department had accepted that editorially *The Sunday Times* should be free to draw attention to the health risks of smoking but felt very badly let down that the paper was also attacking the advertising of cigarettes and thereby appearing to undermine its own efforts to raise revenue.

Further discussions followed in the upper reaches of *The Sunday Times*. The Board debated whether or not the paper should refuse to accept cigarette advertising as a matter of policy. There was not a majority in favour of such a ban and Harold Evans suggested that such a majority was even more unlikely given the takeover of *The Sunday Times* by the Australian newspaper tycoon, Rupert Murdoch (which had happened in the middle of the colour supplement row). Nevertheless Evans drafted a statement to outline *The Sunday Times'* policy on cigarette advertising—meeting the request for a clarification of policy originally suggested by Imperial's Trevor King. Mr Evans informed me he made four points: first, that it was *The Sunday Times'* policy to cover issues without fear or favour regardless of the advertising content of the paper—and that applied to cigarettes as well; second, that brand names should be published whenever smoking was covered (as indeed Oliver Gillie had done in his heart transplant article); third, that although the paper might occasionally criticise some aspects of cigarette advertising, it was *not* running a campaign against cigarette advertising *per se* (Evans pointed out that such a campaign would be hypocritical in a newspaper which accepted cigarette advertising); and fourth, that the advertising sections of the newspaper were just as free to state product values as the editorial columns were to point out the health risks of smoking.

Oliver Gillie, however, did not agree with the draft and took issue with the suggestion that *The Sunday Times* should *not* run a campaign against cigarette advertising. Gillie sent a sharp response back to Evans saying that the subject was crying out for a major campaign by a newspaper willing to take the consequences and stressing that it was wrong to give an undertaking *not* to campaign on the issue: to do so, Gillie admonished, would signal a sad crumbling of *The Sunday Times'* editorial integrity in the face of advertising pressures.

But the matter was never resolved. After Rupert Murdoch took over Times Newspapers, Harold Evans became editor of *The Times*, and many of the paper's advertising executives left to seek work elsewhere. Imperial moved away from *The Sunday Times* too. They took nearly half a million pounds worth of advertising with them by not rebooking the spots for the coming year. Nick Hill and his colleagues saw this move as a direct result of all that had gone before. Imperial's marketing manager, Brian Cloake, said that the company had decided to switch its advertising to the new *Sunday Express* colour magazine while the future of *The Sunday Times* was 'shaky'.[17] Imperial insisted that the decision was 'wholly commercial', denying the allegation made in the *New Statesman* that it used 'blackmail' to neutralise one of its most effective potential opponents.[18] But Imperial's defection was only temporary. The *Sunday Times* Magazine continued to draw extensively on cigarette advertising revenue. Two and a half years later (July 24th, 1983) the Magazine carried five pages of cigarette advertisements (Imperial one; Rothmans one; BAT one; and Gallahers two) out of a total of thirty-three pages of advertising. Cigarettes were still safe.

These pressures may be subtle, but when the media threatened the image of Philip Morris' Marlboro Cowboy, the response was swift and decisive. The threat was all the more powerful because it came not from newspapers or magazines but from television, which could match Marlboro cowboy for cowboy and image for image. The television programme was called 'Death in the West—the Marlboro Story', and was made by myself and

Director Martin Smith for Thames Television in 1976.[19] This is
how the American TV critic Terry Ann Knopf summed it up:

> The film deals a devastating blow to the Marlboro Man. Taking
> the image-makers at their word, Taylor went out and
> interviewed six real life American cowboys—prototypes of the
> Marlboro Man—who were all one-time heavy smokers and
> now in various stages of dying from cancer or emphysema . . .
> The interviews with the cowboys were followed by statements
> from their doctors attributing their diseases to heavy smoking
> . . . The documentary derives additional force from the icy
> exchanges between reporter . . . and two representatives of
> Philip Morris . . . it stands as a powerful commentary on the
> human toll of Madison Avenue's glamorous portrayal of
> cigarette smoking.[20]

Shortly after 'Death in the West' had been shown in Britain, CBS
'60 Minutes' expressed interest in showing the film on the
American television network.[21] Philip Morris took out an
injunction in the High Court in London, preventing Thames
Television from selling the film or showing it again.[22] Thames and
Philip Morris subsequently agreed to an out of court settlement
and, by consent order, all copies of the film bar one, which was to
remain locked in Thames' vault, were handed over to Philip
Morris.[23] The settlement was to remain a secret.[24] 'Death in the
West' was quietly consigned to Boot Hill. No one attended the
funeral. Between transmission and injunction, the Editor of the
'This Week' series, David Elstein, made it clear to the US
publication *Advertising Age*, that the film was not aimed at
Marlboro alone, but at all cigarettes: 'Our concern was to draw
an exceptionally simple contrast between the view of the
manufacturers and the facts of life out on the range.'[25]

What follows is a mosaic of 'Death in the West' compiled from
press reviews and news stories.

> The scene shows a handsome, rugged, virile cowboy enjoying a
> cigarette as he rides into the sunset. While the majestic theme
> music plays, a deep-voiced announcer says, 'Come to where the
> flavor is. Come to Marlboro Country'.[26]

On the beautiful Western plains, the sun is setting over a majestic mountain backdrop, and a handsome, square-jawed cowboy is stoking a campfire. For the cowboy, Bob Julian, the last roundup was almost over. 'I started smoking when I was a kid following these bronco busters,' he says in a raspy voice. 'I thought that to be a man you had to have a cigarette in your mouth. It took me years to discover that all I got out of it was lung cancer. I'm going to die a young man.' He was right. He died a few months later at 51.[27]

'In my opinion, Mr Julian has lung cancer directly as a result of his smoking,' said the doctor.[28]

The film's message is blunt. One moment, the Marlboro man gallops across the screen. The camera cuts then to a long distance shot of cowboy John Holmes riding the range. Gradually the viewer can make out the oxygen tank draped over his horse, the tubes running into Holmes' nose. Holmes, who smoked a pack a day for 45 years, suffered from emphysema.[29]

Holmes, a New Mexico cattleman, describes how it feels to suffer from emphysema. 'I just have to stop and gasp for breath and it feels like someone has their fingers down in my chest cutting all the air passage off.[30]

Taylor ... then follows these with interviews with their doctors. 'Cigarette smoking, I'm sure, is the cause of John Holmes' pulmonary emphysema'.[31]

Montana is Marlboro country too, the film's narrator says. Ray Madson is a Montana cowboy, a loner, a drifter, a smoker. He had an operation for lung cancer, but his physician tells the interviewer that 'Ray's chances of survival are zero'. 'And the other day I saw this young kid smoking and I told him he shouldn't start what I got into,' Madson tells the interviewer. 'I showed him my scar. It didn't seem to bother him any.'[32]

One champion rodeo rider tells how he struggled for years to quit smoking, then finally collapsed one day and crawled into the barn spitting blood. He had lung cancer.[33]

Another lung cancer victim, a former Wyoming wilderness guide, barely has the strength to speak as the mountain birds twitter in the background. 'He's got no strength, no hope and he doesn't care now,' says his wife.[34]

Philip Morris ... executives were interviewed extensively about the health hazards of cigarettes.[35]

Dr Helmut Wakeham, Philip Morris vice-president for science and technology, is asked 'Can you say that cigarettes do no harm to the cigarette smoker?' The doctor replies 'I'm not in a position to say that. I don't know what harms the cigarette smoker and what doesn't harm him. You must be trying to get me to admit that smoking is harmful.'[36]

Dr Helmut Wakeham (Philip Morris Inc.): 'Anything can be considered harmful. Applesauce is harmful if you get too much of it.'

Question: I don't think many people are dying from apple-sauce.
Dr Wakeham: They're not eating that much.[37]

'I think that if the company as a whole believed cigarettes were really harmful, we would not be in the business,' says Dr Helmut Wakeham. 'We're a very moralistic company.'[38]

Another Philip Morris vice-president, James Bowling, is asked whether cigarettes are harmless. 'I don't know that,' he replies, 'I don't know whether they're harmful or harmless. What I'm saying is, I think somebody should find out.'[39]

Taylor: Is it possible that your refusal to accept the evidence [that smoking is a health hazard] may be coloured by the fact that you make cigarettes?

Bowling: Is that possible? Well, of course that's possible, Peter. I think I'm a fairly reasonable human being and not anyway removed from the others of society. I certainly wouldn't be in the business if I thought cigarettes were harmful to people. I think it's important that there be a lot of us around who are trying to keep the research honest and open. I think the real dishonesty is telling people things that are not so.[40]

[56]

Meanwhile, Philip Morris have engaged a Kansas City law firm who managed to track down the ageing cowpokes ... The lawyers in their report suggest that there is considerable doubt that any of the six were cowboys.[41]

Philip Morris is attempting to discredit the film by saying some of the men weren't really cowboys. 'It was a hoax,' Paul Gibson, a company spokesman, said from New York.[42]

The company obtained an injunction against Thames Television, the producer, charging deception and claiming it was 'sandbagged and double-crossed'.[43]

The nub of the suit was that the cigarette company had been duped into permitting its commercials to be used in a film it thought would depict cigarette smoking more favourably.[44]

In the summer of 1982, I retraced my trail through Marlboro Country. The only surviving cowboy was John Holmes,[45] the owner of a small ranch near Cimarron, New Mexico, whom we had filmed with oxygen cylinder strapped to the saddle,[46] rounding up his cattle. (The others had all died shortly after the film had been shown.) John was now hooked up to his oxygen supply for twenty-four hours a day. Four great cylinders stood in the corridor outside his bedroom and a fifth by the side of his bed, the humidifier bubbling constantly as it fed the oxygen through a thirty-foot rubber tube to which John is now permanently attached. The lifeline is just long enough to enable him to move around his small wooden ranch house. When he steps outside, he takes his 'Linde Walker' with him (a small portable oxygen supply). The day I arrived was just like the day we had filmed with John and his wife, Colette: a clear blue sky over the great plains of Cimarron and thunder clouds rumbling over the distant mountains. We sat eating 'son of a gun' stew which John had prepared. On the wall of the small dining-room was a 'Thank you for not smoking' sign. He reminisced about his days as a smoker. 'I did start early, when I was about seventeen, and stayed with it for forty years. I used to inhale. That was the glory of smoking. You inhale and you can feel it going down. It gives you a "lift", especially in the morning—much as I expect dope would give you today.' I asked him how he felt nowadays. 'It hurts like hell when you get short of breath, and you get to heavin' and tryin' to push the air out and get some more air in. There's hardly no way I can describe it.' (John quit smoking eleven years ago, on the way home from the hospital the day the doctor told him he had emphysema.)

He told me that on November 30th, 1976, he and his wife Colette had had visitors. 'I was out in the yard one day, sitting out by the tractor, enjoying the sunshine. A car pulled into the driveway and two men got out and asked for John Holmes. I told them they were looking at him.' (John didn't have to wear his breathing apparatus all the time in those days.) 'They started asking me questions: What did I think had caused my emphysema? How did I make my living? I said I'd been ranching here for twenty years since I bought the place—I taught school in the winter and raised cattle in the summer time. They tried to prove I'd done other things and wasn't a *bona fide* cowboy. They were trying to trap me. I was just as much a cowboy as anybody could be. You try to fool with cattle and not be a cowboy and you're in trouble! I had to ask them several times who they were and what they were questioning me for. They just said they represented a law firm in Kansas City, and they were out here checking on the film. One took notes while the other asked questions. After Colette came, they finally admitted they worked for Philip Morris.'

Colette recalled the unexpected visit. 'When I drew up, I saw John in serious conversation with two persons. I had to drag the Philip Morris connection out. I looked one of them directly in the eyes and asked him three or four times, "Are you with Philip Morris? Are you representing Philip Morris?" He avoided it as long as he could. In order to continue the conversation he had to say "yes". They were very reluctant to admit it. They were very polite and businesslike. They weren't belligerent—that wasn't their style.'

Both John and Colette had been greatly upset at what had happened to the film. 'I thought it was going to be used to keep people from smoking—especially younger people,' said John. 'I felt frustrated. They probably had all the money and the smart lawyers.' Colette felt the same way. 'I was so excited about the potential,' she said, 'and then it disappeared. It was like a dream.

It was very powerful evidence based on truth and on peoples' lives. There's nothing more powerful than that. They were intimidated by it and wanted at all costs to prevent its showing. They had the power, the lawyers and the funds to do that. It's just wrong.'

John, despite his infirmity, still farms 170 acres and raises fifty head of cattle. 'I'm gonna have to get rid of some of them,' he reflected, 'but I won't till I have to—even if I'm a little money out of pocket. It gives me something to do. I want to keep moving. I don't want to sit around and die off slowly.'

On my way to New Mexico, I visited Mrs Beatrice Farris[47] in Mustang, Oklahoma, the widow of 'Junior' Farris, the champion rodeo rider. Junior's youngest daughter, Terry, and his oldest son, Bill, met me at the airport and took me to Wheatlands Cemetery where he was buried in the family plot next to his father. A single white geranium grew alongside a marble slab that simply said: 'Maurice Seabron "Junior"—February 12, 1914—July 11, 1977'. Engraved at the side was a horse's head. All the family had gathered at home to meet me, sitting round a television set from which 'M.A.S.H.' flickered silently. Little had changed since my earlier visit in 1976. The mantelpiece was still stacked high with 'Junior's' rodeo trophies. Mrs Farris produced a leather wallet full of her husband's memorabilia: pictures of him with one of the prize 'quarter' horses which he used to breed; photographs of him chasing a calf at full tilt at an indoor rodeo. Some of the family wept quietly as we sat round and talked. 'If there was anyone in the world who could have overcome lung cancer, "Junior" Farris would have done it,' said Mrs Farris defiantly. 'He enjoyed his smoking, he really did,' she reflected. 'He'd go into his nicotine fits. He had a problem. He couldn't stop. He had a heart attack and the doctor said, "You light up one more, and we'll have to throw some dirt in your face".' Mrs Farris mentioned that 'Junior' had also had two visitors after the film. 'I believe two attorneys asked him questions and followed him around. I believe "Junior" said they were from a tobacco company.' I asked the family if they thought he had been a 'cowboy'. 'What do you call someone who works with horses and cattle? A livestock person?' said Bill. 'He may not have been a movie cowboy, but in my estimation he was a true cowboy. He rode horses, he rounded up cattle, he roped, he branded. What more is there to being a cowboy?' There was real anger about the suppression of the film. 'I thought it was going to be shown in schools and all over the place to the kids,' said Mrs Farris. ' "Junior" would have loved to have seen it.' As we left for the airport, Terry said, as if to herself, 'Dad said he was going to die with his boots on. He didn't.'

Nor did Bob Julian, the brand inspector from Wyoming whom we had filmed sitting by a campfire as the sun went down. He told us he thought he was going to die a young man.[48] Bob died the following year. 'He used to be a terribly heavy smoker,' his widow Dixie Julian told me, when I visited her in Kemmerer, Wyoming.[49] 'He used to smoke them right down. I never knew how he took the last puff without burning his nose. Whether cutting sheep or working cows, he always had a cigarette in his mouth. He never gave the health risks a thought. They advertise plenty for the cigarettes, but not about the risks. He started when he was eleven, rolling his own. They used to smoke cedar bark off the fence posts until his father finally bought him some tobacco. I thought it was a real shame the film was never shown again. I think it should be shown to the kids in school.'

The Kansas City attorneys also visited Bob Julian. I asked his widow how she reacted to the suggestion that her husband was not a 'cowboy'. 'That really made me mad,' she said. 'He'd worked with livestock all his life, not only cattle but sheep and horses. I can remember him talking about running cows in off the range with his brothers. They were raised out on the ranch. That's the way they lived. To my sense, he was a real cowboy. I never did figure out what Marlboro figured was a cowboy.'

As Bob's condition deteriorated, he went to Salt Lake City, three hours' drive away, for cobalt radiation treatment. The family now had an oxygen cylinder in the car, as his breathing was becoming increasingly difficult. 'We'd have to go past the cemetery once in a while,' remembered Mrs Julian. 'Whenever he saw somebody being buried he'd say, "There's a lucky one. That ought to be me". He was getting really depressed. It was very, very hard. He kept working right to the end. He fought it. He'd inspected a truckload of horses out in front of the house that morning before we left.' It was Bob's last trip to Salt Lake City. 'When we got down there, his lungs had filled up with fluid. I

wanted to stay. He wouldn't let me.' By the time Mrs Julian got
back to Kemmerer, Bob was dead. 'I didn't cry at the funeral,' she
told me. 'People thought it was strange. I'd done all my crying in
the eight months before. When he died, it was a blessing for him.'
Mrs Julian took me to his grave, on a hillside overlooking the
railway track. A sagebrush was growing over it. 'Bob always said,
"You can plant a sagebrush on my grave." A lot of Wyoming
people always take sagebrush with them when they move.'

I then drove a hundred miles across Wyoming through the real
Marlboro Country of the advertisements, to Pinedale. In La
Barge, a stop on the way, the lady in the tiny US Post Office told
me that Marlboro had made some of their commericals in the
neighbourhood. 'They brought their own cowboy and borrowed
local horses,' she said. 'They wanted them with long tails, so they
looked wild. I know, because they used some of ours.' Pinedale
was also the home of the most famous Marlboro Cowboy of them
all, Darrell Winfield,[50] the man with the moustache, whose
rugged, weatherbeaten face is familiar the world over. The small
dusty town nestles at the foot of the Bridger Wilderness, among
some of the most spectacular mountain scenery in North
America. Harold Lee had been one of its mountain guides.

I went to see his widow, Mrs Freda Lee,[51] who had described
her dying husband so movingly in the film: 'He's just a poor little
old man. No strength, no hope, he just doesn't care.'[52] In summer,
Harold used to take visitors from all over the United States on
fishing trips in his sixteen-foot flat-bottomed boat, along the
Green River which flows from the mountains down onto the
Wyoming plain. Harold Lee died on October 19th, 1976, a few
days before Bob Julian. 'He died in his own home,' Mrs Lee told
me. 'It just looked like he lay there and starved. He couldn't eat
anything. He said, "Why me? There's millions of people that have
smoked all their lives." I think Harold knew over the years that
cigarettes were just one more nail in his coffin.' His daughter
Linda added, 'Daddy said when he was still lucid, "You know,
they're going to have a cure for this in three to five years." But they
haven't. There is no cure.' They took me down to the Green River
and showed me the spot where Harold used to keep his boat. 'The
Green River was his love,' they said. 'He could get fish out of that
river when nobody else could. They loved to go fishing with him

because they always brought fish home.' When Harold died, Mrs Lee and Linda went down to the Green River with the family Bible and sprinkled his ashes on the water, as he had always wanted. 'That was his wish,' said Linda. 'He wanted to be cremated and put on the Green River. Mummy read the Lord's Prayer at the place he used to put his boat in, and I scattered the ashes. It was almost as if the river was talking to us. It was Daddy's day. He's probably happier now than he ever was—the best fishing trip ever. That's how he told me to think about it.' The Kansas City attorneys arrived in Pinedale a few days after Harold Lee died.

But 'Death in the West', though legally dead, was still breathing. On December 1st, 1981,[53] a brown envelope arrived in the San Francisco office of Dr Stanton Glantz, an associate professor of Medicine at the University of California, and a non-smokers' rights activist. Inside was a videotape of 'Death in the West'. I have no idea who sent it. After months of legal consultation, Dr Glantz turned the film over to the California Nonsmokers' Rights Foundation, which had been formed by a coalition of anti-smoking groups in the state. Dozens of copies of the tape were made and sent to newspapers and TV stations all over the country. On May 11th, 1982 'Death in the West' was given new life by the NBC affiliate station in San Francisco, KRON-TV. KRON showed the whole film followed by a half-hour discussion of the issues it raised. The response was so great (3,000 calls jammed the switchboard[54]) that the station showed it again. I was not involved in any of these screenings or in any of the subsequent transmissions of the programme. Once KRON had broken cover, other TV stations across the country followed, transmitting the film either in full or in part: KGO-TV in Los Angeles; WCVB-TV (Channel 5) in Boston (where it won the highest rating of its time slot)[55]; the CBS Evening News; and NBC's 'Monitor' programme which conducted an in-depth investigation into the fate of the film and its repercussions. It was also shown in Washington State (on KING-TV in Seattle), in Chicago (on WTTW-TV), in North Carolina—Tobacco Country—(on WBTV in Charlotte), and in Wichita, Kansas—Marlboro Country. Dr Glantz was even flown to Rome to discuss the programme on Italian television.

But the real vindication of 'Death in the West' was still to come. One of the main reasons why Ray Madsen, 'Junior' Farris, John Harlin, Bob Julian, Harold Lee and John Holmes had agreed to participate in the programme was the hope that their suffering might serve as a warning to young people, in particular those adolescents who, like themselves, had taken up the habit at a very early age. They had told me in moving terms how they hoped that schoolchildren would see the programme. Seven years later they did. In the spring of 1983 Dr Stanton Glantz, and two other academics—Dr Alan Schnur and Herbert Thier of the Lawrence Hall of Science at the University of California, Berkeley— collaborated in the production of a thirty-page curriculum for upper elementary and junior high school students based on 'Death in the West'. The curriculum was designed to be used in conjunction with a videotape of the programme which would first be shown to the class. (According to Dr Glantz, seventy to eighty per cent of teenagers who smoke, smoke Marlboro.) KRON-TV, the station which had first aired the programme, helped finance the curriculum and launched the schools project by showing 'Death in the West' for the *third* time on May 26th, 1983. According to Dr Glantz, 'the response surpassed everyone's wildest expectations'. By the time the Bay Area schools broke up for the 1983 summer vacation, 88,000 schoolchildren had watched the programme and completed the curriculum. The subsequent evaluation conducted by Dr Glantz and Dr Schnur strongly suggested that the project had 'changed those attitudes that lead to smoking among youth, thereby preventing many youngsters from beginning to smoke'.

'Death in the West' also became a cult in Australia. In Melbourne the videotape came into the hands of an organisation called Mop-Up (the Movement Opposing the Promotion of Unhealthy Products) which had been formed to oppose Marlboro's sponsorship of Australian tennis. Mop-Up was a coalition of doctors, teachers, academics and community health workers. The film was first shown at a public meeting attended by about fifty people who raised $1,000 (Australian) in a collection at the end to finance further distribution of the programme. An explanatory pamphlet was printed and sent out to schools, colleges and health centres across Australia. It read:

For teenagers in Australia and the world over, the Marlboro brand has a well-proven appeal. The image of toughness, independence and open space has been a winner for the Philip Morris Co. This film goes beyond the romance, to the reality. It blows the Marlboro myth apart . . . we need to help kids to de-code advertisements, to help them understand the manipulation involved . . . It should, we believe, be shown to every school student in Australia.

Copies of the tape (and a teacher's guide) were offered for sale at $25 apiece—a price heavily subsidised by the $1,000 raised at the initial public meeting. By the summer of 1983, six hundred tapes had been sold in the state of Victoria alone.

It is interesting to speculate what might have happened if the film had never been suppressed. Would it have become the object of such controversy? Would it have been seen by tens of thousands of shoolchildren? Would it have raised issues wider than those of smoking and health? Certainly if 'Death in the West' had travelled its natural course, it might have been seen by Ray, 'Junior', John, Bob and Harold before they died—and by John Holmes before he became still more infirm. However, thanks to the efforts of Dr Stanton Glantz and dozens of television stations, most of their widows have now watched the film they thought had been buried for ever. Those I spoke to were moved by what they had seen and proud of what their husbands had done. In particular they were gratified by the educational use to which the programme was now being put—which had always been their husbands' wish. Time ensured that the wish was granted.

4

The Golden Goose

Defending the tobacco industry in a debate in the European Parliament in 1980, the British Euro MP and Chairman of Rothmans International, Sir David Nicolson, reminded his listeners that tax returns from tobacco throughout the European Community were almost as great as the total European budget. Sir David declared:

> I think we must realise . . . that one of the prime activities of this industry is in effect to act as a tax collector for the government concerned. This is something we are very much aware of and something which I believe the governments are very much aware of also. I therefore think that they will proceed very cautiously before they kill the goose which lays such a big golden egg.

Sir David added that there were no less than 180,000 people employed in the tobacco industry within the EEC, and that these were economic facts which were 'relevant to any future debate on the subject of public health policy'.[1]* Sir David was right. No one knows better than the chairman of a tobacco company how

---

* The EEC Member States also pay around $650 million a year in subsidies to the Community's 225,000 tobacco growers in Italy, Greece, Germany, France and Belgium.[2]

tightly these economic facts and figures bind governments to the Smoke Ring. They also provide the industry with a reservoir of support from across the political spectrum, not just from politicians who represent areas where tobacco provides thousands of jobs, but from trade unionists, obliged to defend the interests of their workers. These are the economic reasons why wealth comes before health. The story is the same all over the world. Later chapters deal with America and the developing countries. This chapter deals with Britain.

The political conflict between wealth and health is as old as tobacco itself. Governments have long condemned it, whilst rubbing their hands at the money it brings into their Treasuries. When King James I came to the English throne in 1603, he described smoking in *A Counter-Blaste to Tobacco* as 'a custom loathsome to the eye, hateful to the nose, harmful to the brain, dangerous to the lungs'. To discourage smoking, he increased the tax on tobacco by 4,000 per cent from two pence a pound to six shillings and eight pence a pound. He then found that tobacco was a source of much-needed revenue which was not being fully tapped because people could not afford to smoke. He slashed the tax to two shillings a pound, and money poured into the royal coffers.[3] Governments have been hooked on tobacco ever since.

Tobacco is the Chancellor of the Exchequer's third biggest source of consumer revenue. In 1981, his total income was £22 billion: £11 billion came from Value Added Tax (VAT); £3.6 billion from hydrocarbon oil; £2.8 billion from tobacco; £2.6 billion from wine, spirits and beer; and £460 million from betting and gaming.[4] An analysis of the cost of a packet of twenty cigarettes shows why governments hold tobacco so dear: the retailer gets roughly ten pence; the manufacturer fifteen pence; and the Chancellor seventy-five pence. It is also the cheapest of all the duties to collect. A notional ring is drawn around each factory, within which cigarettes can be manufactured and moved around duty-free. The moment they are delivered to the retailer, the duty becomes payable. Her Majesty's Customs and Excise, the government department which collects the revenue, give the manufacturers thirty days in which to pay up, to allow them time to get the money back from the retailers. On the fifteenth day of every month, they dip into the manufacturers' bank account

[66]

through direct debit and take out the millions of pounds which the companies owe the government according to computerised records.

Cigarettes are the government's simplest and most effective mechanism for raising money. In 1981, faced with a back bench revolt over the budget, when MPs refused to ratify an increase in the duty on diesel oil, the Chancellor simply added an extra three pence to the price of a packet of twenty cigarettes as a way of making up the difference: this was in addition to the increase of fourteen pence which he had already announced in his budget. (Despite this double increase, cigarettes were still cheaper in real terms than they were in 1962 when the British Royal College of Physicians published its first Report.) But governments know they walk a fine line, and must avoid increases which lead to a drop in revenue as well as a drop in consumption—the number of cigarettes sold. Between 1977 and 1981, cigarette consumption in the United Kingdom dropped from 126 billion cigarettes to 110 billion[5] as a result of a series of heavy tax increases. In the same period, despite this dramatic drop, governments still raised an additional £1 billion in revenue.[6] Governments know that the goose is a hardy creature but have no wish to see it stop laying the golden eggs. (Throughout the 1970s, British governments did much to ensure the industry's continuing prosperity, with £25 million worth of regional assistance grants and over £5 million in interest relief grants for modernisation of plant and machinery— see Appendix 1.)

Every year statisticians and economists from the Customs and Excise Planning Unit go into purdah and emerge with a figure which represents a probable drop in consumption which would follow the duty increase they propose to put forward to the Chancellor. The Planning Unit generally assesses its tobacco package on the basis of the annual rate of inflation, and then sends it over to the Chancellor, who usually tells them to double it. The tobacco companies obviously want the government to keep the increases down to a minimum. At the end of every calendar year, they send their marketing directors and accountants round to Customs and Excise headquarters for a meeting with officials. They invariably predict disaster if there are further duty increases, leading to further drops in consumption. They point to the figures, and tell the officials how many redundancies the previous year's increase led to, and the threat of closure which now may hang over a particular factory. They remind the tax men how important the industry is to the country's economy, not in the belief that the officials are in a position to do anything about it, but perhaps more in the hope that some of their message may rub off as they prepare their package for the Treasury. 'They don't miss a trick,' remarked an insider.

The industry recognises the need to cultivate senior civil servants, not just from Customs and Excise, but from all government departments concerned with tobacco, and has the resources to ensure that such relationships are developed in the most desirable surroundings. While Imperial entertains at the Glyndebourne Opera, BAT invites its contacts to the Wimbledon Tennis Championships. Between 1978 and 1981, BAT's guest list at Wimbledon included thirty-six civil servants from government departments which included Customs and Excise, the Treasury, the Department of Industry, and the Cabinet Office. One of BAT's high-ranking guests was Sir Douglas Lovelock, the Chairman of the Board of HM Customs and Excise. Sir Douglas attended strictly in accordance with the terms of the Civil Service Pay and Conditions of Service Code (see Appendix2). In response to a question submitted by the Director of Action on Smoking and Health, David Simpson, at the company's AGM on June 17th, 1981 (ASH holds one share in each of the tobacco companies which enables it to ask questions on these occasions), BAT's Chairman, Sir Peter McAdam, explained the reasons for the Company's hospitality:

We take the view that it is important for us to maintain good and cordial relations with a wide variety of business contacts. On a number of occasions, and Wimbledon is one of them, each of our Operating Groups entertains important overseas and domestic customers, suppliers, government officials and diplomatic representatives. In our view, the maintenance of good relations in the areas I have just mentioned is very much in the interest of our shareholders.

The issue remains sensitive within the civil service. 'They're a very hospitable industry,' one civil servant told me. He said that after a question on the matter had been asked in the House of Commons, he had been rung up by his Permanent Secretary and asked if he had been to Wimbledon. He said he had, paid £8.50 for his own ticket, and never been anywhere near the BAT tent. He said he had also been offered a helicopter ride to the Marlboro British Grand Prix at Brand's Hatch. 'We're very circumspect,' he said sagely. A civil servant in another government department told me that tickets were offered for the Benson & Hedges cricket final at Lords. I asked if they were accepted. A press officer intervened and forestalled the answer. He said the question was not significant. Another civil servant in a further department that dealt with the industry said, 'They're super efficient. They have resources. They are powerful, and they're listened to.'

But the real lobbying is done at the political level, where the same tried and tested economic arguments are used. The industry's most potent political defence is that the country (which means the governments who run it) simply cannot afford to be without tobacco. In difficult economic times such arguments tend to fall on receptive ears. In 1981, a time when cigarettes were under attack from health ministers anxious to put health before wealth (see Chapter Eight), the industry marshalled its economic defence through a study commissioned by its trade organisation, the Tobacco Advisory Council. It was called 'The UK Tobacco Industry: Its Economic Significance'[7] and was carried out by two Scottish economists, Professor Donald Mackay and Ronald Edwards. They concluded that tobacco provided: £4 billion worth of government revenue; 35,000 manufacturing jobs, and 264,000 jobs overall associated with tobacco; a trade surplus of £245 million on the balance of payments (twenty-two per cent of all cigarettes made in the UK are exported); and consumer expenditures of £4.8 billion—nearly four per cent of all the money people spent in Britain. This is the economic ammunition which the industry supplies to its political allies in the House of Common's. They number around a hundred MPs and include the companies' paid parliamentary consultants, such as Imperial's Sir John Langford-Holt (until 1983) and BAT's Sir Anthony Kershaw; those with constituency interests in tobacco, such as Harvey Proctor, MP until 1983 for Basildon, where Rothmans employ around

1,000, and James Molyneaux of Northern Ireland, where
Gallahers employs 3,400; those with trade union connections,
such as Glasgow's Michael Martin, former shop steward, for
whose constituents Imperial provides valuable jobs; those whose
constituents depend on jobs provided by Imperial's many
subsidiaries, like Dr Gerard Vaughan of Reading, where Imperial
has one of its largest Courage breweries; those who have interests
in marketing and consultancy, like former Labour Minister for
Sport, Denis Howell; and those such as Conservative Martin
Stevens, who have strong ideological reasons for supporting the
industry on the grounds that the state should not 'nanny' the
individual. (Mr Stevens was also a consultant to the advertising
agency Wells O'Brien—until it went into receivership in June
1983—although he had no connection with any cigarette
account.) This powerful political coalition which spans all parties
from left to right is the industry's eyes, ears and mouthpiece at
Westminster. It is well briefed on the need to preserve the health of
the golden goose.

Michael Colvin formerly the Conservative MP for Bristol
North-west (where Imperial employs 4,600), and now MP for
Southampton (Romsey and Waterside), told me how the
Chancellor would be lobbied in the long run-up to the budget. He
would first have a word with his Labour colleagues from Bristol,
such as Chief Whip Michael Cocks, and discuss strategy. They
would agree to corner the Chancellor in the Division lobby which
MPs enter to vote. Members have eight minutes to go in and six
minutes to get out. 'You can mix it with him if three or four of you
spread yourselves out and ambush him,' he explained, 'I say to
him, "Quite honestly, you can't go on clobbering the tobacco
industry the way you are, because the time is going to come when
the industry isn't going to be able to bear it any longer. Sales have
really dropped. What are you going to do next year? The time is
coming when you're going to get less revenue back. Honestly, give
the tobacco industry a breather. Go and clobber someone else for
a change." ' This would be Stage One of the operation, carried out
just before Christmas. Stage Two would come in the New Year as
the time for the spring budget approached. Mr Colvin said he
would probably meet with Imperial and might even get his
colleagues together and go and see the Chancellor as an official

delegation, just to talk about the industry. 'We M Ps get through to Ministers more easily than Imperial,' he said. 'They get through to civil servants.'

These economic arguments are effective because they confirm what governments know already. But those concerned with public health argue that governments are misguided and misled: that the calculations are wrong; that the real cost of cigarettes to the nation is far greater than the economic benefits they bring. In its 1971 Report, 'Smoking and Health Now', the Royal College of Physicans said:

> It appears that the government's failure to take any effective preventive action is based on the fear that the country can neither afford to lose the revenue derived from tobacco taxation nor tolerate the economic consequences of running down the tobacco industry. Unofficial assessment, however, suggests that this fear may be mistaken.[8]

The Report recommended that the government should carry out an official inquiry into the economic consequences of a decrease in cigarette smoking and publish a full account of the balance sheet. The government accepted the recommendation and set out a special working party of senior officials from government departments concerned with tobacco to make 'a realistic assessment of the economic and other implications of a reduction in cigarette smoking'. The inquiry was chaired by a senior official from the Cabinet Office and included officials from the Treasury, Customs and Excise, the Department of Trade and Industry and the Department of Health and Social Security. The result of their investigation was never published. The document they produced called 'Cigarette Smoking and Health—Report by an Inter-departmental Group of Officials' was marked 'Confidential' and never saw the light of day until a copy came into the hands of *The Guardian* nearly ten years later. The newspaper published a detailed account of its contents on May 6th, 1980.

The officials based their calculations on a twenty per cent and forty per cent reduction in the smoking population. They estimated that if there was no reduction in smoking, around one and a half million people would die prematurely by the year 2000.

If there was a twenty per cent reduction in smoking over the next three decades, they calculated that a quarter of a million lives would be saved: if there was a forty per cent drop, the number would be doubled. There would also be a considerable reduction in the number of days lost at work through sickness. The officials then calculated the effect on various government departments. The Department of Health and Social Security, which might have been expected to have been the main beneficiary of a drop in smoking, was in fact a loser in purely economic terms. Because people live longer, there would be a significant increase in the retired population whom the state would have to support, and the Department of Health and Social Security would have to pay the bill. Although they calculated that a twenty per cent reduction in smoking would save the government £4 million in health care costs by 1981, increased social security payments would mean that the reduction would be costing an *additional* £12 million by the year 2001. A forty per cent fall would cost the government even more in the long term—an extra £29 million by the turn of the century. The officials concluded that, contrary to what was sometimes suggested, some small savings in health expenditure would in the end be more than offset by increased social security payments.

They then considered the effect on revenue. In 1971, tobacco duty yielded just over £1 billion. On the principle that people would spend what they saved by not smoking on other taxable consumer goods, they calculated that in five years the net loss to the revenue, resulting from a twenty per cent drop in smoking, would be £150 million: the loss for a forty per cent drop would be £305 million. The net loss, they said, was inevitable because taxes on cigarettes (then sixty-nine per cent) were more than three times the taxes on other consumer items (mainly taxed at twenty per cent), on which ex-smokers would now spend their money. They said that the notion that there would be a saving as there would be fewer tobacco imports, was false. Many of the goods on which people would be likely to spend their money would be imported which would lead to an additional burden on the balance of payments. They calculated that a twenty per cent reduction in smoking would lead to an increased trade deficit of £50 million at the end of the five-year period: a forty per cent reduction would double it. Increased domestic demand would outweigh the savings on tobacco imports.

They also considered the effects on employment. They said they would be minimal as the numbers involved, around 46,000 (in 1971), were not large. But they warned that there might be factory closures, in particular in areas which already had high rates of unemployment—involving Gallahers in Northern Ireland, Imperial in Scotland, and Rothmans in the North-east.

If all these economic consequences were bad news for the government, they were even worse for the tobacco industry. The officials concluded that a forty per cent reduction in smoking would 'virtually wipe out' the industry's profits and possibly lead the parent companies of Gallahers and Rothmans to withdraw from the United Kingdom altogether. The message from Whitehall was clear: the government could not afford to do without cigarettes.

In ten years, little has changed. The sums still work in the industry's favour. In 1982, tobacco revenue of £4 billion (including VAT) paid for nearly a third of the cost of the National Health Service (£14 billion). The cost of smoking-related diseases to the NHS (£165 million a year) remains a fraction of total tobacco revenue. Even taking into account the fifty million working days a year lost through illnesses caused by smoking (experts have tried to calculate the cost but failed), the total cost of cigarettes to the nation is estimated to be considerably less than half the £4 billion revenue which tobacco brings in. Wealth beats health every time.

Because of the precious jobs it creates, the tobacco industry inevitably draws trade unionists into the political battle, thereby acquiring some unlikely ideological allies. These include not just members of the Tobacco Workers Union, which is left wing on most issues except tobacco, but some of Britain's biggest and most powerful trade unions: the Transport and General Workers Union, which organises in Bristol and Northern Ireland; the General and Municipal Workers Union, which organises in Nottingham; and the Association of Scientific, Technical and Managerial Staffs (ASTMS), many of whose members hold white-collar jobs throughout the industry. With over three million unemployed, the trade union movement is anxious to preserve every job it can. The city of Glasgow is an illustration of how important tobacco is to trade unionists and the MPs who support them at Westminster.

Nearly two-thirds of Scotland's tobacco workers are employed in the city whose prosperity was once built on tobacco. Glasgow's links with the trade go back to the seventeenth century, when Scottish ships were given access to the new English colonies in Virginia. Many of the early city fathers were tobacco barons. The Mitchell family was to Glasgow what Wills were to Bristol and Players to Nottingham. They were great public benefactors too, and gave Glasgow one of the finest public libraries in Scotland. At the turn of the century, the city's prosperity was built on heavy engineering, shipbuilding and tobacco. Today, the first two great industries are in decline, and even tobacco faces an uncertain future. Imperial's Alexandra Parade factory is all that is left of the heritage and it too is shedding workers. Cigarette production is being transferred to Bristol under the company's new rationalisation plans, leaving Glasgow poorer by another 400 jobs by 1984. Alexandra Parade will then only make cigars and pipe tobacco. Imperial's factory is one of the few left standing in an area devastated by unemployment. The leather works, the chemical works, the carpet factories and the engineering firms have all closed down. The east end of the city where the factory is located is what social workers call 'an area of multiple deprivation', with no jobs, bad housing, crime and all the social problems which such conditions breed. Alexandra Parade was built in the 1950s and expanded to meet the increasing demand for cigarettes. Whole families use to work there. People queued up to get in. A job at Alexandra Parade seemed a job for life. For years, the Tobacco Workers Union tried to halt the natural slippage in jobs by ensuring that a new person was taken on for every one who left. The union has now given up the struggle and accepted the inevitable. In the summer of 1982 there were 2,652 people without work in the Bridgeton area,[9] which normally provides the factory with its workforce. Nor is there any escape to find work in the south of the city. The jobs have gone there too. The Clyde Iron Steelworks is an empty shell, and sections of the Clydebridge Steelworks have been bulldozed into the ground. Redundancies are everywhere, from the Hoover factory to the 'Chunky Chicken' plant.

Michael Martin, the former shop steward and Labour MP for Glasgow Springburn, the area where Imperial's factory is located, has tried unsuccessfully to persuade Imperial to bring some of the other things it makes into the constituency. 'The wealth of the Imperial group was created by tobacco workers,' he told me. 'We help them when they need us. Imperial use me and other MPs with constituency interests when they've got problems at Westminster. Now it's time for them to help us. It's damaging for someone's health to be on the dole.'

The story is the same in other parts of the country, in Belfast, Liverpool, Newcastle and the North-east. Many workers in these areas found jobs in tobacco when they had been discarded by the industries in which they had once worked. In South Wales, many tobacco workers were former miners; in Newcastle and Stirling they had once been miners too; in Spennymoor and Darlington they were redundant textile workers; in Glasgow, Newcastle and Liverpool they were former shipyard workers. The National Executive of the Tobacco Workers Union bears testimony to the huge industrial upheaval of the 1970s. Two of its members were once officials of the National Union of Mineworkers; one is an ex-steel worker; another an ex-boilermaker; another a former dyer and bleacher.[10] Understandably, these workers do not want to see the tobacco industry die and their jobs disappear as they had done before.

Charles Grieve, General Secretary of the Tobacco Workers Union, and himself once a worker at the old Mitchell factory in Glasgow, placed the redundancies in perspective. 'Before the war, the tobacco industry was very secure, and from the late Fifties onwards it was more secure than most. You could only get a job through family connections. It was great in the boom period. Wages were good. But it's all changed now. Back in the Thirties, in the Depression, people could still afford to smoke. Most workers would buy five Woodbines between two lads. People can't afford to smoke now. Cigarettes are the first thing people cut out when times are hard—except for the women. They need them to cope with the stress when the men are on the dole.' But he did not blame anti-smoking organisations like Action on Smoking and Health for the job losses. 'When the industry argues its case with the government, they always use the issue of jobs, which is quite natural. But from our point of view new technology has meant more job losses to our members than the smoking and health issue. But there's no statistic we can pin down. There's no way that we can find out that Joe Bloggs has lost his job because sales have dropped another million a week.'

The General Secretary of the Tobacco Workers Union is a strange ideological bedfellow for the tobacco industry. On the mantelpiece in his office stands a bust of Lenin and a plaque of East Berlin. Alongside them is a photograph of a Right to Abortion rally in London's Trafalgar Square, with Charles Grieve on the platform. The Tobacco Workers Union has always espoused 'progressive' causes: it was one of the founders of the Campaign for Nuclear Disarmament (CND) and the anti-apartheid movement. Tobacco workers have a long tradition of militancy, going back to the nineteenth century when cigar workers fought for equal pay for women. Charles Grieve did not recognise any contradiction between fighting for these 'progressive' causes, and fighting to preserve the health of the tobacco industry. He said the union had a duty to represent the interests of its members. What about the health issue? He catalogued his union's achievements: it had pioneered leave for pregnant women; it had introduced breast screening and cervical smear testing in the workplace; its safety record was second to none. But were not all these laudable health concerns all the more reason for the union to be aware of the dangers of smoking? 'Every time we try to put a "sensible approach", we are pooh-poohed,' he replied. 'We've questioned some of the health evidence when it's repeated by those who aren't experts. There are so many pundits on the scene now. Our line is the truthful one. We're not qualified. We do read and study all the viewpoints. The companies give us an unwritten guarantee they'll provide us with any material we can't afford because of the cost. They're good at giving us assistance.'

But despite the jobs at stake and the interest of some of its most powerful members the Trades Union Congress (TUC) has publicly taken a strong anti-smoking line as well as trying to tackle the problem at shop floor level. But it too has run into problems in trying to get its message across. In December 1981, in response to a resolution passed at its annual Congress earlier in the year, the TUC prepared for battle. Its Social Insurance and Industrial Welfare Committee (SIIWC) drew up a confidential document entitled 'Smoking and Health'. The committee reported that more days were lost through smoking than through industrial action, and that the issue was of concern to trade unionists because fifty-six per cent of smokers were unskilled manual workers. They recommended a smoking control programme:

To change the behaviour of the smoker and the potential smoker;

To change the cigarette smoked so that it is less harmful;

To change the cultural background of society against which cigarette smoking is often viewed as a status symbol representing success and sophistication;

To establish the realistic view, which is that cigarettes are both unnecessary and hazardous;

To establish the right of the non-smoker to clean air;

To change the economic and legislative climate so that cigarettes are less readily available, that pressures promoting smoking are ceased and education programmes are supported and reinforced.

The Tobacco Workers Union got hold of a copy of the SIIWC document and were angry that they had not been consulted. They dismissed it as a 'scandalous state of affairs', and said it was 'little more than a rehash of propaganda'.[11] They saw it as a direct attack on their industry which endangered their members' jobs. They asked whether the TUC would have dared draw up such a document if the industry and jobs affected had been those of railwaymen, steelworkers or miners. They attacked the Committee's report as the work of 'ill-informed and dictatorial zealots'. They said the attempt to change smokers' behaviour was:

. . . a chilling expression which might perhaps be appropriate for the treatment of psychopathic inmates of Broadmoor, or what one expects from the gaolers in Pinochet's concentration camps which is surely alien to the TUC.[12]

One of the Tobacco Workers Union's strongest allies was ASTMS, which has 5,000 members working in the tobacco industry around the country. But ASTMS' support was far from unanimous. Its flamboyant General Secretary, Clive Jenkins, is an outspoken anti-smoker and the union has many more members working in the National Health Service and the medical profession than it has in tobacco. The Health and Safety Officer for one of the union's Birmingham branches, Mr D. J. Brooks, said scathingly, 'I notice ASTMS have joined the Tobacco Lobby', and accused the union's national organiser of peddling 'every phony argument put forward by that unprincipled body of profit-seekers'. He concluded:

I, for one, would prefer my union to spend its time and money on some worthier cause than supporting the tobacco manufacturers in their desperate attempts to justify the unjustifiable. Instead let our officials, lay representatives and sponsored MPs divert themselves to supporting the current TUC campaign against smoking.[13]

Despite support from sections of other trade unions, the Tobacco Workers failed to torpedo the SIIWC document. At the TUC's annual conference in September 1982, its recommendations became official TUC policy. It was a notable victory for the health lobby, and in particular for Action on Smoking and Health which had done much work behind the scenes in collaboration with the Health Education Council.

But it was not a victory that could readily be translated to the political level. Although jobs were at stake, they concerned only a handful of Britain's twelve million trade unionists. There was no revenue involved. The industry had few friends to call on within the TUC. For once health had a clear run—at least until it ran into Labour party politics. Given the TUC's endorsement of the Social Insurance and Industrial Welfare Committee report, health campaigners had every reason to believe that the Labour party would include a clear statement of its intention to ban cigarette advertising in the health policy document it drew up in preparation for the 1983 General Election. They were disappointed. There was no reference to legislation, only a promise to 'act', although Labour's Shadow Health Secretary, Gwyneth 'Gunboats' Dunwoody (a formidable lady) was personally committed to banning all cigarette advertising. 'If I'm Minister, there'll be direct action,' she assured me. Did that mean legislation? She said of course it did—and not just to ban all cigarette advertising but all tobacco sponsorship of sports and the arts. So why was this not spelt out in Labour's policy document? Had the party been under pressure from the Tobacco Workers Union and its other trade union allies? 'No,' she said emphatically, 'the pressure wasn't necessary with Michael Cocks [Labour's Chief Whip and Bristol MP] sitting there on Labour's Campaign Committee, worrying about jobs in Bristol.' She pointed out that the same concern naturally extended to other Labour MPs who represented areas besides Bristol where tobacco provided much-needed jobs. Mrs Dunwoody however never got the chance to translate her words into deeds as Labour lost the election.

History will show whether any politician can deliver in power what he or she promised in opposition on the smoking and health issue. As the following chapters show, the chances are that, on the record of the past twenty years, even the brave and the bold will be scuppered—'Gunboats' or not—by powerful forces which are difficult to overcome and politically dangerous to resist.

5

Refusing the Medicine

The main political battles on smoking and health fought in Britain in the twenty years which followed the publication of the Royal College of Physicians' first Report in 1962 involved attempts made by three Health Ministers to use legislation to restrict the advertising and promotion of cigarettes. Each planned to attack these vital links in the Smoke Ring. The Ministers concerned were Kenneth Robinson in the 1960s, David Owen in the 1970s, and Sir George Young in the 1980s. This chapter deals with the battles of Kenneth Robinson and David Owen. A later chapter deals with those of Sir George Young.

The industry fiercely opposes legislation of any kind as it sees it as a prelude to a total ban on the advertising and promotion of cigarettes. Throughout this period, it argued that it would co-operate with the government in a series of voluntary agreements in which it would take into account concerns over smoking and health and adapt its products and its advertising and promotion accordingly. On the first count, the industry did make great efforts. Tar yields were nearly halved and by 1982 low tar cigarettes accounted for nearly twenty per cent of the market.[1] The companies even spent millions developing tobacco substitutes, only to see them fail in the marketplace. But on advertising and promotion, their efforts were less than wholehearted. Health Ministers turned to legislation because the industry was not prepared to tolerate the kind of restrictions which they were determined to see. But governments were not prepared to tolerate them either as Kenneth Robinson was the first to find out.

Kenneth Robinson was Minister for Health from 1964 to 1968, in Britain's first Labour government for nearly fourteen years. The last Labour government had set up the National Health Service in 1948. 'I'm an addict of fifty-five years' standing,' Kenneth Robinson told me as he lit up another cigarette. 'I've always smoked Players. One of them used to last nine minutes. One only lasts about four minutes now. I feel guilty all the time. It's not something one does unconsciously any longer.' When he was a Health Minister, he never smoked in public. He remembered the agonies which one of his predecessors, Iain MacLeod, had gone through in the early 1950s when he gave an early press conference on smoking and health. 'MacLeod was a chain-smoker,' he said. 'I remember him vividly telling me that he didn't know what the hell to do as all the journalists knew he was a chain-smoker. If he didn't smoke, there might be panic; if he did, they might not think that he took it seriously. In the end he lit up.' When Kenneth Robinson became Minister, cigarettes were on his 'shopping list'. The climate after the Royal College of Physicians' Report favoured some action, but he never felt there would be legislation and believed that prohibition was completely out of the question. 'There's an unspoken conflict between Ministers of Health and Treasury Ministers. It was never overt,' he said. 'In my day, revenue from tobacco duty almost exactly paid for the hospital service. One was just aware that if, by some miracle, one cut smoking down by fifty per cent, the economy would be in a dicky position. My job was not to look after the economy but to try and do something about public health.'

The industry as well as the government knew that it too would have to make some response to the Royal College of Physicians' Report. Within a month of publication, it had voluntarily agreed to be bound by a code which excluded advertisements which over-emphasised the pleasures of smoking, featured conventional heroes of the young, and which appealed to manliness, romance and social success. The industry was to police its own code. Judging by advertisements more than a decade later, the policeman was off-duty most of the time. The industry also agreed to protect young children by not showing television cigarette advertisements before nine p.m. Television was the medium on which the companies spent most of their money, as it was the most powerful and effective way of getting their message across. Television was Kenneth Robinson's first target.

The subject cropped up in general conversation with his Cabinet colleague, Tony Wedgwood Benn, who, as Postmaster-General, had political responsibility for broadcasting. Robinson said he thought the government really ought to do something about cigarette advertising. Benn agreed. Both knew there would be a 'great hou-ha' if they tried to legislate but then realised that Benn, in his capacity as Postmaster-General, could ban cigarette advertising on television without any recourse to Parliament. 'All it probably required,' remembers Robinson, 'was a word from Benn to the ITA*, saying, "I've discussed the matter with the Minister of Health and we think that on health grounds it would be desirable to exclude cigarette advertisements on television." The ITA took the necessary action. It was probably no more than a circular. It was done without any great public debate or fuss. And it stuck.' Robinson and Benn hatched their 'little plot' and cigarette advertisements disappeared from Britain's television screens on August 1st, 1965.

The companies reacted to the television ban by employing new means of promotion, including pouring their money into gift coupon schemes. When the Royal College of Physicians' Report was published in 1962, the industry was spending £13 million a year on advertising. By 1966, it was spending £41 million—well over half of it on gift coupons.[2] The schemes were wildly successful, encouraging people to smoke more to collect more coupons to collect more gifts. Between 1965 (the year of the television ban) and 1966, consumption soared by 6 billion cigarettes.[3] Imperial was one of the first to introduce the scheme and watched its coupon brands, Embassy and Players No. 6, increase its already dominant share of the market. Rivals, Gallahers and Rothmans, were forced to join in the give-away schemes, although with no great enthusiasm, to prevent Imperial

* The ITA is the Independent Television Authority, which controls the Independent Television network (ITV). It later became known as the Independent Broadcasting Authority (IBA).

swamping them completely. Kenneth Robinson was anxious to move against the smoking bonanza, but knew he was limited in what he could do. 'It would have been a hell of a thing to get legislation,' he said. 'It was the first time the Labour party had been in power for fourteen years and we had a list of prospective legislation as long as your arm. I thought we should try and get a voluntary agreement to reduce the level of advertising. Advertising must have some effect, constantly bringing cigarettes in front of potential new smokers.' He entered into 'marathon' negotiations with the cigarette companies. 'We had meeting after meeting after meeting. They probably went on for nearly two and a half years.' The air was thick with smoke, with heavy smokers on both sides of the negotiating table. 'There was always a slight hint that the government could legislate, a hint of blackmail in the background. I used it progressively as the talks went on and on. I used to throw up my hands and say, "Gentlemen, if you can't agree, you leave me no alternative." They knew we meant business and feared that legislation might bring a total ban— which is not what we were seeking.' The negotiations went on for so long not because the companies were trying to keep the government at bay, but because they could not agree among themselves on the concessions they were prepared to make. 'They were all ready to accept restrictions,' said Robinson, 'but I could never get all of them to agree on the same restrictions. Imperial would agree to virtually anything, provided they were allowed to continue with coupons. Rothmans said that as long as coupons were banned, they would agree to almost anything else. Each one didn't want to give way on the form of promotion they reckoned they gained most by. It was commercial rivalry more than anything else which prevented agreement being reached. I got madly frustrated because we went on and on. I had to get tougher and tougher, saying, "If you can't reach agreement, you've only yourselves to blame if the government brings in legislation that you find unpleasant." '

Robinson knew he was chancing his arm on his ability to persuade his Cabinet colleagues to legislate. 'I had an uphill struggle persuading them. It wasn't easy.' The last thing the Prime Minister, Harold Wilson, and his Leader of the House of Commons, Dick Crossman, wanted was a row over cigarettes in the run-up to the next General Election. In the autumn of 1967, the Labour government had quite enough problems. In two by-elections earlier in the year, it had lost a seat in Scotland (Glasgow Pollock) and narrowly held on to its traditional stronghold, the Rhondda Valley in Wales. Labour was not popular with its grass roots supporters. The 'Breathalyser', introduced by Transport Minister Barbara Castle to deter drinking and driving, had caused great resentment amongst Labour's grass roots: the prospect of legislation against cigarettes was thought likely to alienate them still further. Booze and fags were the pleasures of the masses. 'We're in danger of becoming known as the government which stops what the working classes really want', wrote Dick Crossman in his Diary.[4] Although Crossman was the Labour Party's leading intellectual and one of the most powerful figures in Harold Wilson's cabinet, he also understood the feelings of Labour's grass roots supporters.

With three crucial by-elections coming up, Crossman thought that Kenneth Robinson's proposals for legislation were the last thing the government wanted. The subject came up before the Cabinet's Home Affairs Committee in October, just before the by-elections were held. Robinson told his colleagues he wanted to introduce legislation to control advertising in general and cigarette coupons in particular. There was an intense debate, mainly on ideological grounds. No one denied the health risks of smoking, but there were strong differences of opinion on the propriety of the state interfering with personal liberties. Robinson argued that the state was entitled to intervene within limits to protect the individual from himself, just as it did with heroin. Crossman took the opposite view, and, ideology apart, insisted that to introduce legislation on cigarettes would be politically unwise. Robinson got his way, and the Cabinet Committee agreed that he should proceed with legislation. 'In the end I got it through with a reasonable majority,' said Robinson, 'but it was harder going than I'd expected.'

Having lost the argument in committee, Crossman insisted that any legislation on cigarettes should be postponed for at least a year, until the fuss over the Breathalyser had died down; and that at the very least, the Minister should hold off making any statement on the government's intention to legislate until after the

voters had gone to the polls in the by-elections. 'But no,' wrote
Crossman in his Diary, 'the Minister of Health had to make his
policy announcement and he chose to do it this morning, thereby
battering the poor Leicester Labour Party with another blow.'[5]*
Crossman's political instincts had not failed him. A rough survey
of around eighty Labour MPs who had been canvassing in the
three constituencies, showed that most of them thought that two
of the biggest issues on the doorsteps were 'Barbara's Breathalyser' and Kenneth Robinson's announcement of legislation
against cigarette advertising. Labour lost two of the three
by-elections.

Nevertheless, Kenneth Robinson ignored the political sirens
and pushed ahead with his proposals for legislation. When they
came up before the Cabinet's Legislation Committee, Crossman
made sure that they were not included in the following year's
legislative programme. The Committee then threw the Bill back to
Home Affairs. Crossman described the scene:

> A vast affair, attended almost exclusively by number twos and
> Ministers interested in a particular item. Sure enough, round
> the great table in the great Ministerial Committee Room, about
> twenty Departments were represented. The only item which
> interested me was Kenneth Robinson's old proposal to forbid
> cigarette advertisers to use coupons ... So here we were,
> discussing the same old thing. Ken was quite brief. Then the
> Lord Chancellor turned to me. I was quite unprepared and
> simply blurted out that this was another of those Bills which we
> simply couldn't afford to pass when we were running up to an
> election because bans of this sort make us intensely unpopular,
> particularly with children and families. If you are going to deal
> with cigarette smoking, you should not try this kind of
> frivolous but intensely unpopular method.[6]

Crossman finally killed Robinson's proposals for legislation when
the Ministry of Health was reorganised in the autumn of 1968 to
become the Department of Health and Social Security (DHSS).

---

* Leicester South-West was one of the three by-elections. The first blow
referred to was the elevation of its MP, Herbert Bowden, to the House
of Lords, as Lord Aylestone, which necessitated the by-election.

Crossman was designated its first Secretary of State. 'When Dick took over,' said Robinson, 'one of the first things he did was to kill my proposals on electoral grounds. He went to Harold Wilson and said, "This is a vote-loser." There was no question about it. It was a decision reached between Dick Crossman as Secretary of State and Harold Wilson as Prime Minister, that this was a vote-loser and we'd better forget it.' But Robinson persisted to the end. He tried to by-pass Crossman before he took over as Secretary of State. Crossman found out and stopped him. He told the Prime Minister that Robinson had tried to go behind his back:

> When I told the story to Harold, he said that Robinson might be trying to get a cause for resignation, but I don't think this is true. No, it's the bloody-mindedness of a man isolated out there at the Elephant and Castle* and sore at being thrown out of his Ministry in order to give place to me. I am more and more aware that if he is left out of the government when I take over it will be very bad for me since he has built up a very high reputation in his four years as Minister of Health. If I seem to chuck him out in order to take his job, it won't do me any good in the National Health Service. On the other hand, everything he is doing now is making it very difficult to avoid just that.[7]

Robinson expressed his regret to Crossman that after all the time and effort, his proposal for legislation had come to nothing. Crossman replied, 'Well, you know I've always been opposed to it. I'm sure it's a loser and Harold agrees with me.'

The industry, and Imperial in particular, were 'absolutely delighted' to see the death of Kenneth Robinson's plans. Crossman, according to Robinson, became 'Bristol's pin-up man'. It was to be nearly ten years before David Owen took over from where Kenneth Robinson left off.

In the general election of 1970, Harold Wilson's Labour government was defeated by Edward Heath. The tobacco in-dustry had little to fear from Heath's Conservative administra-tion. The new government was happy to pursue the system of

---

* The headquarters of the DHSS is located at the Elephant and Castle south of the River Thames and is somewhat cut off from all the other Ministries in Whitehall.

[86]

voluntary agreements which Kenneth Robinson had found so ineffective and frustrating. The new Secretary of State for Social Services, Sir Keith Joseph, believed that legislation regarding cigarettes was 'a significant and dangerous diminution of corporate and personal freedom'.[8] Nor was he convinced that a ban on advertising would reduce the consumption of cigarettes. The worst blow the industry suffered was at last having to put a mild health warning on cigarette packets: 'Warning by HM Government: Smoking Can Damage Your Health', and the words 'Every packet carries a Government Health Warning' in the small letters at the bottom of every advertisement. Also in 1971 the industry's voluntary code on advertising was slightly revamped.

In Britain, it had taken nearly ten years for a health warning to be put on a packet. Sir Keith complimented the industry on the 'responsible and helpful way' it had conducted its discussions with the government.[9] Sir Keith Joseph's successor at the Elephant and Castle in 1974, when the next Labour government came to power, was the same Barbara Castle whose Breathalyser had precipitated the revolt amongst Labour's grass roots. Mrs Castle, like Kenneth Robinson, was a heavy smoker. As Minister for Transport, she had once sent a circular round all her Cabinet colleagues, asking them to make sure that they wore their seatbelts when riding in their official cars. Kenneth Robinson sent her a memo in return with the message, 'When you give up smoking, I'll wear my seatbelt'. But if the industry thought that Mrs Castle was a friend because she was a smoker, it was wrong. She favoured strong action, just as much as Kenneth Robinson had done. She entrusted the campaign to her young, ambitious Health Minister, Dr David Owen, who as a medical man himself, believed that some form of legislation was necessary to tackle the smoking-related diseases which he said were 'of epidemic proportions'.[10] 'Voluntary agreements are not worth the paper they're written on, unless the industry knows the Minister of Health has the power to legislate,' he told me. 'A Minister needs to know before he goes into negotiations, and the industry needs to know it too, that he has the power to legislate. Then you can have a serious discussion. Their experience tells them that all governments back off legislation. And the record is true. They do.'

The industry knew that Dr Owen meant business, as an insider described: 'The only time I saw anybody frightened in the industry was with David Owen. We had a meeting with him, a very big meeting. We went along to the House. He started off by saying, "Well, ladies and gentlemen, we all know the problems with smoking. We're not going to talk about that. We know that smoking causes a lot of diseases. We all have wives and children, so we're all men concerned with this problem." Owen frightened the life out of the industry.'

Dr Owen described his negotiations as 'pretty civil but very tough'. He was not planning to ban advertising altogether, and accepted the industry's view that a total ban would prohibit the advertising of the low tar brands which it was now government policy to encourage people to smoke. But he did want to bring advertising under some kind of legal control to make up for the inadequacies of the voluntary agreement. (In fact in 1975 and 1977 the images used in cigarette advertising were further curtailed when the Advertising Standards Authority—the body which polices advertisers and their advertisements—tightened its cigarette code: for example, by the end of the 1970s, the Marlboro cowboy had finally ridden into the sunset—at least in Britain.) In the belief that the industry would never make any meaningful concessions as long as they knew the Minister had no clothes, Dr Owen proposed to dress tobacco in the Medicines Act, which the previous Labour government had introduced in 1968. The suit, as Dr Owen saw it, was hanging on a peg labelled 'Section 105' and just waiting to be taken down. The Section empowered the Minister to include by order in the Act any substance which, while not in itself a medicine, nevertheless 'if used without proper safeguards, is capable of causing danger to the health of the community'.[11] In theory all the Minister had to do was table an Order decreeing tobacco to be such a substance and, unless it was defeated in the debate which would in this case inevitably follow, was then free to use the Medicines Act to control cigarettes. This would enable the government to control not only the tar, nicotine and carbon monoxide content of cigarettes, but also health warnings and 'the restriction of promotion and codes of practice for advertising and sponsorship'.[12] The amended Medicines Act would give a Health

Minister everything he wanted. To the industry it was clearly the thin end of a very dangerous wedge.

Imperial argued that the voluntary agreement was successful and that legislation was both unnecessary and unwarranted; it added to bureaucracy and government expenditure; the long-term results would be the prohibition of advertising and promotion; it placed 40,000 jobs at risk, many of them in areas of high unemployment; legislation detrimental to the tobacco industry was also detrimental to the overall employment prospects of about a quarter of a million people. The economic guns were fired off again.

Dr Owen steered his proposals for hi-jacking the Medicines Act through the Cabinet Health and Social Services Committee, but not without opposition. 'We knew we would have objections from the Department of Trade, as we routinely did. They were against it on grounds of "undue interference",' he said. 'The Department of Industry were also against it because of jobs—and we knew that we would have objections from the Minister of Sport, Denis Howell.' But the expected opposition from the Treasury did not materialise, at least not from its Ministers, Financial Secretary Robert Sheldon, and Chief Secretary, Joel Barnett who, despite customary departmental objections, personally endorsed their Cabinet colleague. 'Bob Sheldon certainly made it absolutely clear as his own personal view, that this was quite legitimate,' said Dr Owen. 'So the Treasury was not absolutely hostile.' But there were grounds for the lack of traditional hostility. 'They'd become convinced that this approach would not deeply damage the revenue and they were also quite glad for our support on health grounds, to increase taxes on cigarettes.' Dr Owen also had to persuade the Department of Health and Social Security in addition to his Cabinet colleagues. 'Although there were some civil servants who were very committed on the issue,' he recalled, 'the bulk of the Ministry was committed to the Medicines Act because of its involvement with the pharmaceutical industry. Sensing this was in the wind, the industry tried to generate the belief that the tactic would damage the credibility of the Medicines Act: that it would make it more controversial and would drag an Act which was working well with the pharmaceutical industry into ill-repute.

You could sense that the lobbyists were trying to get the pharmaceutical industry to argue against using the Medicines Act.'

To counter these arguments, Dr Owen had to convince two other important figures, Sir John Butterfield, the new Chairman of the Medicines Commission, and Dr Robert Hunter, Chairman of the newly established Independent Scientific Committee on Smoking and Health, whose job was to advise the DHSS on the development of low tar cigarettes and tobacco substitutes. Dr Owen went to see them both personally, and convinced them of the propriety of what he proposed to do, pointing out that it would not adversely affect their work. 'I bullied or convinced the Ministry, I'm never quite sure which, to use the Medicines Act,' he said, 'so that by the time we went to the Legislation and Social Services Committee, I had the DHSS loyally on board.' But Dr Owen knew that it would not be easy to get the legislation through Parliament—or even through his own party.

From 1974 until 1979, Labour never had an overall majority in the House of Commons and only governed with the agreement of minority parties. The government survived as the result of a series of deals with the Ulster Unionists and the Liberals, two of the main minority parties in the House of Commons. These deals were carefully glued together by the then Leader of the House of Commons, Michael Foot. The job of Labour's Chief Whip, Michael Cocks, was to see that the deals stuck when MPs marched into the voting lobbies. Michael Cocks was a Bristol MP and, according to Dr Owen, against the proposed legislation. 'He was a vehement opponent and would have done his utmost to defeat it,' he said. The Ulster Unionists too were unlikely to view it favourably, with Gallahers' plants in Northern Ireland providing 3,400 jobs and Rothmans' factory at Carrickfergus providing another 800 (now the only major employer in the town after the closure of the ICI and Courtaulds textile plants had made nearly 5,000 people redundant). The legislation would not only have upset many of Michael Cocks' Bristol constituents, but many of those of the MPs whose support the Labour government needed to survive. Nevertheless, Dr Owen was confident that he could get his proposals through the House of Commons. But before proceeding, he wanted to test the water, not just to indicate parliamentary concern on the issue, but also as a way of putting additional pressure on the industry with whom he was still negotiating. In order to do so, he asked one of his Labour colleagues, Robert Kilroy-Silk, to introduce a Private Member's Motion on smoking. Kilroy-Silk introduced the debate on his Motion with the admission that he was 'a relatively heavy smoker' and then proceeded to attack the system of voluntary agreements:

> What the industry has accepted has been what it believes will not be substantially detrimental to its interests. The industry has made certain voluntary agreements, but they have been pin-pricks in terms of the scale of the problem. They have proved difficult to obtain and, when obtained, have been given grudgingly and unwillingly by the industry and frequently subsequently flouted and broken . . . It is not my aim to prohibit smoking. As a smoker myself, I should resent that most deeply. I am not seeking to ban, prohibit or impose curbs on the freedom of the individual to live his own life in his own way . . . I would be the first to challenge any attempt to restrict my self-acknowledged addiction, but it is important to try and make smoking safer for those who smoke and to persuade other people not to start . . . It is no exaggeration to say that cigarette manufacturers are merchants of death and retailers of disease.[13]

There were even more savage attacks to come, in particular from one of the Labour party's doctors, John Cronin, MP for Loughborough, and a consultant surgeon:

> There are no grounds for soft pedalling in the attack on tobacco manufacturers. They are, in effect, mass killers. They are committing genocide by their products. I know that they are members of the establishment. They are people whom some would regard with respect. One of their chairmen was knighted in the New Years Honours List. One has grown accustomed to the activities of the tobacco manufacturers, but in simple scientific terms, they are killing 100,000 people in this country every year and they are causing massive ill health. I suggest

there are no grounds for treating them with any special consideration.[14]

Two of the Conservative MPs who came to the industry's defence, Dr Gerard Vaughan and Kenneth Clarke, both later became Health Ministers in Mrs Thatcher's government. Dr Vaughan knew Imperial well. He had one of their largest breweries in his Reading constituency, had been on a two-week fact-finding trip to Malawi in 1973 to see their tobacco operations, and had been one of their guests at the Glyndebourne Opera. Neither visit was of course in any way improper. Dr Vaughan always made it clear to the company that, as a doctor, he accepted the medical evidence. He also urged greater diversification. At one meeting over lunch at Prunier's in St James's, he asked Imperial what long-term plans they had to diversify out of tobacco altogether and was astounded when his question was met with 'total incredulity'.

Dr Vaughan became Minister of Health in 1979. In the smoking and health debate in 1976, he said:

I suggest that even today the Minister has failed to explain satisfactorily why legislation is necessary. He is dealing with an industry which is wholly willing to co-operate with him and that has shown this since 1971 in a whole series of agreements . . . I suggest again and again that there is no need to legislate in this area. The Medicines Act was never intended for application to tobacco . . . I ask the Minister not even to consider going ahead with these proposals. I suggest that he goes back to the industry and allows further voluntary agreements to develop.[15]

Dr Vaughan also took the opportunity to remind the House of Commons of how important the industry was to the country:

. . . the tobacco industry comprises a major part of our economy. It employs large numbers of people. It produces substantial revenues—£16,000 million a year to the Exchequer . . . The tobacco industry is a major supporter of sport . . . half industry's contribution to the Arts—£250,000—came from the tobacco industry. Therefore for many strong reasons, although we must try to make smoking safe, from the point of view of our general community economy and our employment position, we must consider very carefully what we do.[16]

Kenneth Clarke, the Conservative M P for Nottingham Rushcliffe (Nottingham is the home of John Player) who succeeded Dr Vaughan as Minister for Health in March 1982, joined in defence of tobacco:

> ... the well being of the area which I represent is very much affected by the well being of the tobacco industry ... I can understand exasperation growing on the part of the tobacco industry, which is manufacturing a lawful product ... It is understandable why it should dawn on many people engaged in the tobacco industry that they are involved in impossible negotiations. They are being asked to give only one concession, but then we go on to the next. There is no finality. They are entitled to feel a little exasperated and to ask how much further they will have to go. They are entitled to ask whether they are simply being had or being induced to go as far as possible voluntarily and whether there will be a statutory power to clobber them still further.[17]

Dr Owen was fully aware of the battle he would face, not only in the House of Commons, but very possibly in the courts, the grounds for the action being that he was acting *'ultra vires'*— beyond his powers. The industry was certainly prepared to challenge him. In the House of Commons debate, Dr Vaughan had also pointed out that when the Medicines Act was debated in 1968, the government had given assurances that it would not be widened and that if any subsequent Minister tried to do so he would be acting *'ultra vires'*. Michael English, another Nottingham M P, had warned of the implications of cigarettes being brought under the Medicines Act when it was being given its second reading in 1968.[18] But Dr Owen remained undaunted. 'The industry was very worried,' he said. 'I would have put the order down and let them bloody well challenge it in the courts. I would have argued that we were acting "*ultra vires*" in a good cause.'

But battle was never joined. There were political changes inside the Labour party. There was another General Election in 1976, which Labour won again. Harold Wilson had retired and James Callaghan became Prime Minister. Barbara Castle was succeeded by David Ennals as Secretary of State for Social Services. Following a Cabinet reshuffle in 1977, David Owen became Foreign Secretary. Roland Moyle became the new Minister of Health. To the disappointment of Dr Owen, the Medicines Act strategy was quietly forgotten. 'It was absolutely tragic that David Ennals let this drop,' he said. 'I think he sensed that Jim Callaghan didn't want it. That Labour government had a majority if it wanted to do something [because it had made a pact with the Liberals] and even though Jim Callaghan showed resistance, there were others who'd have got that through.' A new voluntary agreement was signed in March 1977. The industry agreed to include the word 'seriously' on the health warning (so it now read 'Smoking can seriously damage your health'), and the government agreed to forget about legislation for the next three years. The high hopes which Dr Owen had raised among anti-smoking campaigners—that legislation might now become a reality—vanished with the Minister and left some bitterness behind. Looking back, Mike Daube, who had been Director of Action on Smoking and Health throughout the Labour government's term of office (1974–79), took a less rosy view of Dr Owen's efforts:

For $2\frac{1}{2}$ years the rhetoric was magnificent . . . The sense of public relations was impeccable. Owen became widely recognised as a Health Minister who was determined to face up to the smoking problem, but the image bore as much relation to reality as the glossiest cigarette ads to the consequences of smoking . . . David Owen had persuaded smoking and health campaigners that the introduction of legislation under the Medicines Act—which he presented as a certainty—would be the thin end of the legislative wedge. Criticisms of Owen were muted while there was a chance that his strategy might work, and ASH tried not to embarrass him, in Parliament or anywhere else. Because it genuinely believed that Owen would implement his strategy, ASH persuaded its supporters not to rock the boat; in retrospect, it might have been better to let the boat sink.[19]

But by the mid-1970s, the focus of the smoking and health debate had switched to completely new ground. In 1977, Britain became the world's testing ground for synthetic tobacco substitutes. If substitutes could be shown to be less hazardous, and if smokers could be persuaded to take to them, they stood to make profits of millions for Imperial, Gallahers and Rothmans, the companies which pioneered them. The development was hailed as the greatest revolution since the filter tip and the greatest advance since James Bonsack's cigarette machine first made mass production possible a century earlier. But despite the ballyhoo, most of the cigarettes launched on to the British market in the summer of 1977 only contained around twenty-five per cent of tobacco substitute: the rest was just ordinary tobacco. In effect, what was on offer was a new form of low tar cigarette. The percentage of tobacco substitute in the new cigarettes was small because companies were frightened of putting smokers off if the taste and flavour were too different when they first tried them.

Imperial, in partnership with Britain's Imperial Chemical Industries (ICI), had invested ten years of research and £20 million in the project, and had constructed a brand new plant at Ardeer in Scotland to produce its substitute, known as New Smoking Material (NSM). Ardeer had ambitious plans to produce NSM in quantities equal to fifteen per cent of all tobacco consumed in the United Kingdom. Imperial's rivals, Gallahers and Rothmans, had embarked on a similar venture with the (American) Celanese Corporation to produce 'Cytrel'. All three tobacco companies had reason to believe they were proceeding with the government's blessing, having shown that a mixture of substitute and tobacco might be less carcinogenic than just tobacco by itself. After four years of deliberation the new substitutes were given qualified approval by the Independent Scientific Committee on Smoking and Health, which had been set up by the government in 1973 under Dr Robert Hunter (known as the Hunter Committee) to advise on (amongst other things) 'less dangerous' smoking in general and tobacco substitutes in particular. The Hunter Committee expressed a qualified verdict on the new cigarettes:

The product may be no more dangerous to health than a similar product containing tobacco only and could prove to be less injurious.[20]

The welcome wasn't rapturous but it did give NSM and Cytrel the go-ahead.

On July 1st, 1977, a dozen new brands were launched. Retailers had packed their shelves, in anticipation of the demand. But the new brands stayed there, gathering dust. Smokers did not buy them. Tobacco substitutes were a monumental flop. After a year, all twelve new brands accounted for less than one per cent of the total cigarette market. Imperial burned 600 million of its new cigarettes, and its fingers as well, as it watched $20 million worth of investment go up in smoke. Its new factory at Ardeer was working at five per cent capacity. Half the workers were laid off. Rothmans' Marketing Director, Rex Van Rossum, observed:

> The introduction of tobacco substitutes into the UK market, which was accompanied by an unprecedented fanfare of publicity, turned out to be the marketing non-event of the decade. Twenty years of research and development took only about two months to be destroyed in the marketplace.[21]

The cigarette companies, particularly Imperial, angrily blamed the government for not only failing to endorse the launch, but for pouring a large bucket of cold water all over it. The new Minister for Health, Roland Moyle, administered the shock personally:

> This is too serious a subject in which to mince words. Cigarettes, with or without substitutes, can be debilitating and ultimately lethal. For the government's part, you can be assured that we will work relentlessly towards the ultimate objective of a smoke-free society.[22]

Roland Moyle had been well briefed by ASH. The manufacturers also blamed the government-funded Health Education Council (HEC) which published a famous cartoon, albeit six weeks after the launch, which showed a man leaping from the Post Office Tower with the caption: 'Switching to a cigarette with tobacco substitute is like jumping from the thirty-sixth floor instead of the thirty-ninth.' The failure of tobacco substitutes was one of the health lobby's clearest and most important victories. They had successfully got across the message that there was no such thing as a 'safe' cigarette. But despite the political recriminations, it was the consumer who gave tobacco substitutes the thumbs-down: they were not significantly lower in tar than any of the nineteen low tar brands currently on the market; they were no cheaper than 'ordinary' cigarettes (the government had seen to that, to protect its revenue); and most important of all, smokers just did not like them.

The industry may well have been justified in laying some of the blame for the failure at the government's door, but the government was consistent in the position it took: to have encouraged tobacco substitutes would have been to encourage smoking, and that was not government policy, as Roland Moyle had made clear. The history of tobacco substitutes is an illustration of the political dilemma which all low tar cigarettes present. In principle, governments welcome them because they appear to reduce the health risks while preserving revenue, jobs and trade: in practice, Health Ministers committed to discouraging the smoking habit as the only really effective way of preventing death and disease, see them as a distraction which encourages smokers to carry on smoking instead of trying to give up.

Lord Hunter (Dr Hunter had become a Life Peer in 1978) whose Committee had approved tobacco substitutes, clearly shared the industry's view. He later called the HEC's famous advertisement 'disastrous' and said: 'The approach of those charged with concern for the health of the people wrecked the initiative.'[23] Lord Hunter firmly believed that governments should have encouraged tobacco substitutes. He believed that people were going to carry on smoking and therefore should be encouraged to smoke less hazardous cigarettes, be they tobacco substitutes or low tar. It was his view that governments should do everything possible to promote this trend but he inevitably came into conflict with Health Ministers who believed that their first priority was to discourage smoking and not to encourage people to carry on with the habit by simply changing their cigarettes. When Lord Hunter's Chairmanship of the Independent Scientific

Committee on Smoking and Health came to an end in 1980, he went on to become an adviser to Imperial Tobacco for 'the normal, modest consultancy fee'.[24] He followed a path taken six months earlier by another DHSS scientist, Dr Andy Nelmes, who left the Department to join Gallahers.[25] Dr Nelmes had also been Scientific Secretary to Lord Hunter's Committee.

When the three-year-old voluntary agreement negotiated by David Ennals expired in 1980 (by which time Mrs Thatcher was installed in Downing Street after her election victory of 1979), there was renewed pressure for legislation to ban advertising. This was encouraged by the 1979 World Health Organisation Report 'Controlling the Smoking Epidemic', which recommended 'a total prohibition of all forms of tobacco promotion'.[26] But the industry's defences had grown stronger too.

The companies increasingly argued that to ban advertising and promotion would not only prevent them encouraging smokers to switch to low tar cigarettes, but would cripple the country's sporting and cultural life which now flourished with the help of tobacco money. While governments had been tinkering with health warnings and restrictions, sponsorship had become firmly established in the Smoke Ring.

6

All in the Game

Throughout the 1970s, overall business expenditure on sponsorship of sport and the arts in Britain grew at around twenty per cent a year, from £15 million in 1973 to over £50 million by 1981.[1] Roughly ninety per cent was spent on sponsorship of sport and the rest on the arts. The tobacco companies, which do not divulge their advertising budgets, were by far the biggest spenders. Sponsorship is a particularly attractive form of promotion: it enables the companies to associate cigarettes with healthy, glamorous and life-enhancing activities; it polishes their corporate image; it creates goodwill among the public; it gives them access to prestigious and powerful people and institutions involved in sport and the arts; it makes financially hard-pressed governments and governing bodies even more dependent upon them; and, above all, it enables them to get round the ban on advertising cigarettes on television. Tobacco sponsorship is designed to change the public perception of cigarettes and the companies who make them. This chapter deals with sport, the following with the arts.

Motor racing is the most heavily sponsored of all sports. On Sunday July 18th, 1982, Britain's Minister for Health, Kenneth Clarke, was entered in the first race at the Marlboro British Grand Prix at Brand's Hatch. Newspapers and billboards all over London carried huge advertisements featuring the Marlboro

Formula 1 racing car, flanked by the red Marlboro cigarette logo promoting what the royal patron of the event, HRH Prince Michael of Kent (the President of the Royal Automobile Club which organised the meeting), called 'the high spot in the motor sport year'. Not to be outdone, other London billboards showed the John Player Special Team Lotus roaring down on passers-by as proof that British cigarettes were still in the race. Brand's Hatch opened its gates at six a.m. Some drivers queued for three and a half hours to get in. Philip Morris' Managing Director, Robert Hermans, promised the crowd of 90,000 an 'unforgettable' day,[2] as the Marlboro McLaren racing team provided excitement on the ground and the Marlboro aerobatic team provided thrills above. The star of the day was the former World Champion, Niki Lauda, whom Philip Morris had just enticed out of retirement to rejoin the team, at a figure rumoured to be around $1 million.

The politicians who were Marlboro's guests for the day did not have to queue up at the crack of dawn. They were met at the Battersea Heliport in London by the wife of Philip Morris' Managing Director and, in a helicopter with a dollar sign on the side, flown directly to Brand's Hatch, where the air was thick with fumes and the sound of Marlboro cigarette commercials being broadcast over the public address system. One of Marlboro's guests for the day, as he had been the year before, was Tory backbencher Martin Stevens, the Chairman of the National Appeals Committee of the Cancer Research Campaign. Mr Stevens told me that under his direction the income of the campaign had increased from £150,000 in 1956 to £17 million in 1982. Was there not a contradiction between his work for the campaign and accepting the hospitality of tobacco companies? 'Not really,' he said. 'It's only a very few years ago that we used to have big boxes of cigarettes on our boardroom table at Cancer Research committee meetings. I suggested that the practice be discontinued. In the course of a year, I guess I'm the guest of 150 commercial organisations of one kind or another, as are my colleagues. I'm not sure it does us any harm. I don't think Members of Parliament should be isolated in an ivory tower.'

Martin Stevens was helicoptered into Brand's Hatch in time to see the Minister for Health, Kenneth Clarke, on the starting line for the first race of the day, alongside the former Minister for

Sport, Sir Hector Monro, and other Westminster notables for the
House of Lords v House of Commons charity race (sponsored by
The Mail on Sunday). Sport beat Health. Sir Hector came fifth.
Kenneth Clarke came eighth. The returning hero, Niki Lauda,
won the big race of the day and with it the special Marlboro
British Grand Prix Trophy: a gold-plated model of a Formula 1
racing car surrounded by a mobile spinning globe resting in a nest
of tobacco leaves.[3] The race was carried live by BBC television
cameras and a half-hour package of the highlights was broadcast
on the network later that evening. One of the BBC's commen-
tators was Barrie Gill, the Chief Executive of Championship
Sports Specialists Ltd. (CSS), the biggest of the sporting
consultancy operations which have mushroomed with the growth
of sponsorship. (Another BBC commentator, Peter West, who
covers cricket, tennis and rugby, is a director of a similar
company, the West Nally Group, which has handled Benson &
Hedges cricket and tennis[4] as well as Silk Cut jazz for Gallahers; it
also helped R. J. Reynolds' sponsorship at the 1982 football
World Cup in Spain.) CSS has handled Marlboro for Philip
Morris, John Player and Lambert & Butler for Imperial, Dunhill
for Rothmans and Kent (the brand it markets in Europe) for
BAT. Among the sports stars in its stable are Barrie Sheene,
Stirling Moss, Frank Bough (long-time presenter of BBC TV's
Grandstand and since the beginning of 1983 presenter of BBC
TV's *Breakfast Time*), the England Test Cricket Team, the
Football League and the Prime Minister's son, Mark Thatcher.

Barrie Gill, a former Ford Marketing Manager, is refreshingly
honest about his business and his tobacco clients. Gill does not
smoke. He remembers smoking himself silly, waiting for Winston
Churchill to die, thought it was stupid and stopped. I asked him
why tobacco had poured so much money—he reckoned about
£25 million—into motor racing. 'It's the ideal sport for
sponsorship,' he said. 'It's got glamour and worldwide television
coverage. It's a ten-month activity involving sixteen races in
fourteen countries with drivers of sixteen nationalities. After
football, it's the Number One multinational sport. It's got total
global exposure, total global hospitality, total media coverage
and 600 million people watching it on TV every fortnight. It's
become the technocrats' Coliseum. It's macho, it's excitement, it's

colour, it's international, it's glamour.' What sort of a return did the tobacco companies get for their £25 million investment? 'I'd say they get £200 million back in return. They get their feedback at about ten to one. You get out of it what you put in. Like all sponsorship, there's no point in putting your money into an event, just sitting back and saying "our sales must go up". It's the way it's used. It's used for promotion, for hospitality, for sales incentives, for exposure. It's certainly image-building. Marlboro picked motor racing as an image-builder. Marlboro is what they call an "achievement" cigarette. It's for people who are achievers.'

The sponsors are quite open about what they get out of it, as a special advertising section on Formula 1 Grand Prix racing in *Newsweek* (March 21st, 1983) indicated: 'But sponsors in Formula 1 get something more for their money than just advertising: the image of the sport rubs off on them,' says Marlboro's Aleardo Buzzi:

> 'We are the Number One brand in the world. What we wanted was to promote a particular image of adventure, courage, of virility. But our sponsorship is not just a matter of commerce, it is a matter of love. We don't just sign a cheque. We support the sport.'

The special section ended with a full page Marlboro advertisement.

I asked Barrie Gill why sponsorship appealed to tobacco manufacturers. 'It's the most versatile, flexible, cost-effective (that means it gets lots of television time for the money) media for promoting anything. Look at it pound for pound. If you wanted to launch an aftershave it's going to cost you nearly £60,000 to make a TV commercial and then about £40,000 a minute every time you put it on the network. So, even with half a million pounds, you're not going to make much of an impact. You give me half a million, and you can have your own League, your own Sunday events. I could give you coverage you just wouldn't believe.' Is it not a way of getting round the TV ban on advertising cigarettes? 'It has proved to be a way of doing that. That's obviously an appealing factor, but it's not the only reason. It's image-building. Unlike any other product, you've got to to remember that that little length of cigarette is the same anywhere. They're all paper with tobacco inside. Every product has to have an image. I think Marlboro has its image first from its cowboy advertising and second from its sport. I think it is linked in the public mind with sport and success and achievement.' He admitted that the tobacco sponsors were not 'entirely altruistic'. 'They're not the Archangel Gabriel. They're there to get visibility. They're there to sell cigarettes.' What about the health issue? 'If we decide as a nation that we cannot in any way promote smoking because we believe it is fundamentally wrong for the future health of our citizens, we've got to find ways of making up the revenue, preserving newspapers and preserving sport.'

Although Grand Prix racing may outsparkle its rivals in glamour and money, it comes well down the list if measured in hours of television coverage. Motor racing is heavily outviewed by more mundane sports like snooker, whose television marathons eat up the hours, command huge audiences, and cost a fraction of motor racing to sponsor. Although cigarette advertisements were banned from television in 1965, the cigarette companies were able to circumvent the legislation, and sixteen years later commanded 247 hours of television time in a single year in which to promote their brands before millions of viewers, through their sponsorship of a whole range of sporting events.[5] Imperial gained the greatest exposure, with 116 hours of screen time for Embassy and John Player; Gallahers, fifty-five hours for Benson & Hedges; and BAT, forty-five hours for State Express. In 1981, three of the four top sporting events which gained most television exposure were sponsored by tobacco companies—they were Embassy and State Express snooker and John Player cricket.[6] (The cricket Test Matches sponsored by the Cornhill Insurance Company topped the list.)

If a London television viewer had the stamina to sit down and watch every minute of every television commercial shown in a year, he would be sitting in front of his set for a total of 510 hours.[7] If he watched every minute of cigarette-sponsored sport as well, he would be there for half as long again. The exposure is massive and costs next to nothing. A minute of network television time for Embassy snooker costs Imperial about £50 (calculated on

the £75,000 needed to stage the event and the prize money of
£150,000).[8] A peak time network commercial lasting a minute,
were the company allowed to buy it, would cost Imperial about
£140,000.[9] As the advertising magazine, *Campaign*, noted,
'Considering the prize money of £150,000, it must rank as the
best media buy of the century'.[10] Imperial also sponsors motor
sport, powerboat racing, cricket, speedway, snooker, darts,
bowls, horseracing, tennis, rugby union, rugby league, badmin-
ton, show jumping, motor cycling and table tennis. Yet the total
amount Imperial spends on sponsorship (including the arts) is
only around two per cent of its total marketing budget, an
indication of sponsorship's value for money.

Tobacco sponsorship creates great problems for the broadcasting organisations, the BBC and Independent Television. In 1981,
the BBC, which is not allowed to carry advertising, broadcast
seventy-two hours of Embassy snooker, thirty-six hours of State
Express snooker, thirty-three hours of John Player cricket, twenty
hours of Benson & Hedges cricket, twelve hours of Benson &
Hedges tennis, twelve hours of Benson & Hedges snooker, eleven
hours of Benson & Hedges golf, eleven hours of Embassy darts,
and nine hours of State Express golf.[11] The BBC recognises the
dilemma sponsorship presents. Some of the events are enor-
mously popular: snooker, for example, has done wonders for
BBC 2's ratings. 'There's no doubt we're being used,' a BBC
executive told me. 'We have to be very strong to make sure we're
not being ill used.' He cited the example of the Rugby League Cup
Final, which BAT had used to launch their State Express brand in
Britain. At the end of the match, a banner bearing the cigarette's
brand name was unfurled behind the victorious team. The BBC
cut the shot. The offending banner was then handed to the team to
carry round the field in their lap of honour. The team declined.
(The executive pointed out that any sponsor could provide a
similar headache.) It's not an easy task to balance television
ratings and public responsibilities. 'The tobacco companies are in
the driving seat,' he said. 'If they pull out, there aren't other
sponsors ready to step in.' Was sponsorship a way of getting
round the television ban on cigarette advertising? 'Yes,' he said.
Would the BBC ever consider refusing to broadcast events
sponsored by tobacco companies? He said realistically he

couldn't see it happening. 'We're in a Catch-22 situation. I don't think there is a resolution. The BBC is hooked.'

There was also concern at the headquarters of the BBC's rival broadcasting organisation, the Independent Broadcasting Authority (IBA), the body which is responsible for Independent Television (ITV). Here the headaches are fewer, given the BBC's virtual monopoly of tobacco-sponsored events. Like the BBC, the IBA has had problems with BAT's State Express. A senior IBA executive told me that eighteen months previously, on the day of a horse race meeting, BAT changed their State Express banners (technically the 'house' name) to '555' (technically the 'brand' name). The contract for the meeting had clearly said 'State Express'. The 'World of Sport' producer on the spot telephoned his office in London, which then rang the IBA. The IBA ordered the banners to be covered up. Shortly afterwards, the Authority received a personal delegation from BAT and a letter of complaint from the Tobacco Advisory Council (the industry's trade organisation whose Chairman, Sir James Wilson, was also a member of the government's Sports Council). The IBA did not change its position. But were not the distinctions academic? 'That's true,' said the IBA executive. Was sponsorship a way of getting round the ban which had been imposed on the Authority in 1965? 'Yes,' he said, 'sponsorship gives them formal entrée into

But tobacco sponsorship is, like cigarette advertising, now subject to government regulation. Until 1977, there was no control of sponsorship although Health Ministers expressed their concern as they equated the issue with health. David Ennals, Labour's Secretary of State for Social Services, made his views quite clear in March 1977 in a speech on Smoking and Prevention:

> It seems to me that this practice is not merely an evasion of the spirit of the ban on television advertising, but that it is grotesque for outdoor sports to be so closely associated with habits that are notoriously dangerous to health. My colleague, the Minister for Sport, shares my concern that the use of sponsorship in this field should be regulated, and we hope the continuing discussions with the industry will soon reach an acceptable outcome.[12]

Shortly afterwards agreement was reached, although to health campaigners it was far from 'acceptable'. Tobacco sponsorship of sport was to be regulated but by the Minister for Sport and the Department of the Environment, *not* by Health Ministers and the DHSS. The Sports Minister, who was given the responsibility of negotiating the new agreement with the industry, was the former football referee, Denis Howell. Health Ministers could offer advice from the touchline, but were not allowed to blow the whistle. Denis Howell negotiated a three-year agreement under which the companies would keep their spending within 1976 levels (in real terms) and would not display their brand names on promotional signs at televised events or on competitors and their equipment. When Denis Howell ceased to be Minister of Sport after Labour's defeat in the 1979 General Election, he became a consultant to Barrie Gill's Championship Sports Specialists Ltd.

Whatever the minor restrictions, the medical profession grew increasingly concerned as tobacco sponsored events grew and dominated Britain's television screens. Doctors paid little attention to the tobacco industry's argument that sport would be the poorer—and indeed some sports like motor racing would collapse—without its munificence. They saw tobacco sponsorship for what it was: another way of promoting cigarettes and giving respectability to the smoking habit. In 1981, as negotiations began to renew the agreement between the industry and the Minister for Sport, the leaders of the country's medical establishment acted together in an unprecedented way and urged the government to ban tobacco sponsorship for sport. A joint letter was sent to Neil MacFarlane, the new Minister, from the Presidents of eight of Britain's royal colleges of medicine: the Royal College of Physicians, the Royal College of Surgeons of Edinburgh; the Royal College of General Practitioners, the Royal College of Pathologists, the Royal College of Obstetricians and Gynaecologists, the Royal College of Radiologists, the Royal College of Physicians and Surgeons of Glasgow and the Royal College of Physicians of Edinburgh. The letter said:

Our concern is, naturally, with the health of the people of this country . . . Cigarette smoking is the single most important preventable cause of death and disability in the United

Kingdom. The DHSS calculates that this is responsible for at least 50,000 premature deaths each year from smoking-related diseases . . . In consequence, we are particularly concerned that sports sponsorship by tobacco interests will tend, in the minds of the young, to establish a paradoxical link between smoking on the one hand and, on the other, enjoyable participation in healthy sports. Moreover, tobacco sponsorship of sport is one method of circumventing the legal ban on the advertising of cigarettes on television . . . It would be all the more regrettable if the efforts of health educators supported by government were to continue being undermined by the contrary influence of the tobacco sponsorship of sport, with its tendency to glamorise, in the eyes of the young, an addictive and dangerous habit.[13]

The Presidents' plea for a complete ban went unheeded. The fears they had expressed that the new agreement might prove 'too permissive and too long term' were well founded. In 1982, a new three-year agreement was signed. Health warnings were to be placed on advertisements promoting sponsored events; house and brand names were to be removed from competitors and their equipment; and expenditure was to be frozen at 1976 levels, allowing for inflation. But whatever the outward appearance, the agreement was no great set-back for the industry. To the chagrin of the BBC, as a quid pro quo for conceding health warnings on advertisements for sponsored sport, the tobacco companies negotiated the right to call an event after the *brand* name of a cigarette. Hitherto they had only been allowed to call it after the name of the '*house*' or *company* which produced it. The event could now advertise the cigarette. When initially consulted, the BBC had opposed the move but in the end the Corporation had to live with its objections.

The industry had an easier ride at the Department of the Environment than it ever would have done at the Department of Health. 'Sport needs all the money it can get,' I was told at the Department of the Environment. 'Smoking tobacco is a perfectly legal activity. Sport is a perfectly legal activity. So there's nothing illegal or undesirable in one legal activity sponsoring another.' Is it not wrong that a product which has been shown to be responsible for 50,000 deaths in the United Kingdom should be associated with a healthy pastime like sport? 'Greater participation in sport must lead to a healthier nation,' came the reply.

'You really can't expect government, which believes in the freedom of individuals to do what the hell they want, to say on a matter of whim that because tobacco is associated with death, and although there's no evidence to show that tobacco sponsorship causes on extra person in this country to smoke a cigarette, nevertheless we're going to ban it. That would be an incongruous attitude for a government to take. If Health Ministers were really convinced, if they were really sure in their minds that it would be in the nation's best interest generally to ban tobacco sponsorship, they would never have gone along with this agreement.' I asked about the 50,000 deaths a year. 'That's an over-simplified statistic,' came one answer. Another followed, 'I'm a sixty-a-day man who hasn't touched a cigarette for the past thirty years. I'm prepared to concede that cigarette smoking may actually be beneficial for a large number of people and therefore may contribute to their health. If they didn't smoke cigarettes, their health might actually suffer in some other way. Tobacco is part of the infrastructure of our society. Western societies use cigarettes or tobacco. They're part of our way of life.' At the Department of the Environment, tobacco is pushing at an open door.

Besides enabling the companies to get round the current advertising restrictions, sponsorship also offers them the opportunity to dig in in the face of restrictions still to come. The industry privately accepts that these are inevitable. In May 1979 BAT executives attended a five-day conference in Germany to discuss these restrictions and consider new opportunities for marketing their products in anticipation of the difficulties they would face in using traditional channels of communication. In the memorandum written after the conference, BAT noted that prospects for 1990 were 'poor':

> ... Among the most important BAT markets, the number completely free of all bans and restrictions will have diminished from eight in 1979 to two. These restrictions primarily affect the persuasive nature of advertising.[14]

Faced with such a gloomy prognosis, BAT and its companies

around the world had to find other means of getting the image of their brands across. One way suggested in the memorandum was for companies to explore the possibility of beaming cigarette advertisements into countries where they were banned:

> As advertising bans tend to fall unevenly on countries within regions, companies should explore the opportunities to co-operate one with another by beaming TV and radio advertising into a banned country.[15]

The company warned, however, that: 'Obviously the political risks of this action must be weighed up and treated with prudence.'[16]

BAT also considered less controversial ways of circumventing the anticipated restrictions by attaching their cigarette brand names to non-tobacco goods and services—a process which has become known by the industry's opponents as 'back door advertising'. BAT's 1979 memorandum stated:

> Opportunities should be explored by all companies so as to find non-tobacco products and other services which can be used to communicate the brand or house name, together with their essential visual identifiers. This is likely to be a long-term and costly operation, but the principle is nevertheless to ensure that cigarette lines can be effectively publicised when all direct forms of communication are denied . . .[17]

The memorandum also stressed that 'The importance of bringing plans to fruition and initiating action well before bans or severe restrictions are imposed is absolutely vital.'[18]

BAT noted that this approach had already been adopted by Philip Morris and Dunhill as well as by its own associated company in Germany BAT Cigaretten-Fabriken.

On July 16th, 1979 BAT Cigaretten-Fabriken licensed an Italian fashion marketing group, Kim Moda of Milan, to use the corporate graphics and colours of one of its best selling brands, Kim. BAT's German company had marketed the brand in various European countries since 1971. Kim, a cigarette aimed primarily at women, is notable for its distinctive livery of red, orange, brown and yellow wavy lines. By the mid-1970s, the brand's success had encouraged various other non-tobacco companies (particularly in Italy) to use the Kim name and colours on products other than cigarettes. This they were able to do because trademark law only protects a product within its own category. The trademark Kim had originally been registered (number 132985) by an Italian clothing company called Sagaf in 1956. The Italian fashion marketing group, Kim Moda, whom BAT licensed to use Kim's corporate graphics and colours in 1979, had acquired the Kim trademark for use in its business from Sagaf in 1976. Now Kim Moda had BAT's brand livery to go with the name.

The next steps came in 1980 and 1981. Kim Moda signed a licensing agreement with another Milan company, Italian Top Fashion, permitting it to use the Kim name and colours on its Kim Top Line range of sportswear. As part of the contract between Kim Moda and the head of Italian Top Fashion, Paulo Bodo, Kim Moda also agreed to provide a number of players who would promote the Kim Top Line range of sportswear. A contract was signed with the International Management Group, the circus of world superstars run by the American impresario Mark McCormack, under which his female tennis stars, Martina Navratilova, Sue Barker, Betsy Nagelson and Diane Fromholz, would wear Kim Top Line sportswear. Such was the complex and circuitous corporate route by which Kim made it to the finals of the Wimbledon Tennis Championships in the summer of 1982, and on to millions of television screens the world over.

Kim was launched in Britain (where nearly half of the country's seventeen million cigarette smokers are women)[19] in the summer of 1982, just before the Wimbledon Tennis Championships. The glossy campaign, designed by BAT's advertising agency, Dorland's, featured an elegant lady in a white hat tied round with a scarf in the Kim colours, the brim pulled down over her eyes. Dorland's said the fact that Wimbledon was on the horizon was pure coincidence. BAT insisted that the launch had nothing to do with Wimbledon but was dictated by the timing of the Chancellor's Budget speech the previous March. When millions of television viewers watched Martina Navratilova win the Ladies' Final wearing the Kim name and colours, BAT denied any involvement and pointed out that Kim was the name of the sportswear she was wearing. The company said it was not responsible for where the insignia appeared as it had nothing to do with the agreement between the Wimbledon champion and the Italian fashion company. The reason for the fuss was that Ms Navratilova had worn the Kim name and colours for about ten hours in front of the television cameras within a month of the signing of the new sponsorship agreement between the government and the industry. The agreement states:

> The display of house or brand names or symbols on participants and their equipment, or on officials or their equipment, actively involved and likely to come within range of the television cameras, is not permitted during the course of a televised activity in the UK.[20]

The BBC were unhappy too. It was not the first year they had complained about Kim. They had protested about Sue Barker wearing the name and insignia the previous year, and had been told she was advertising sportswear and not a cigarette. (Kim had not been launched in the UK at that time.) The BBC complained again in 1982, when the brand had been launched in Britain, but to no avail. I asked a BBC executive if they had threatened not to cover the final. 'The threat is possible in principle but not in practice,' he said. BAT's rivals were also angry at the apparent exploitation of the loophole in the agreement before the ink was dry on the paper. Barrie Gill, of Championship Sports Specialists said, 'That's rocking the boat. That's silly. We put great big pieces of adhesive tape over our drivers' insignia when they're being interviewed, and there's somebody on TV for over two hours!' The advertising magazine, *Campaign*, editorialised:

> ... It is difficult to believe British American Tobacco's disavowals of involvement except in the most literal way ... At the very least, BAT can scarcely have been unaware of the promotional implications of the display of the logo throughout the Wimbledon fortnight in a medium that is otherwise legally barred to it. A more plausible explanation is that the company has cynically exploited a loophole in the rules on tobacco

advertising . . . It is not a particularly honourable way for a tobacco company to behave . . .[21]

Questions were also asked in the House of Commons. In the end, BAT apologised to the Minister for Sport, Neil MacFarlane. They said Ms Navratilova was a very superstitious lady who had insisted, despite their pleas, on wearing the same outfit as she had worn while winning earlier tournaments. The Minister accepted that BAT had made 'reasonable efforts' to prevent a breach of the Code.[22]

I asked one of the executives of the International Management Group which handles Ms Navratilova's promotional affairs about the incident: 'Why do you want to drag all that up again?' he said. 'Was she a superstitious lady?' He laughed. 'Most sportsmen and women I know are.' 'Did she know Kim was a cigarette?' 'Of course she does.' 'Does she mind advertising cigarettes?' 'She's not advertising cigarettes. Kim's the name of sportswear.' But with the same name and colours as the cigarette? 'Our contract is with the clothing manufacturers. It's got nothing to do with cigarettes. Who's worrying anyway? If Martina thought it was a cigarette, she probably wouldn't have worn it.' The Department of the Environment, which had just negotiated the new agreement, was also embarrassed and muttered about legislation if this kind of thing went on.

Ms Navratilova played again (and won) at Wimbledon in 1983. Her outfit still carried the Kim logo and colours but not the name. This time the word Top Line was emblazoned above the logo. Again there were protests from ASH and the British Medical Association. The Minister for Sport, Neil Macfarlane came down firmly in BAT's court, ruling that the Top Line name with the Kim colours did not constitute a breach of the voluntary agreement on sports sponsorship. A BAT spokesman said:

We do not regard the Kim Top Line controversy as having anything to do with tobacco sponsorship because the promotion was run by a fashion company. Navratilova has been playing with the name Top Line rather than the name Kim this year because there was clearly a misunderstanding last year and we wish to avoid that.[23]

But where sports sponsorship is concerned the tobacco companies have little to worry about. Most of the nation's legislators are disciples of Richard Crossman when it comes to passing laws which interfere with the nation's pleasures. It is no accident that tobacco has now become synonymous with sport so that an attack on one is seen as an attack on the other. It will take more than a storm in a tennis cup to uproot tobacco from sport. Even if Parliament were to heed the medical profession and legislate, the industry can always increase its sponsorship of the arts where there are no restrictions whatsoever.

7

Polishing the Image

When tobacco companies sponsor the arts, they buy not television exposure but prestige and respectability. They buy it cheaply, effectively and without any of the restrictions they face in sponsoring sport. The £1 million a year they spend on the arts may be only a fraction of what they spend on sport, but it is enough to enhance their image as public benefactors as well as selling cigarettes. Tobacco becomes the patron of orchestras and theatres, of opera and ballet, of singers and painters, the saviour of the arts in difficult financial times. As a result of their generosity, the tobacco companies win a place in the esteem of those influential figures and institutions which run the arts in Britain. Even many of those who attack tobacco's sponsorship of sport are prepared to tolerate its creeping invasion of the arts, as if somehow the issue was different. But there are some who are not deceived.

On a warm August evening in the summer of 1982, Labour's shadow Minister for the Arts, Phillip Whitehead, was walking through London's new Barbican Arts Centre. He heard the sound of an open air concert and made his way to the piazza where it was being held. 'It upset me,' he said, 'to be met by a female huckster giving away cigarettes.' The cigarettes on offer were Rothmans' Peter Stuyvesant. The event they sponsored was the Peter Stuyvesant Pops, played by the London Symphony Orchestra.

Three of London's main orchestras are sponsored by tobacco companies: the LSO by Rothmans' Peter Stuyvesant, the London Philharmonic by Imperial's John Player, and the London Philharmonia by BAT's du Maurier (known to its cigarette rivals as 'The du Maurier Band').

The Peter Stuyvesant Pops ran at the Barbican for a fortnight, offering its audiences Gilbert and Sullivan Pops, Ballet Pops, Viennese Pops and Panpipes Pops. The series of concerts began with Pops in Space, conducted by John Williams, the composer of the themes from *Superman*, *Close Encounters*, *Star Wars*, *The Empire Strikes Back* and *E.T.* Mr Williams conducted his greatest hits in a white tuxedo with a cream silk collar, the only person on the stage not wearing Peter Stuyvesant colours. The LSO all wore the Peter Stuyvesant uniform: powder blue blazers, white shirts, and ties striped with Peter Stuyvesant's gold, red and blue, with a PS logo at the bottom. Behind the orchestra was draped a huge illuminated banner, reminding the audience they were watching the Peter Stuyvesant Pops. Four Peter Stuyvesant flags occasionally stirred in the breeze above the podium decked out in the Peter Stuyvesant livery. At each side of the stage were two more giant posters, telling the audience, lest they forget, that these were the Peter Stuyvesant Pops.

There were many young people and children in the audience, some of them sitting on their fathers' shoulders as they listened to their favourite music from *Superman*, *Star Wars* and *E.T.* I had a word with a member of the orchestra in the interval. 'If they've got to put their ill-gotten gains into something, we'd rather they put it into music,' he said philosophically. The Manager of the LSO, Peter Hemmings, agreed with him. 'If they're going to spend their money on advertising, they may as well spend it on us,' he said. I asked him how he felt about being sponsored by a tobacco company. 'A great many of our great industrial firms, oil for example, have side effects which people may find unpleasant. I think we're getting into very deep water. You could say governments shouldn't sell arms, but they provide jobs for thousands of people. Our job is to make the orchestra work.'

The Barbican concerts were designed to mark the twenty-first anniversary of Peter Stuyvesant's association with the LSO, which had been the first ever commercial sponsorship of a British orchestra. The birthday treat cost Peter Stuyvesant £100,000. But the LSO's survival does not depend on Peter Stuyvesant. The orchestra's running costs work out at around £2.5 million a year. It is expected to find about sixty per cent (£1.5 million) of this from the box office. The balance is made up of a government grant of around £600,000 via the Arts Council and £400,000 from commercial sponsors. In 1982, Peter Stuyvesant's contribution of £100,000 was twenty-five per cent of total sponsorship, but only four per cent of the overall cost of running the orchestra. I asked Mr Hemmings what the LSO got out of the deal. 'A fortnight's work for the orchestra, something new for the Barbican and money.' And what did Peter Stuyvesant expect in return? 'They expect to see a commercial return. They expect to sell more cigarettes.' But such commercial justification cuts little political ice with its critics. 'I find it deeply distasteful,' says Phillip Whitehead, 'that something which is banned from TV screens and is only shown on hoardings with a government health warning, should be attached to artistic events so that the event itself is seen as a brand. We all appreciate good works, but I do believe that tobacco kills people. I don't think they ought to be able to buy respectability for things which ought not to be respectable.'

Imperial is the biggest spender in sponsoring the arts, as it is in sport. It puts money into the English, Welsh and Scottish National Operas, the National Theatre, the Glyndebourne Festival Opera, the London Philharmonic, Sadlers Wells, the Ballet Rambert, the John Player Portrait Awards and John Player classical records. Rothmans sponsors opera scholarships besides the London Symphony Orchestra. Gallahers sponsor the Benson & Hedges Music Festival at Aldeburgh and the Gold Award for singing. BAT sponsors the Philharmonia du Maurier concerts, du Maurier classical records, and du Maurier commissioned orchestral works. The range may seem wide but the sums of money involved are droplets in the advertising ocean: £300,000 over three years for the Philharmonia du Maurier concerts; £350,000 for the National Operas; and £240,000 for the National Theatre. In 1980, Imperial spent nearly £15 million on advertising and promotion, most of it on the launch of John Player Special. The investments may be small, but the return in goodwill and image is immense. 'Sponsorship makes us all good guys,'[1] noted one of BAT's du Maurier executives. Sir Anthony Kershaw, who has been BAT's paid Parliamentary consultant since 1976, told me, 'It's an area which needs an awful amount of money, and it's an area where there are quite a lot of influential people who know leaders of the tobacco industry. Of course it's a prestigious thing to do amongst the select people of the country. I shouldn't think it makes very much impact upon ordinary people, the fact that BAT sponsors an orchestra. I think it's very important that tobacco companies are not only seen to be, but actually are a caring sort of outfit which has got the interests of the nation at heart. It's very bad if they seem to be hard-faced people who don't give a hang about how many people died every year.' And is that image improved by sponsoring the arts? 'Oh, absolutely!'

Kenneth Robinson, who as Labour's Health Minister in the 1960s, and Chairman of the Arts Council (the public body through which government funds the arts) in the 1970s has seen the problem from both sides. 'In sport, they get TV advertising at second hand. With the arts, it's image,' he said. 'They know jolly well that as purveyors of a potentially lethal substance, they've got to watch their public image the whole time. Whereas sponsorship of sport to some extent endears them to the masses, sponsorship of the arts is something which endears them to the opinion formers. It all helps the image. It's as simple as that.' I asked him whether he had any objections in principle to the arts taking money from tobacco. 'None whatever,' he said. 'The Arts Council is not in the position of making moral judgments of this kind. I remember once telling Lord Goodman [a former Chairman of the Arts Council and one of Britain's most prominent public figures] that I knew somebody who thought they could get the betting and bookmaking fraternity to do something about arts sponsorship, and I wondered whether he had any objection in principle. "None whatever," he said. "I will take money for the arts, sir, be it from murderers, rapists or anybody." ' Robinson laughed and then added, 'Of course, they've got to do it with reasonable discretion because of the audience they're appealing to and the milieu in which they're operating. I mean, you wouldn't have John Player T-shirts in the chorus in an opera.'

Nowhere is tobacco sponsorship more discreet than at the Glyndebourne Festival Opera, which has given 167 performances of productions sponsored by Imperial Tobacco. Glyndebourne is the beautiful Elizabethan mansion in the Sussex Downs which is the home of the Christie family. Over the past fifty years Glyndebourne has earned an international reputation for opera of the highest quality performed in the 800-seat theatre which the Festival's founder, John Christie, built and opened to the public for its first season in 1934. John Christie's aim was to present opera in an undisturbed atmosphere, with unlimited time for rehearsal, and with the purpose of doing 'not the best we can do, but the best that can be done anywhere'.[2] He even designed the ladies' toilets backstage with doors wide enough to cope with crinoline dresses. Leaving Jaguars and Mercedes parked by the Lambert & Butler* Marquee (helicopters may land by permission), the opera-goers in evening dress, some spectacularly attired like Italian divas, make their way past the tennis courts (where some of the cast may be limbering up before the performance), to the gardens and croquet lawn where they park their hampers and coolers of champagne ready for the interval. Two hours later they return for their seventy-five minute feasts, sitting quietly on their collapsable chairs and eating decorously round their picnic tables, pretending (at least on the evening I was there) that English summer evenings are warm by trying not to shiver. They sit gathered round ice buckets, strawberries covered in cling film and jars of Hellmans mayonnaise. The figures are part of the landscape.

Although Glyndebourne has many other sponsors, including Peter Stuyvesant, Imperial is by far its most generous benefactor. John Player has financed six new productions in six years, *Don Giovanni*, *The Magic Flute*, *Fidelio*, *Der Rosenkavalier*, *The Barber of Seville* and *Orpheus and Eurydice*, thereby relieving Glyndebourne of half the cost of the two new productions it mounts every year. In 1984, Glyndebourne's 50th anniversary, Imperial sponsored the first production at Glyndebourne of Strauss' *Arabella*. The orchestra, the London Philharmonic, is also sponsored by John Player, whose JPS logo is emblazoned on

* Lambert & Butler is one of Imperial's most up-market brands.

the side of the huge black transporter which carries the orchestra's instruments the fifty-four miles from London to Glyndebourne. But in recent years Imperial has not only financed these glittering productions but has also met most of the bills for the upkeep of Glyndebourne's magnificent house and grounds which give the Festival its unique character and sense of occasion.

Unlike John Player's National Opera scheme or the du Maurier Philharmonia concerts, or the Peter Stuyvesant Pops, or the Benson & Hedges Music Festival at Aldeburgh, Glyndebourne is not concerned with selling cigarettes. Discretion is the order of the day. The only place you see a brand name is over the Lambert & Butler Marquee (renamed the John Player Special Marquee in 1983)—for picnics on wet evenings—and in the cabinet in the Long Bar, which displays Lambert & Butler classical records— Elgar's First Symphony and Tchaikovsky's Fifth—as examples of 'the well established association between Glyndebourne and Britain's leading tobacco company'. But tobacco is represented in higher places. Imperial Tobacco's former Chairman and Managing Director, Tony Garrett, sits on the Board of the Glyndebourne Arts Trust (the Festival Opera is a charity and has no state support) alongside the wife of Britain's former Minister of the Arts, Paul Channon, the former Director-General of the BBC, Sir Ian Trethowan, and a dozen other notables from Leopold de Rothschild to former Governor of the Bank of England, Lord Richardson of Duntisbourne. Glyndebourne also helps Imperial foster its political connections. Most years, during the May to August season, Imperial invites dozens of MPs to be its guests for an evening at the opera. The company declined to name the politicians who had accepted invitations over the years, but they included several politicians who later became Health Ministers: Patrick Jenkin, who became Conservative Secretary of State for Social Services in 1979, was a guest when he was shadow Minister (he declined the invitation when he joined the government); David Ennals, who became Labour's Secretary of State for Social Services in 1977 (he told me he was against tobacco companies sponsoring sport, but had fewer objections to them supporting symphony orchestras)—again, like Patrick Jenkin, he went before he became a Minister; and Dr Gerard Vaughan, who became Conservative Minister for Health in 1979 ('I hadn't even seen it as a tobacco exercise, frankly. I'd seen it as a major interest in my constituency and I'd always had great interest in its prosperity'). Imperial invited MPs who were not only its friends but those who might be its future allies, in particular in the battles over cigarette advertising. One of its guests in the summer of 1980 was the Conservative MP Martin Stevens, the Chairman of the Cancer Research Campaign's fund raising committee, who'd attacked government interference with cigarette advertising in a smoking and health debate earlier that year with the words:

> There's a great danger in seeking to put pressure on the tobacco industry interests ... we are big boys now ... whenever politicians try to interfere with human nature and change its course, they fall flat on their fannies.[3]

I asked Mr Stevens about his night at the opera. 'You're given drinks beforehand in the Christies' drawing room; then you see the first act; then you have dinner in the restaurant; and then you drive home. I can't pretend that anything "cigaretty" occurs in the course of the evening.' That came later. Some time afterwards, Mr Stevens said he was visited at the House of Commons by Imperial's Political Affairs executive, Peter Sanguinetti,* whom he had met at Glyndebourne, and who now gave him material related to consumption and cigarette advertising, presumably as further ammunition against those who sought to ban it. Sometimes, Imperial's political investments at Glyndebourne take time to mature. I asked Patrick Jenkin how he felt about having been Imperial's guest at Glyndebourne when he was shadow Secretary of State for Health. 'I was concerned at that stage to have a good relationship with the company and it was one of the ways one could do that in order that I could conduct negotiations in an atmosphere of cordiality rather than in an atmosphere of hostility. I'm never somebody who likes to make war on people. If I can get what I want by ear stroking, then that's what I will do.' I asked whether Glyndebourne afforded the industry an opportunity to stroke his ear as well. 'It might have been,' he said, 'but they

---

* Mr Sanguinetti left Imperial and joined the British Airports Authority in September 1983. He said he was head-hunted and made an offer he could not refuse.

knew where I stood. You may say my ear was stroked and I was persuaded, in the sense of "persuaded", on the advertising "switching brands" issue. I've always been persuaded on that [i. e. that advertising encourages brand switching, not more smokers]. I know there are quite a lot of people who say that is an absolutely minute consideration as against the rest. It may be that I've been overpersuaded. But certainly that's one of the points which the companies made to me very early on, and I took the point.'

Sponsorship of the arts also brings the industry powerful institutional connections. In October 1980 Peter Sanguinetti was one of the delegates who paid £140 for a two-day conference on arts sponsorship at Leeds Castle in Kent, where B A T later held one of its du Maurier concerts. The conference was designed to 'give leaders of industry from both sides of the Atlantic an opportunity in spectacular surroundings to discuss, explore and expound on the theory, philosophy and practice of corporate responsibility towards the Arts.'[4] Tobacco was well represented both in the audience and on the platform. One of the speakers the delegates heard was Philip Morris' Vice-President for Corporate Relations and Communications, Frank Saunders (whom the company had once seconded to Jimmy Carter's presidential campaign as Director of Business Liaison).[5] Mr Saunders told them how arts sponsorship had helped give Philip Morris a different image and how it was both good citizenship and good business. The Leeds Castle conference was held under the auspices of ABSA—the Association for Business Sponsorship of the Arts—which was founded in 1976 by, amongst others, Tony Garrett, the Chairman of Imperial Tobacco. 'Basically, the idea was to set up an organisation to encourage industry and commerce to sponsor the arts and to give us "presence" when dealing with government and other national bodies.' Mr Garrett told me, 'Frankly, I thought, too, that it would do no harm to the "image" of Imperial Tobacco Ltd. to be associated with such a body.' (Mr Garrett subsequently became Deputy Chairman of ABSA's Council, sitting with colleagues every bit as distinguished as those with whom he served on the Glyndebourne Arts Trust. The Council's Chairman was Lord Goodman: other members included Robin Leigh-Pemberton who subsequently became Governor of the Bank of England, Lord Howard, the

Chairman of the BBC's Board of Governors—who was succeeded by the BBC's new Chairman Stuart Young in 1983—and Lord Thomson, the Chairman of the Independent Broadcasting Authority.) ABSA points out in its handbook that arts sponsorship enables companies to make contact with 'Legislators and "opinion formers" at national and local level' and states, for example, that the Imperial Group sponsors the arts in order to make contact with people who would otherwise be inaccessible.[6] To impress the potential sponsor, the handbook also lists a number of case studies, among them the Imperial Tobacco Portrait Award which is run in collaboration with the National Portrait Gallery. The former Chairman of Imperial Tobacco, Andrew Reid, explained the reasons behind the event:

> For a number of years we have felt strongly committed to supporting the arts because the cultural life of this country has greatly influenced the way in which we, as a nation, have developed. It also gives us in the tobacco industry an opportunity to make contacts outside the industry—an activity which greatly enhances the everyday running of our business.
>
> I think that support for up-and-coming talent in Britain is a particularly desirable objective and it is for this reason that the Imperial Tobacco Portrait Award was created. I was greatly impressed by the views of the very eminent panel of judges who clearly considered that both the standard and the extent of the competition entries were of a very high level. They obviously felt that this particular competition would stimulate interest in the art of portraiture and we have thus decided to continue our support for this award for the foreseeable future.[7]

Peter Sanguinetti, then Imperial's External Affairs Executive, spelled out the commercial advantages:

> This competition is a totally new development in arts sponsorship, and although we thought it would have a wide appeal, we were most gratified by the overwhelming response. Of course we do need to attract publicity for a number of well orchestrated reasons. These awards have already received television, radio and press coverage and the final stage, of

unveiling the commissioned portrait, should attract considerable interest. A great deal of credit for our success must go to the enormous amount of effort and commitment by all those involved.[8]

The Portrait Award cost Imperial Tobacco £10,000.

Tobacco is very much a part of ABSA, and has been represented on its Management Committee by Peter Sanguinetti of Imperial and John Weait, BAT's Senior Executive, Group Public Affairs. As in the ABSA handbook, Mr Sanguinetti made no secret of what his company expected from the sponsored.

We want the arts people we pick to work hard to give us publicity. We don't talk about 'giving' money on sponsorship —the recipient gets the money, we get the publicity.[9]

ABSA flourished under the leadership of its young Director, Luke Rittner, who before his appointment in 1976 had been a councillor on Bath City Council and an administrator of the City's Arts Festival. In five years as ABSA's Director (the organisation has its headquarters in Bath), he increased the number of arts events and organisations sponsored from 267 in 1977 to 1,444 in 1981 and doubled the number of companies sponsoring them from fifty-three to ninety-eight.[10] I asked Mr Rittner about tobacco and the arts: 'When we started, there were lots of arts organisations that said to us they had no intention of ever accepting money from a tobacco company. It's amazing what a recession can do.' He said the vast majority of sponsorship was corporate public relations, 'image in one form or another', but there were changes in the wind. He cited BAT. 'Du Maurier were the first to embark on a major piece of art sponsorship which was commodity marketing oriented. There's such a strong identification of the product with the event.' He had been to a du Maurier concert at the Royal Festival Hall. 'The programmes are very smart and look like packets of cigarettes. As you sit there, you sense the whole thing has a feeling. It's just very, very well dressed up. And it's effective.' How did he know? 'I've one personal experience to suspect that it *is* effective in terms of selling cigarettes. Last year my wife was driving up the M4 and was getting tired. To keep herself awake, she stopped to buy some cigarettes. She'd no idea what to ask for as she doesn't smoke. She immediately asked for du Maurier because she'd been to a du Maurier concert. That was the first name that came into her mind.' Had he any reservations about taking tobacco money? He laughed. 'Ab-so-lute-ly none what-so-ever,' he said, stressing every syllable.

I asked him to convince me, assuming I was a tobacco company, that I should put money into the arts.

'It would give you the ability to choose the people you wish to make your number with, and to have an event at which it can be done successfully. If prestige and the altering of a perception is what you're trying to do, then the arts can achieve that, and not necessarily very expensively.'

'What sort of people could I meet if I got into arts sponsorship?'

'Presumably you've mentioned that the tobacco industry is got at quite a lot and therefore government is important to you and Parliament is important to you.'

'I've already got a parliamentary consultant. I pay him several thousand pounds a year.'

'Right, but it would also presumably be useful to offer him the opportunity of actually showing off the company at first hand. He can meet politicians in their own surroundings. He can take them out to endless heavy lunches. What he can't do is involve a man and his wife in a very pleasant evening out.'

'I'm interested.'

'And that's what the arts can offer.'

'But are they going to come?'

'If you choose the right event they won't refuse.'

'But we're dealing with very intelligent, sophisticated people. Aren't they going to be suspicious if we invite them to one of our sponsored events?'

'They're used to having their ears yanked off in every direction. They develop a thick skin so they're not going to be conned; they're not going to think they are there for any other reason than the reason you have brought them there for. That doesn't necessarily mean to say that they're not also going to be susceptible, as a result of a first hand meeting, to change what might hitherto have been a prejudiced view of you.'

Unlike sport, there are surprisingly few voices raised in opposition to tobacco sponsorship of the arts, perhaps mainly because the connection is one of spiritual not physical well-being. Most directors and managers of Britain's theatres and orchestras are only too grateful for the money on offer from tobacco. Defending the National Theatre's acceptance of nearly a quarter of a million pounds from John Player, the National's Director, Sir Peter Hall, said: 'It's a free country. And I notice the government itself earns a lot of money out of smoking'.[11]

But there are a few lone voices in the business who object to seeing their profession used to the greater glory of tobacco. Actor Warren Mitchell attacked the National Theatre's decision in a letter to *The Guardian* in 1982:

> The tobacco industry is desperate for new smokers. The National Theatre throngs with young people who, at an impressionable age, can be shown the wonder of our art linked with the products of the Imperial Tobacco Company. How then can they be persuaded of the harmfulness of smoking? 'Tis pity, Sir Peter, that the National Theatre must whore in this way.[12]

Tobacco also had an opponent at the very top of the British arts establishment, although few knew because protocol prevented him from speaking out as long as he was in office. Until his retirement in 1983, Sir Roy Shaw was the Secretary-General of the Arts Council, the public body which decides how to allocate the £90 million a year which the government spends on the arts. On the eve of his retirement, he told me what he had never been able to say publicly before. To have done so would have caused a storm. 'The arts are life enhancing. I find it very ironical that they should be linked with a product which is life denying. I'm surprised that many leading figures in the arts world appear to have no qualms whatever about taking money from tobacco companies. I'm concerned about the intrusion of all advertising into every area of life, but particularly of tobacco advertising. I don't want to forbid people to smoke, but I do think the demand for cigarettes should be completely unstimulated. There should be no advertising. People who want them can get them, but they shouldn't be persuaded to get them. I reject the argument that advertising does not stimulate demand, that it stimulates only brand competition. The tobacco industry's image is tarnished by overwhelming medical evidence. The image of places like the National Theatre is bright, so the tobacco companies are moving in there to cover up their own tarnish with the brightness of the sponsored organisation.' But was not tobacco money helping the arts survive? 'Public subsidy of the arts by central and local government is about £500 million. The most optimistic estimate of business sponsorship is around £8 million of which tobacco contributes about £1 million a year, so I don't think it's going to make a life or death difference to the arts. In the case of the Philharmonia, it gives them more money than they really know what to do with. It just about doubled their income—an enormous boost. Obviously if you're going to take that amount of money, it must help. If the IRA had given money, that would also help. It all comes back to your assessment of the morality of the source, not the effectiveness of the money.' I asked him if he was equating tobacco sponsors with the IRA. 'Of course not,' he said emphatically. 'I'm simply saying that the IRA would be an immoral source—and without equating the tobacco companies with the IRA—I would say they are an immoral source of a different kind.' He pointed out that companies tended to sponsor established successes. 'Subsidy is not related to need, by any means. They consider "What am I going to get out of this organisation?" Most of the regional theatres could use the subsidy much more than the National Theatre. The more successful organisations attract the sponsors because of their prestige.' I asked if he ever discussed the ethics of tobacco sponsorship with the tobacco people he met. (He had attended the launch of the du Maurier Philharmonia and the John Player Opera schemes.) He said he had not as it would be 'quite inappropriate', in his role as Secretary-General of the Arts Council. 'I had a cordial relationship with Peter Sanguinetti of Imperial, and I have had *ex officio* to conceal my own views. I think he's a charming man. I just happen to think he's in a lousy business. He told me that there was much more money to be forthcoming from the tobacco industry if we could get away from the idea that sponsorship was for general prestige advertising and public relations. What he wanted to get from there to was direct selling, promoting the brand—which in the past had not been the main objective of sponsorship. He thought that if the advertising people could see sponsorship as something which actually sold their cigarettes, then they'd put more money in.' Most sponsors, said Sir Roy, now regarded arts sponsorship as an advertising medium, and a very cheap one at that. The issue had only ever been raised once at Arts Council meetings. 'The Arts Council view, as far as it has one, is that tobacco sponsorship is all right. The only time it has ever been raised was by the one medical man—a neurologist—on the Council. He expressed great misgivings about arts organisations accepting tobacco sponsorship. The then Chairman, former Minister of Health, Kenneth Robinson, said that until the government outlawed smoking, it was no business of the Arts Council to act against cigarette advertising.' I asked Sir Roy if the trend could be reversed. 'I think everything depends on the government's attitude to the advertising of cigarettes. My impression is that they have sold out to the tobacco industry and are unlikely to do anything very effective to control cigarette advertising.' I finally asked him why he thought the government didn't act? 'I suppose because they care more about business and money than they do about health,' he said.

There was a long and bitter political struggle within the Arts Council over the selection of Sir Roy's successor. The appointment was finally announced in January 1983. The new Secretary-General was to be Luke Rittner, the thirty-five-year-old Director of ABSA. Tobacco's most active supporter in the arts had replaced its most bitter critic. Tobacco had now made it to the very top of Britain's arts establishment. Like sport, arts sponsorship had now become a permanent fixture in the Smoke Ring.

8

The Freedom Fighters

Sir George Young, the junior Health Minister in Mrs Thatcher's Conservative government of 1979, was more committed to breaking the Smoke Ring than any of his predecessors. Unlike Labour's Health Ministers, Kenneth Robinson and Dr David Owen, who favoured legislation to restrict advertising, Sir George favoured a *total* ban on all cigarette advertising and sponsorship. Dismissing arguments about revenue, jobs and trade, he pushed ahead, determined to destroy the industry's power to perpetuate its myth about cigarettes. Sir George put public health first. But in doing so, he aroused opposition within his own party, not just from tobacco's known supporters, but from many Conservative backbenchers who embraced the industry's argument that Sir George was attacking freedom not cigarettes. Mrs Thatcher moved him before the damage was done, and replaced him with a Minister who posed the industry little threat.

When Mrs Thatcher's Conservative government was elected in May 1979, the tobacco industry had every reason to feel content. The new government presented itself as a beacon of the free enterprise system, which the Prime Minister so fervently supported, and as a defender of the personal freedoms which were so dear to her heart. (In 1979–80 BAT Industries and the Imperial Group had both made financial contributions to right wing 'freedom' organisations which supported the conservative cause: BAT had given £7,500 to Aims of Industry and £1,000 to the Centre for Policy Studies; and Imperial had given £7,000 to the Economic League which questioned the political power of the British trade unions.)[1] The political climate seemed propitious for the negotiation of a new voluntary agreement to replace the one reached with David Ennals (under which advertising of higher tar brands had been phased out and the word 'seriously' inserted in the health warning), which was due to expire in 1980. At least most of the omens looked good. The industry thought it had friends in the new health team at the Elephant and Castle. A good relationship had already been established with the new Secretary of State for Social Services, Patrick Jenkin, through contacts at Glyndebourne and meetings with Andrew Reid, who became Imperial Tobacco's Chairman in 1979, and Dr Herbert Bentley, who became its Managing Director in 1981. While in Opposition, Mr Jenkin had successfully had his 'ear stroked' by the industry on its need to advertise in order to persuade smokers to switch to low tar cigarettes. The new Minister for Health (the Number Two at the Department) was Dr Gerard Vaughan, who had Imperial's Courage brewery in his Reading constituency, who visited Malawi in 1973 to see the company's tobacco-growing operations, and had been one of their guests at Glyndebourne on several occasions. The only cloud on the horizon came from the third and most junior Minister at the Department of Health and Social Security, Sir George Young, the Under-Secretary of State.

The thirty-six-year-old Sir George, with his pedigree of Eton and Christ Church, Oxford, might have seemed a pillar of the Tory establishment, although few knights of the realm rode to work with a ministerial despatch box strapped on the back of a bicycle. The tall, thin, bespectacled Sir George was committed to preventive medicine, had already made a number of speeches in Parliament highly critical of the tobacco industry, and had been 'a stalwart member', according to ASH's then director Mike Daube, of ASH's all-party group of MPs.[2] Normally the presence of a junior Minister on the bottom rung of the DHSS ladder would not have caused the industry much concern, but when Patrick Jenkin made him responsible for preventive medicine and in particular for government policy on smoking and health, the alarm bells must have started to ring. The industry had not been totally successful in its war for Jenkin's ear. Sir George had bent it too, and strengthened the Secretary of State's conviction that political action was necessary on the basis of the medical evidence which he had long accepted. Mr Jenkin made it clear to the industry that legislation was always at the back of his mind. He told me, 'I've never made any secret of my views, that I think they've got to move fast if they were going to keep ahead of the pressure on Ministers to legislate. That was always the threat behind negotiations. I'd always been totally persuaded by the medical evidence, persuaded by people like Charles Fletcher [of the Royal College of Physicians], Rodney Smith [of the Royal College of Surgeons], even by such libertarians as Reginald Murley [also of the Royal College of Surgeons], and Douglas Black and his predecessors at the Royal College of Physicians. I've listened to a lot of the evidence and become wholly convinced that the objective must be to reduce the damage which is done by smoking. It's not just cancer, it's heart disease and bronchitis. Sir George said when we both joined the Department, "Look here, the Department aren't asking for enough." He was very much instrumental in strengthening my resolve but he was pushing at an open door.'

Nevertheless, unlike Sir George Young, Patrick Jenkin did not favour a total ban of advertising, for reasons which the industry had made clear to him. 'I've never accepted the absolutist view, that you should have no advertising at all,' he said. 'I've always accepted the view that advertising is one of the ways to get people to move to lower tar cigarettes. Therefore one needed a longer term strategy. We never had any idea of simply cutting out all advertising except point of sale like ASH want.* I always accepted the argument that there was a case for persuading people to switch to lower tar brands.' But as far as the industry was concerned, such distinctions were academic. Any legislation was seen as the first step on the road to a complete ban. Sir George Young believed it was necessary to move in that direction for two main reasons. 'Firstly, the government is responsible for the National Health Service, and we spend over £10 billion a year

---

* In fact ASH, like the British Royal College of Physicians, call for the abolition of all forms of tobacco advertising including point of sale.

trying to improve the nation's health. The return we are now getting on each extra billion pounds of investments in new hospitals, in more doctors and more medicine, is getting less and less. Traditional curative medicine is reaching the point of diminishing returns. The real step forward to be made in improving the nation's health lies not in acute medicine but in preventive medicine, in encouraging people to take more care of themselves. I fully realise that this raises political as opposed to medical questions, but they cannot be ducked. The second reason is that you simply can't leave the advertising of a lethal product to the free market. I am a Conservative and believe passionately that decisions about health should be taken by individuals. But they cannot take decisions which are balanced unless they have all relevant information. Clearly the tobacco industry will never do this. So you either say, we're not going to let them advertise their products at all because they're lethal, or we're going to put some resources in to present the other side. It seemed to me that when I went to the Department, it was all too one-sided. People were getting one side of the argument about why they should smoke, but not hearing the other side. To my mind, any responsible government which is interested in health has to put that balance right. That's what I was trying to do at the Department of Health.'

A month after taking office, Sir George flew to Stockholm to deliver a speech at the Fourth World Conference on Smoking and Health. At the First World Conference in New York in 1967, Senator Robert Kennedy had warned prophetically:

The industry we seek to regulate is powerful and resourceful. Each new way to regulate will bring new ways to evade . . . Still we must be equal to the task. For the stakes involved are nothing less than the lives and health of millions all over the world. But this is a battle which can be won—I know it is a battle which will be won.[3]

Twelve years later, with victory nowhere in sight, Sir George declared his intention to fight on in the belief that he was now in a political position to bring the victory closer:

The solution to many of today's medical problems will not be found in the research laboratories of our hospitals but in our Parliaments. For the prospective patient, the answer may not be cure by incision at the operating table, but prevention by decision at the Cabinet table . . . Historically, a nation would look to its doctors for better health. Now they should look to their Members of Parliament . . . my top priority is to draw up a long term strategy which has as its own objective the reduction and eventually the elimination of disease caused by smoking.[4]

The new Minister was well chaperoned by his civil servants. 'You must stop considering Sir George as "your" man,' one of them warned Mike Daube, the former ASH director, who had also been invited to address the conference. New Ministers traditionally rely heavily on the advice of their civil servants (known in Britain as the 'Yes Minister' syndrome, after a popular BBC television series), and often find it difficult to wrench the bureaucracy off a comfortable course which it has been happy to pursue for years. Voluntary agreements were one such course. They, of course, produced disagreements, but no great political confrontations, as neither Kenneth Robinson nor Dr David Owen had got beyond first base in their attempt to get legislation. Sir George Young clearly spelt trouble for any cosy relationship with the industry. 'When Sir George arrived at the DHSS,' one insider told me, 'officials weren't actually that keen on preventive medicine, on smoking. They were quite relaxed and didn't want to stir it up.'
    Some civil servants in the Department did not want Sir George to go to Stockholm. They pointed out that no other Ministers (presumably from the United Kingdom) were going, his predecessor had not been asked, and he had been invited as a backbencher, not as a Minister. They advised him not to make the speech and, if he insisted on doing so, wanted him to make one *they* had written, not one he had written himself. Sir George wrote his own speech and showed it to his officials. They warned him that he was about to start negotiating with the industry and was blocking himself in by taking that line. It was likely to make life difficult for the Department's relationship with the industry. When Sir George made it clear he was going to go ahead and deliver the speech, they did not want it published and distributed back home. But Patrick Jenkin supported Sir George and the objections were overruled.

The Stockholm speech was delivered and published. Within weeks of coming to office, Sir George Young had declared war on the tobacco industry.

The industry made its dispositions accordingly. It knew that, even without the presence of Sir George, the pressure for increased restrictions on advertising was growing. The industry's tactic (learned in America) was to confuse the issue by shifting the ground of the argument from cigarettes and health to civil liberties and freedom. At its marketing conference on future advertising restrictions held in Germany a few weeks after the new Conservative government came to power, BAT had tried to anticipate the problems ahead, and evolve ways of dealing with them in advance. In its memorandum, written after the conference, it listed a series of 'factors' which might lead to a ban on advertising:

1. Absence of serious civil and political unrest, leaving politicians free to indulge in so-called reforming practices.
2. The presence of ambitious politicians, a growing bureaucracy, an autocratic government with weak or no opposition seeking to make a name for themselves by adopting striking social measures.

BAT warned:

It is important for the tobacco industry, and BAT above all, to be alive and responsive to the influence of such men.[5]

As BAT recognised, encouraging opposition on 'freedom' grounds was one way of fighting back. Certainly this was the tactic most likely to evoke a response in the ideological climate which Mrs Thatcher encouraged.

The industry ensured that 'freedom' had a voice by financing a lobbying group in opposition to ASH, called FOREST—the Freedom Organisation for the Right to Enjoy Smoking Tobacco. FOREST was the idea of its Chairman, former Battle of Britain fighter pilot and Commander-in-Chief of RAF Germany, Air Chief Marshal Sir Christopher Foxley-Norris. When he retired from the Forces at the age of fifty-six, Sir Christopher decided to carry on his fight for freedom on behalf of the 'harassed' smoker. He discussed the idea with two friends, Andrew Reid, the Chairman of Imperial Tobacco, and Kirkland Blair, a Director of Rothmans. A lunch was arranged in London with senior executives of the tobacco companies, under the auspices of Sir James Wilson, the Chairman of the Tobacco Advisory Council (the industry's trade organisation), who had been one of Sir Christopher's contemporaries at Winchester. Sir Christopher also had separate meetings, mainly at board level, with senior executives from Imperial, Gallahers and BAT. Sir Christopher likened his relationship with the tobacco industry to that between a general and the government: he was the general, the industry was the government. FOREST was launched at the Union Jack Club in London on June 18th, 1979, when Sir George Young and most of Britain's anti-smoking lobby were in Stockholm for the Fourth World Conference on Smoking and Health. Sir Christopher stressed that FOREST was not 'an organisation to promote the sale of tobacco or to boost the numbers of people who smoke'. He said its aim was:

> . . . to restore and establish freedom of choice. (It is the word 'freedom' that is important in our title; and the word 'right' and the word 'enjoy'.) There are a growing number of people in central government and local government, people in authority and people without authority, except self arrogated, Jacks in office and Jacks out of office, experts and self-styled experts, who apparently have decided to eradicate what has been an accepted element of our way of life for three centuries and more; and to persecute those who practise the pastime of smoking by falsely representing them as some sort of anti-social, undesirable minority of social parish outcasts.

On the health issue, Sir Christopher declared: 'We are medically unqualified to comment or make judgments.'[6]

Sir Christopher was the industry's perfect public defender but he lacked any political expertise in the ways of Westminster. The companies agreed to give FOREST more money—around £50,000 a year—so that it might become a more effective lobby. FOREST simply sent the industry most of its bills. It opened an account with one of Britain's most successful public relations agencies, Good Relations, and through it found a full-time Director, Stephen Eyres. Eyres was a Tory right-winger who had once edited *Free Nation*, the newspaper of Norris McWhirter's right wing 'Freedom Association'. He came to FOREST with extensive political contacts, having once been resident tutor at Swinton College, the Conservative Party's political training centre for candidates, agents and constituency workers. Introducing himself to FOREST's members (the organisation claims 30,000, each paying at least £1 a head), the new Director warned:

> I've never cared much for fashionable causes . . . I don't smoke . . . but I do care about personal freedom . . . and what a fundamental right it is to choose to smoke. We are pro free enterprise—and what finer examples than Britain's tobacco firms, accountable to their shareholders, competing to serve their customers' demands . . . Be on your guard, you do-gooders.[7]

Eyres also had an insider's knowledge of the workings of Westminster, having been official Research Assistant to Nicholas Ridley, who became Financial Secretary to the Treasury. He had also done research for Ian Gow, who became Mrs Thatcher's eyes and ears as her influential and powerful Parliamentary Private Secretary. Under Stephen Eyres' direction, FOREST spread the word amongst like-minded MPs. 'Ideologically we draw heavily on the "anti-Nanny state" wing of the Tory party,' he told me. FOREST also drew support from Labour MPs with constituency interests 'worried about jobs and working class values which include smoking'. Eyres reckoned, 'We could guarantee to produce up to fifty people who would politically oppose what they regarded as unsupportable attacks on the freedom of the individual to smoke.'

FOREST enabled the industry to broaden its political defences in the House of Commons under the guise of freedom not cigarettes. But FOREST was only one of the organisations the industry used to get its message across. Gallahers paid Welbeck Public Relations (part of Foote, Cone & Belding) around £40,000 for services which included identifying and making

[135]

contact with useful politicians and hosting meetings with them. The Tobacco Advisory Council opened an account with Good Relations, worth around £100,000. (In June 1981, FOREST also became a client.) Good Relations' Managing Director, Maureen Smith, had connections with the hierarchy of the new Conservative government. Before the 1979 General Election, she had a meeting with Lord Thorneycroft, the Chairman of the Conservative party, and, with the help of one of her colleagues from Good Relations, had helped three Conservative shadow Ministers brush up their image. The Ministers were Patrick Jenkin (who became Secretary of State for Social Services in Mrs Thatcher's 1979 government and Secretary of State for the Environment in her 1983 administration), John Nott (who later became Secretary of State for Defence), and Tom King (who became Secretary of State for the Environment and then Secretary of State for Employment in 1983). The work was unpaid. Maureen Smith assured me it was done in a personal capacity and not on behalf of Good Relations. The company's brief from the Tobacco Advisory Council was to help the industry present its case more effectively (the 'freedom' issue was to be used against those who sought to restrict smoking in public places) and, on the political front, to assess what support it had in the House of Commons.

At the beginning of 1980, support among the 'freedom' lobby in the House of Commons was assessed as a result of a question posed by another public relations company with a tobacco client. The Conservative MP Martin Stevens was asked by a friend who worked for the company to provide some political feedback on several issues, including the question of whether MPs would legislate to reduce cigarette advertising. Although Mr Stevens admits he has many friends in the tobacco industry, and has been Imperial's guest at Glyndebourne, and Philip Morris' at the Marlboro Grand Prix, he is at pains to point out that he is Chairman of the Cancer Research Campaign's National Appeals Committee. 'The idea that I'm some sort of proponent of the tobacco industry is exactly the kind of untruth which is built up by pressure groups who crucify anybody who doesn't obsequiously fall in with the whole of their platform,' he said. 'I'm a libertarian. I didn't come into politics in order to stop people doing things. I came into politics to leave them free. I hope everybody will stop smoking tomorrow, but I don't think the state should impose rules about these matters.'

On February 7th, 1980, Stevens sent a letter to all Conservative backbenchers. Under the heading 'Tobacco Advertising and Promotion', he warned that the Department of Health seemed confident that both government and Parliament would 'unquestionably' accept new, severe restraints on cigarette advertising and sports sponsorship. He asked where it would all end:

Already alcohol advertising is under pressure; next no doubt it will be sugar, butter, aerosols, synthetic fibres ... any substance taken to excess is—after all—dangerous. Milk, fish and chips ...There will always be enthusiastic lobbies for banning otherwise legal human activities. Surely Conservatives should lean against the wind in resisting such pressures, not to mention attempts by government to define 'socially acceptable' behaviour?

At the end of the letter he asked his colleagues whether they agreed with the proposition:

With regard to the proposed further limitation on tobacco advertising and the prospect of growing interference in otherwise legal activities by governments of both parties, this House believes that the encroachments of the Nanny State are increasing, have increased and ought to be diminished.

He received replies from around a hundred Conservative backbenchers, eighty per cent of whom supported the proposition. According to Mr Stevens the results of his poll were then brought to the attention of the Conservative Chief Whip, Michael Jopling, who was left in no doubt that many Tory backbenchers were strongly opposed to what the government's Health Ministers were trying to do.

The negotiations for the new voluntary agreement had begun in December 1979. The industry's worst fears were confirmed when Patrick Jenkin read out his Department's shopping list at the first meeting. There was to be an end to all poster advertising; an end to all remaining cinema advertising; a fifty per cent reduction in all remaining advertising; a new health warning.[8] 'Our first opening bid when we first met them was a package which really took their breath away,' Patrick Jenkin told me. 'They were very deeply shaken. There was a stunned silence. The meeting broke up shortly afterwards and they said, "We'll have to go away and think about this." They certainly hadn't expected anything like as tough a regime as we started by asking for.'

FOREST reflected the industry's shock with a cartoon at the back of its newsletter, showing Sir George Young in German SS uniform. In his hand was a whip. On his tunic was an armband with the letters 'DH-SS'. The negotiations between the government and the Tobacco Advisory Council (which acted for the industry) dragged on for almost a year—a time-honoured industry tactic as far as the anti-smoking campaigners were concerned. The DHSS team grew weary of hearing the sporting analogies of the TAC's Chairman, Sir James Wilson, who was not only a member of the government's Sports Council but also wrote football reports for *The Sunday Times*. The industry was not anxious to preside at its own funeral. Sir James, according to one of the DHSS negotiators, could never understand 'what the Tory party was doing in this particular field. It went against everything he'd ever learnt about it.' From the beginning, Sir George Young, who handled most of the negotiations for the DHSS, recognised that his interests and the industry's were totally incompatible. The industry wanted to sell more cigarettes and he wanted them to sell fewer. Unlike Patrick Jenkin, Sir George refused to accept the industry's argument that it needed to advertise to get smokers to trade down to low tar. He believed that their objective in advertising was to reinforce the social acceptability of cigarettes and the habit of smoking. He also questioned the companies' insistence that they were not interested in selling to young people. Halfway through the negotiations, the driver of Sir George's official car (which he used when he was not on his bicycle) showed him an invitation which his son had just received through the post on his eighteenth birthday. His son had been invited to join Philip Morris' Club Marlboro. In return for ten Marlboro pack tops, he was entitled to:

Free or half price entry to dozens of top UK clubs and discos.

Hundreds of current albums and tapes at really cheap prices.

Special terms on tickets to Brand's Hatch or Silverstone race meetings.

Discounts off sports and hi-fi equipment.

Information on learning skiing, hang gliding, scuba diving, wind surfing, sailing and many other sports.

Both Sir George's driver and his son were non-smokers and resented the unsolicited intrusion through the letter box.

Sir George used the example during the negotiations as an illustration of how the current agreement was being breached, and suggested it did not bode well for any new agreement. Patrick Jenkin made the same point to the House of Commons when he said that such promotions were 'blatantly out of accord with the whole spirit of the agreement . . .'⁹ Shortly afterwards Philip Morris abandoned its Club Marlboro promotion.

For months both sides dug their heels in. 'I'm a good friend of Sir George's,' Sir Anthony Kershaw, BAT's Parliamentary consultant told me, 'He's a terribly stubborn negotiator. He really doesn't negotiate at all. He says A, B and C, and after you've talked to him for six weeks, it's still A, B and C. He doesn't negotiate. He doesn't know how!' After nearly twelve months, agreement was finally reached in November 1980. 'They caved in at the end,' Sir George said. 'They feared legislation and thought there was going to be something in the Queen's Speech [which outlines the government's legislative programme for the next session], so they settled.' There was to be a thirty per cent reduction in poster advertising; a series of new, though scarcely dramatic warnings ('Most Doctors Don't Smoke' was one of them); and restrictions on promotions aimed at young people and on promotional offers in general. The industry also agreed to provide £1 million for research into the effect of low tar cigarettes. But if there was any victory, it was the government's. The industry had been anxious for at least a four-year agreement, to carry them beyond the next election. The new agreement was only to last twenty months, until July 1982. But ASH's Director,

David Simpson, was not impressed by the result of a year's labour:

> The main point about this new agreement is the unmistakable demonstration that the voluntary agreement system of trying to reduce smoking is a complete failure. Even after a year's hard fighting by Ministers, the cigarette companies have not conceded anything remotely capable of beating Britain's biggest avoidable cause of death and disease ... It's like the Home Guard trying to fight off a nuclear attack.[10]

Patrick Jenkin and Sir George Young now decided that when this short agreement expired in twenty months' time, they would have to use legislation to obtain the restrictions which the industry was not prepared to concede under any voluntary agreement. But the move had to be made with great care. Patrick Jenkin knew he would have 'the utmost difficulty' in persuading his Cabinet colleagues to accept government legislation. He knew the industry was convinced on the basis of its parliamentary contacts that no legislation on cigarette advertising would ever get through the House of Commons, but he believed the assessment was wrong. The strategy the Health Ministers devised was to introduce government legislation which could then be amended. The practice was quite constitutional and not uncommon. The vehicle was to be the Health Services (Miscellaneous Provisions) Bill—a vacuum cleaner piece of legislation which was designed to tidy up many legislative odds and ends left lying around the Elephant and Castle. At the industry's own request, amending legislation to the Medicines Act was needed to block a loophole on imported tobacco. When the Bill came before the House, the plan was to have a backbencher (David Ennals was prepared to do it) table an amendment to the Medicines Act, giving the government power to control cigarette advertising. The mechanism had been tried and tested before. An amendment concerning the compulsory wearing of seatbelts, an issue which raised many of the same 'freedom' issues as smoking, was added to a government Transport Bill: a clause controlling sex shops was added to a Local Government (Miscellaneous Provisions) Bill; and the clause bringing Scottish homosexual law into line with that of the rest of Great Britain was added to the Criminal Justice (Scotland) Bill. 'Because the government has an interest in the Bill, it will see it gets through, even with the Private Member's clause,' explained Patrick Jenkin. Both Ministers made it clear that they would support such an amendment on a free vote. The Bill was cleared by the Cabinet's Legislative sub-committee in November of 1980. But the strategy hit an unexpected obstacle.

When Francis Pym replaced Norman St John Stevas as Leader of the House of Commons in January 1981, he looked at the line of government Bills in the queue and decided there were too many. Mr Pym took out his pruning knife. The Health Service (Miscellaneous Provisions) Bill was one of the casualties, and with it the plan to bring in legislation on cigarette advertising when the short voluntary agreement ran out. 'That was our strategy up the spout,' lamented Sir George Young. But the Ministers were not daunted. They planned to try the same technique the following year when the twenty-month agreement expired in July 1982. But much water was to flow under Westminster Bridge before then.

Patrick Jenkin had already hinted to the House of Commons that the government would not stand in the way of a Private Member's Bill on cigarette advertising:

> I have made it clear to the industry that the House must be free to continue to express its view on smoking and initiate such action as it might see fit; but I have indicated to the industry that I can give no undertaking on behalf of the government to obstruct legislation in the meantime.[11]

In the House of Commons, individual MPs as well as the government of the day can initiate legislation in the form of Private Member's Bills. They are able to do this under a number of complex procedures: they may enter a ballot from which twenty names are drawn (time is allocated for the discussion of the winners' Bills on twelve Fridays of the parliamentary session); they may make an advocatory speech under the 'Ten Minute Rule' after Question Time on Tuesdays and Wednesdays (only fifteen Bills have become law in this way since 1945); or they may introduce the Bill under a special Standing Order (No. 37). Private Member's Bills are rarely successfull: in the 1981–82 session only eight out of seventy-two became law.[12] Labour M P, Laurie Pavitt, deserves a place in the *Guinness Book of Records*, having tried sixteen times in sixteen years to get an anti-smoking Private Member's Bill on the Statute Book, mainly involving advertising restrictions. The industry's supporters are benignly dismissive of his efforts. 'His campaign is looked upon as a bit of a joke,' said the former Conservative M P for Bristol North-West, Michael Colvin. 'On balance, because the industry is so responsible, there'll be no attempt by any government to stop the advertising of tobacco products.' Laurie Pavitt's fifteenth Private Member's Bill, which he had carefully steered through its First Reading, would have given the Secretary of State statutory power to reduce cigarette advertising to whatever level he thought right, and would have virtually eliminated tobacco sponsorship of sport and the arts. The Bill was due to come up for its Second Reading on Friday, June 12th, 1981. Private Member's Bills seldom prosper except when they are faced with no concerted opposition and a government prepared to give them a fair wind. Patrick Jenkin had already indicated that the wind was blowing in Mr Pavitt's direction. There would, of course, always be opposition from the industry's supporters in the House, but it did not seem insuperable, given government support at the time.

One tactic opponents of any Private Member's Bill can use is to talk out the Bill which is listed before it, so that there is no time left for debate on the Bill they wish to kill. This was the tactic the industry's parliamentary supporters used to defeat Laurie Pavitt's fifteenth Private Member's Bill. The effort was made because, on the face of it, Pavitt stood an outside chance of being fifteenth time lucky, through the government's tacit blessing. On Wednesday evening he went to the Commons vote office to pick up the papers for the Friday debate. Friday is early closing day at Westminster, as all debates end at two thirty p.m. Pavitt looked to see if his Bill was likely to be squeezed out by the deadline. The omens seemed good. The Bill which came before it, on licensing private zoos, seemed uncontentious enough and, as he looked through the papers, likely to go through fairly quickly as there were no amendments attached. On Thursday morning, Pavitt checked again. There were still no amendments. The Zoos Bill was unadorned. When he came to check again on Friday morning, the day of the debate, a correspondent from one of the medical papers said, 'You realise you've been clobbered again.' Pavitt looked at the order paper again and said he saw over 160 amendments. Thirty of them had been tabled by the Bristol MP Michael Colvin, and twenty-seven by BAT's parliamentary consultant, Sir Anthony Kershaw. Most of them were single word modifications. Laurie Pavitt's Bill was talked out. The Zoos Bill ate up all the time. It was a triumph for animal welfare.

I asked Sir Anthony Kershaw how he became involved in zoos. 'I've always been interested in animals,' he said, 'but I didn't want, neither did any of the hierarchy in the House want, to see Laurie Pavitt's Bill go through, because it was early in the session and it might have come up for its Third Reading. If it had made progress, we'd have gone to the government and said, "Are you going to stick to your position [and abide by the voluntary agreement] or are you going to let this Bill go through. If you do, then all bets are off as far as the tobacco industry is concerned."'

Having concluded their short voluntary agreement with the industry in November 1980, Patrick Jenkin and Sir George Young then turned their attention to the negotiation of a new agreement on sports sponsorship. Although they exercised no right of veto over the agreement, which since 1977 had been the preserve of the Department of the Environment and not the DHSS, they were consulted as an interested party. The previous agreement, which had been negotiated by Sports Minister Denis Howell in 1977 (under which the companies had agreed to control their spending and keep brand names off signs at televised events) was due to expire in December 1980, but had been extended a further year, until December 1981, because Sir George and his colleagues did not want to see a 'soft' agreement on sport while they were fighting to get a tough agreement on advertising. The Conservative Minister for Sport at the time was Hector Monro, who had once been a Scottish Health Minister. Patrick Jenkin tried to convince him of the need for a tough agreement. 'I tried to persuade Hector Monro that he ought to pitch the thing very high. He simply said, "Well, we simply have to have the money for sport." David Ennals ran into exactly the same problem vis-à-vis Denis Howell. Denis Howell had an agreement which ensured continued money for sport, and it went quite contrary to the

Ennals' agreement. The same happened under this government. I asked Hector Monro that he should make it a condition that they did not advertise brand names [in the title of the event]. They could advertise the company but not the brand.' (In other words, the Benson & Hedges final would become the Gallahers Final, the John Player League would become the Imperial League, and the Marlboro British Grand Prix would become the Philip Morris British Grand Prix.) 'He refused to accept that. He said, "You'd never get the money." He didn't accept my pressure.'

Sir George Young and his colleague, the Scottish Health Minister Russell Fairgrieve, also tried to persuade Hector Monro to take a hard line with the industry. They had no more success than Patrick Jenkin. Sir George said, 'We had a chat with Hector beforehand and tried to explain this aspect to him. We reminded him that he'd been a Health Minister in the previous government. But Hector wasn't going to turn off the tap. Health was peripheral. I explained that the companies were getting round all our restrictions by bombing money into sport. We made very little progress.' Russell Fairgrieve explained how irreconcilable their positions were. 'The conflict of interest was clear. We wanted to cut down sponsorship, while it was in the Department's interest to have more sport. The tobacco companies didn't sponsor sport unless they assumed it would help the sale of cigarettes.' But there was pressure from the other side too.

In July 1981, while Health Ministers were trying hard to lean on the Sports Minister, there was a reception held at No.10 Downing Street. One of the guests was the Minister for Health, Dr Gerard Vaughan, who was a personal friend of the Thatchers. (He had not been directly involved in any of the negotiations with the industry.) The *Daily Mirror* subsequently reported that Denis Thatcher, the Prime Minister's husband (and a keen sports fan) was alleged to have pointed out to Dr Vaughan:

' . . . that sport could lose a lot of money if the Health Department kept up its tough line on tobacco companies' sponsorship of sporting events.'[13]

Adam Raphael of the *Observer* carried the same story and went on to say:

Dr Vaughan reported this conversation with the Prime Minister's husband at the Department and recommended that Ministers should take a more relaxed view about the whole issue of tobacco sponsorship of sport.[14]

In response to the story, a Downing Street spokesman said: 'We do not comment on scurrilous gossip like this. We do not go into what people do or do not do at a private function.'[15] The DHSS stonewalled with the statement: 'The Department cannot comment on alleged private conversations involving Ministers.'[16]

A few weeks after the Downing Street reception, on August 5th, 1981, the Prime Minister and her husband were shown tobacco's contribution to sport at first hand, when they flew into Norwich airport in a private Cessna jet, chartered by the chief of Lotus Cars, the late Colin Chapman.[17] On the tarmac to greet them stood the black and gold John Player Special team Lotus, in its full cigarette livery with brand name on the bonnet. The Thatchers looked over the car while Colin Chapman explained the refinements. The Prime Minister had a special interest in motor sport as her son, Mark, was a racing driver who was on the books of Championship Sports Specialists, which handles sponsorship for a number of major companies including Imperial's John Player Special racing team.

By the summer of 1981, the Prime Minister was aware of the growing opposition within her own party to the course on which Sir George Young was embarked. She had already assured the House of Commons that she believed in the voluntary agreement and had added: 'I believe we should be very slow indeed in thinking of imposing any statutory regulations.'[18] Ideologically, Margaret Thatcher was as opposed to the 'Nanny State' as almost any member of the freedom lobby on her back benches. Instinctively, she too would be opposed to any legislation which appeared to interfere with the right of an individual to make his own choice. Nevertheless, despite the warning signs from the Tory back benches, Sir George was determined to press ahead. He had already begun to turn his mind to the next voluntary agreement, which would have to be negotiated when the current one expired in July 1982. Sensing that the industry was unlikely to make any greater concessions in 1982 than it had in 1980, he once again prepared legislation, either to concentrate the companies' minds or to put into practice if the threat failed to have the desired effect.

Plans were made to use once again the Health Services (Miscellaneous Provisions) Bill in November 1982 as a way of leaving the door open for legislation. But the plans never got beyond the drawing board. The government did not share Sir George's enthusiasm for the fight, or his view of national priorities and, as governments always do, backed away from a showdown with the industry. With nearly three million unemployed, the last thing the government wanted was a political storm on what it regarded as a peripheral issue involving one of Britain's most successful industries, much valued provider of jobs and source of greatly needed revenue. Sir George Young was prepared to do more than just pay lip service to the smoking and health cliché, 'the biggest preventable cause of death and disease': he was on the point of taking political action on the basis that the words actually meant what they said. But in the political and economic climate of the day words seemed more prudent than deeds as far as cigarettes were concerned. Sir George was moved to the Department of the Environment in Mrs Thatcher's government reshuffle of September 1981, where he was subsequently given special responsibility for Britain's ethnic minorities. With Brixton still smouldering from the race riots earlier that summer, the Prime Minister probably decided that Sir George's proven energies could be put to better and safer use elsewhere. Russell Fairgrieve, the Scottish Health Minister who shared Sir George's conviction and determination, returned to the back benches with a knighthood. Patrick Jenkin was promoted to the Department of Industry, as Secretary of State, the Ministry officially responsible for sponsoring tobacco, although he made it clear that his views had not changed. The only survivor at the DHSS was the Minister of Health, Dr Gerard Vaughan. Tobacco's opponents were removed at a stroke and with them the plan to introduce legislation. When the Health Services (Miscellaneous Provisions) Bill resurfaced to go through Parliament in 1983, the clause which Patrick Jenkin and Sir George Young had proposed to use as a vehicle for legislation was no longer part of the Bill.

Reflecting on the revolution, Russell Fairgrieve said, 'We in the Health Ministry were not looking at it from the point of view of promoting sport, not looking at it from the point of view of revenue, not from the point of view of jobs. We were looking at it, single-minded, from the point of view of health. Our position was that cigarettes caused 50,000 deaths a year. We had to act. We were tough. We were committed. We did pose a threat.' The Ministers who succeeded Patrick Jenkin and Sir George Young posed the industry no threat. Ideologically they were in sympathy with the freedom lobby which had been largely responsible for the removal of Sir George Young. Sir George was replaced by Geoffrey Finsberg who, in his first speech at a conference of European Ministers responsible for public health, declared:

My government does not welcome the use of regulatory or legislative measures in order to control the legitimate commercial freedom of tobacco companies.[19]

Patrick Jenkin was replaced as Secretary of State by Norman Fowler who, as Minister of Transport, had opposed the seatbelt legislation on ideological grounds.[20] (The new seatbelt law was estimated to have saved a 1,000 people from serious injury or death in the first two months of its operation—February and March 1983.) Mr Fowler said he was not convinced that legislation curtailing cigarette advertising would lead to a decline in smoking, and therefore it was:

. . . legitimate to weigh the possible but unproven benefit to the nation's health against other factors such as the need to avoid unnecessary interference in the activities of private industry . . .[21]

Dr Gerard Vaughan was later replaced as Minister for Health by Kenneth Clarke, the Nottingham MP who had defended the industry and its sponsorship of sport in the House of Commons in 1976. He had warned:

I can understand the exasperation growing on the part of the tobacco industry which is manufacturing a lawful product . . .

in the attacks on sports sponsorship there is the serious danger
of grave damage being done to sport in this country purely in
the interests of anti-smoking.[22]

(The Parliamentary Private Secretary to the new Minister of
Health, David Trippier, was one of FOREST's fifty guests, along
with the new Sports Minister, Neil Macfarlane, at a reception
held at the House of Commons in June 1982.)

Mike Daube, a Senior Lecturer in Community Medicine and
former Director of ASH, called the revolution the beginning of 'a
new dark age for preventive medicine':

> It was almost certainly an accident that Sir George found
> himself at DHSS; it is no accident that as soon as he looked like
> succeeding, he was replaced by a hard line opponent. It is a
> measure of the power of the industry and the lack of
> importance attached by politicians to prevention, that the move
> was so easy to make and attracted so little attention.[23]

The freedom fighters savoured their victory. I asked three of
them about Sir George's fate. Sir Christopher Foxley-Norris,
FOREST's Chairman and founder, said:

> He's a classic example of how over-enthusiastic, ill informed
> critics of smoking can damage the anti-smoking campaign. In
> fact the government got rid of him eventually. They moved him.
> They went and put in some sane and less excitable people.

Conservative MP Martin Stevens, who circulated the 'Nanny
State' letter amongst Tory backbenchers, said:

> I am quite pleased that he's no longer responsible for that
> particular area of activity. I think we've now got a much more
> balanced and rational approach and one that is willing to listen
> to arguments and evidence.

Sir Anthony Kershaw, BAT's parliamentary consultant, said:

> I got the impression that unless he was overruled, the voluntary
> agreement would go for a burton. He was moved. He was

causing a lot of perturbation at a time when industry was getting awfully nervous about the recession. It could have been a very large self-inflicted wound for social reasons which didn't command a great deal of enthusiasm. It was not politically sensible. There would have been a major political row about a peripheral matter at a time when the government was deeply unpopular and the recession was very bad. This is the political reality. You don't run head-on into a brick wall. You stop.

With Sir George Young out of the way, the wheels ran smoothly again. In 1982, a new sponsorship agreement was signed by the new Sports Minister, Neil Macfarlane. Shortly afterwards a new voluntary agreement was reached between the industry and the new Health Ministers at the DHSS. The agreement was an indication of the revolution which had taken place. Health warnings were changed—back to the old one: 'Warning: Cigarettes Can Seriously Damage Your Health'. The size of the warnings on posters and advertisements was increased—by six per cent. The industry was to give £11 million over the period of the agreement for health promotion research, especially among young people—provided the research was not 'designed directly or indirectly to examine the use and effects of tobacco products'.[24]

I asked Geoffrey Finsberg, who had taken over Sir George Young's responsibilities in negotiating the agreement, why there had been a retreat on the health warning. He said that he personally had wanted a stronger warning, featuring the word 'death', but the companies were not prepared to accept it and he was not prepared to push it. 'I'm perfectly satisfied with the one we've got,' he said. Why exclude smoking from the health research, especially when it was particularly concerned with young people? 'The companies who are putting up the money have to consider the interests of their shareholders. It will be quite understandable if they were not prepared to finance something that was directly against their interests. There is such an enormous field to be covered by the way of health research that anyone who turns down 11 million quid is an idiot.' Did he fight the exclusion? 'No, because it's common sense.' Hadn't he boxed himself in by saying in advance that he didn't favour legislation? 'No. All I was doing was putting into words what has in fact been the policy of successive governments. No government has in fact legislated because in a free society you can't legislate. And there's no proof that legislation actually reduces the amount of cigarettes actually smoked. All it seems to do is to cause brand switching. It doesn't cause people to smoke. I think the agreement we got this time is a major advance.'

Not surprisingly, the health lobby saw the agreement as a huge step backwards. Dr Keith Ball, ASH Vice-President, said:

We are distressed that the Government has accepted the industry's offer of £3 million [a year] for research on health promotion but not on smoking. This is less than the cost of a single cigarette brand launch, and is likely to be used as a smokescreen to obscure the unparalleled dangers of smoking compared to other health risks. It is beyond belief that the tobacco industry has the sheer effrontery to claim an interest in health promotion when it excludes from research the major avoidable cause of ill health in Britain today.[25]

I asked Sir George Young if he agreed with his successor's view that the agreement was a major advance. 'No comment' came the sharp reply. Appropriately, when Laurie Pavitt tried yet again in 1982 to get his Private Member's Bill through for the sixteenth time, Michael Colvin, the Bristol MP, said it was ' . . . a misguided attempt by the anti-smoking lobby to drive a nail into the non-existent coffin of the tobacco industry'. 'The tobacco industry is well,' he assured the House of Commons. 'It is getting fitter every day'.[26]

The tobacco industry was 'well', because the Smoke Ring had protected it from the most serious and concerted political attack it had faced in twenty years. The claim that it was 'getting fitter every day' was a measure of the industry's confidence in the ability of the Smoke Ring to protect it for the next twenty years. As the following chapters will show, the Smoke Ring has proved to be equally effective on the other side of the Atlantic.

9

The Golden Leaf

In America the politics of tobacco are rooted deep in its soil and history, because the Golden Leaf is grown there. The tobacco industry never fails to point out the fact, in the hope that people will associate tobacco with the good things instead of the millions of premature deaths from smoking-related diseases. The Tobacco Institute, the industry-financed lobbying and propaganda organisation, ran double-page colour advertisements in national magazines, showing America's agricultural heritage—corn, wheat, cotton and soya beans—lying on America's first-ever cash crop—tobacco. Beneath the caption 'There's a lot of America in each of these crops' were the words:

They feed, clothe and give pleasure to peoples around the world. And, in doing so, they bring us all that much closer together.

Each has its own separate history, far longer than man's recorded history.

Tobacco was our first cash crop, the salvation of the strugging Jamestown Colony 350 years ago. It was our first step into the international trade in which all of these now excell.

Wherever in the world they go, and they go nearly everywhere, they say something good about us as a country. Because they are the finest of their kind.[1]

There was a government health warning in the corner. The economic importance of the crop and the political power exercised by those elected to defend it have made the Smoke Ring even more impenetrable in America.

The economic contribution tobacco makes to the country is enormous: it provides $57 billion of the gross national product; $14 billion of total federal tax revenue; $7 billion of total state and local tax revenues; and a $2 billion net surplus on the balance of payments. In addition, it creates jobs for nearly half a million people directly employed in the industry, and for nearly two million overall in tobacco and related industries.[2] As in the United Kingdom, on a purely financial basis, the economic benefits of tobacco far outweigh the health care costs. Smoking related diseases are estimated to cost over $8 billion—nearly eight per cent of America's total bill for health care.[3] (Lung cancer alone costs $3.8 billion in lost earnings, $380 million in short-term hospital costs, and $78 million in physicians' fees.)[4] Federal and state revenues for tobacco of $22 billion cover nearly three times that amount. (No direct comparison with the United Kingdom can be made in terms of cost to the national exchequer because most health care costs in America are paid for by private medical insurance, not a National Health Service.)

The source of this vast wealth is generated by 600,000 tobacco farm families, mainly concentrated in the Southern states of North Carolina, Kentucky, Virginia, South Carolina, Tennessee, Georgia, Florida and Alabama. This is where the politics of tobacco in America begin. To see why they are such a powerful force, I visited Pitt County in North Carolina, which the locals proudly call 'the largest tobacco producing county in the largest tobacco producing state in the largest tobacco producing nation in the world'. The result of the labours of Pitt County's 2,500 tobacco farmers is, according to one of them, 'A wide array of safe and healthy tobacco products for the consumer's choice to be found on store shelves across the nation and around the world.' Pitt County lies amidst the fertile plains of Norfolk sandy loam soil in which the tobacco plant flourishes, to the east of the town of Raleigh, where Buck Duke sold his first tobacco after the American Civil War. Tobacco country gradually creeps upon you as the tall stalks with their broad green leaves begin to fill in the gaps between the fields of American maize which line the highway. (Even in the heart of tobacco country, corn often covers five times the acreage of tobacco. There are legal restrictions on the amount of tobacco a farmer may grow: there are none on growing corn. Corn brings in nearly $250 an acre; tobacco brings in over four times that much.)[5] Broken-down curing barns of rain-washed wood dot the landscape, their rusty tin chimneys still clinging to the roofs. (Tobacco leaves are dried in barns heated by a hot flue. Flue-cured tobacco is what most people smoke.) Weeds and ivy choke the abandoned shacks where tobacco workers once lived. Just outside the hamlet of Farmville, there is an old truck stop station with a faded 'Philips 66' sign in the forecourt, which has not seen a truck in years. Tobacco farming is not what it used to be. Gas-fired curing barns and mechanical harvesters have stripped Pitt County of many of its workers, and with it much of the traditional romance of tobacco. Many farmers in the county have been growing tobacco for generations. James Clarence ('J.C.') Galloway's family has farmed there for nearly 200 years. The records only date back to the beginning of the last century, when the courthouse was burned down, and the county's history with it. 'We've had a rough time keeping records,' says J.C.'s son, Jim Junior. 'First your guys came [the English] and burned out our courthouse, and then the Yankees came and did it again.' In 1840, J.C.'s grandfather, John Bryant Galloway, traded two slaves from his farm for a slave who had worked as a ship's carpenter and belonged to a friend in the seaport of Wilmington. The slave came to Greenville, Pitt County, and built the family farmhouse, which still stands today, although empty, on the edge of the Galloway's eighty acres of tobacco. 'It's built of pitch pine,' says J.C. proudly. 'It'll never rot.' Behind the white wooden house stand the skeletons of old curing barns which had been set well apart from each other so that if one burned down, the others wouldn't go up in smoke as well. I asked Jim Junior how old they were. 'About fifty to seventy years. They didn't used to get real old, they burned down so fast.'

In front of the house is a row of new curing barns, like metal mobile homes, now fired with liquid propane gas. They cure twice as much tobacco with half the labour and do it much faster than the old wooden barns at the back. On the wall of J. C. Galloway's study is a wooden plaque with the inscription: 'Warning: the tobacco industry has determined that the Surgeon-General may be dangerous to your health.' By the overflowing ashtray on the desk is a pile of 'Pride in Tobacco' (a public relations slogan designed by R. J. Reynolds) mailing stamps, to remind everybody that 'tobacco pays over $50 billion in taxes each year'. I asked father and son about smoking and health. J.C. waved his cigarette in the air and said he was trying to cut down from three packs a day. He was now smoking low tar. 'See this,' he said, 'there's four milligrams of tar and four-tenths of a milligram of nicotine there. I've smoked all my life. The damn reason I'm smoking this is because I'm trying to quit smoking.' I smiled. 'Yeah, I'm trying to cut my throat. I switched to these to cut down and try to quit, but I smoke twice as many to get the tar and nicotine my body's got the demand for. Look at that,' he said, pointing to the ashtray full of cigarette ends. I asked him why he wanted to quit. 'I just feel that at my age, and as much as I smoked, it's detrimental to my health maybe a little bit.'

Jim Junior interrupted. 'We as average citizens don't argue the health question. We leave it up to the medical people. They're supposed to know. My contention is that as long as tobacco is going to be a legitimate product and is going to be consumed, we should make every possible effort to maintain our place in the market. If eventually the medical authorities are successful in their efforts and they reduce smoking, then we'll have to reduce our production. But we wouldn't stop people smoking if we farmers in North Carolina didn't produce another acre of tobacco. It's gonna be produced. It's gonna be brought in anyhow. We're experiencing this in marijuana right now. Our coast down here is just lousy with the stuff. It's coming in in boatloads and boatloads. If we didn't grow it, tobacco would still come in.'

'Take liquor,' his father added. 'There was a time when the government outlawed it, but we drank just as much. [North Carolina is famous for its 'moonshine'—alcohol brewed in illegal stills.] But the government wasn't getting a thing from it. The Mafia was making all the money, so we legalised it again. Why outlaw tobacco and go through it all again. People are going to smoke anyway.'

Although tobacco farmers are obviously worried about

[154]

smoking and health, because in the end it affects the demand for their crop, they are far more concerned about the survival of the federal price support system which for half a century has ensured that the leaf has remained 'golden'. This, more than any other single issue, is the driving force behind the politics of tobacco in America. Tobacco survives not just because 53 million Americans smoke a total of 635 billion cigarettes a year,[6] but because the federal government *guarantees* the tobacco farmer a greater return on his investment than on almost any other crop. In 1981, a US Department of Agriculture survey found that it cost a farmer on average $1.41 to produce one pound of tobacco. At market he was guaranteed at the very minimum £1.59 a pound—a clear profit of eighteen cents on every pound of tobacco he produced.[7] To the 44,000 tobacco farmers in North Carolina, the price support programme is sacred. When you look at the figures, it is easy to see why. In 1979 the net profit for tobacco in North Carolina was $1,198 per acre, compared to $233 for peanuts and $72 for soya beans.[8] The tobacco price support programme is a gold-plated insurance policy. It is ironical that the federal government guarantees the profitability of a crop whose product it then discourages people from using. The administrative cost of the support programme alone, $13 million in 1981,[9] is equal to the amount the government spends on educational programmes designed to persuade people not to smoke.

The tobacco price support programme has its origins in the 1930s, when tobacco farmers all over America were going broke. Too many farmers were producing too much tobacco and the companies were buying it up for next to nothing. For generations, fathers had divided up their land amongst their sons so that farms became smaller and smaller. Many depended on the tobacco patch for survival. When the marked collapsed, thousands of small farmers went out of business and, like Joad in John Steinbeck's *The Grapes of Wrath*, left the land for an uncertain future elsewhere. In Pitt County, farmers flocked to mass meetings in Greenville and demanded political action to stop the disaster. A delegation of a dozen tobacco growers was sent to Washington. One of its members was James Cleveland Galloway, J.C.'s father. Similar delegations arrived from all over the country and lobbied the Congress and President Roosevelt to restore order to the market by guaranteeing the price of their crop. The government agreed to provide the farmers with a floor price guarantee of seventeen cents a pound, and the farmers agreed to cut back their production of tobacco by a quarter.[10] The price support programme was a kind of agrarian socialism. The government set up the Commodity Credit Corporation, a form of state agricultural bank which borrowed money from the US Treasury and let it to farmers at preferential interest rates, whether they raised wheat, cotton, corn, sugar, hogs or tobacco. The money was channelled to the farmers through grower co-operatives which were established in every county. When the farmer took his tobacco to auction, any which failed to fetch one cent above the government support price was automatically bought up by the co-operative and put into storage to be sold another year. (Tobacco properly stored maintains its quality for many years.) The farmers then repaid their loans to the co-operative, and the co-operative repaid its loans to the Commodity Credit Corporation. When, and if, the tobacco put into storage was sold, the proceeds went to pay off the loan for which it had been the collateral.

In 1939 the voluntary agreement to restrict production broke down, and farmers planted thousands more acres of tobacco (1,159,000 pounds compared with the average of 709 million pounds of the preceding ten years).[11] The market was flooded. When the British, who were one of tobacco's main customers, stopped buying as Britain entered the Second World War, there was economic chaos once again. To stabilise the situation once and for all, the government imposed a legal restriction on the amount of tobacco which could be grown. Each farmer was allocated an acreage 'allotment' of tobacco, which was tied for ever to the land to which it was given. If the land was sold, the allotment went with it. In the forty years since the tobacco programme was started, land has changed hands many times, and much of it has passed out of agricultural use altogether. Jim Galloway Junior showed me houses which were being built where a farm once stood. He said that the builder who bought the plot would have leased the tobacco allotment which came with it to a farmer who wanted to grow more tobacco. He explained that half the eighty acres of tobacco which he and his father grew were allotments they had leased from other people. 'The allotments are only a piece of paper,' he said.

In 1981, computer records showed that North Carolina had an exclusive 'club' of 116,098 allotment holders,[12] whose members ranged from truck drivers and construction workers[13] to huge institutions and corporations. The US Department of Agriculture estimates that fifty-eight per cent of allotment holders lease their tobacco allocation to farmers for roughly $1,000 per acre per season.[14] America's tobacco farmers are thought to pay $279 million a year[15] to allotment holders, which inevitably pushes up the price of US tobacco. Among North Carolina's 50,000 non-farming allotment holders are: 151 doctors who own a total of over 500 acres; nineteen churches; twenty-five public bodies; Richard Nixon's Alma Mater, Duke University (named after Buck); the Carolina Power and Light Company, owner of over 200 acres; the Raleigh YMCA, owner of five acres; and Mrs Dorothy Helms, the wife of US Senator Jesse Helms, who inherited two acres after her father's death (she gives the proceeds to the church). This semi-feudal system of tobacco growing has been readily seized upon by Washington's growing army of tobacco programme critics, but their main point of attack is the programme's cost. Despite the insistence of tobacco supporters that there 'is no tobacco subsidy', the programme has cost the American taxpayer millions of dollars. The Report of the US Comptroller-General[16] which provides the most official and authoritative figures available, shows that although the programme in theory pays for itself, because the farmers repay the federal loans when their tobacco is sold, the losses on principal and interest charges have been considerable. Since the programme began in the 1930s, $57 million in loan principal have been lost through tobacco staying in storage and never being sold: and until April 1981 (when the practice was stopped) at least $591 million had been lost in interest charges, because the Commodity Credit Corporation borrowed the money from the US Treasury at the prime rate and let it to the farmers at a special cheap rate. The Report states:

The Department's estimates indicate a $591 million difference between the Corporation's interest payments to the US

Treasury ($845 million) and its interest income ($254 million) from the inception of the programme . . .[17]

It concludes:

The tobacco price support programme has incurred substantial unreported interest cost expenses . . . additional losses can be expected on loans made at below market interest rates before April 1981.[18]

In addition to these subsidised losses, the administrative costs of the programme were still running at $7 million a year in 1982 (after President Reagan's Budget Director, David Stockman, had cut the $13 million running costs of the year before). Tobacco politicians, like Senator Walter Huddleston of Kentucky, insist that the tobacco programme is:

. . . the best, most efficient, least costly programme that has ever been devised to assist in the agricultural product of this country.[19]

Critics like Senator Mark Hatfield of Oregon points out the anomaly of subsidising a commodity which causes its consumers such harm:

Since 1938, the Federal government has been participating in support of tobacco while at the same time, because of the associated health problems to the consumer, is spending millions of dollars to discourage the use of tobacco products. I find this to be an offensive paradox, a tragic comedy of moral and fiscal irresponsibility. It is time to re-evaluate our policy towards this commodity.[20]

Given the glaring paradox, it might seem surprising that the tobacco price support programme has survived for so long. The fact that it has is a tribute to the political skill and power of the tobacco state politicians. Tobacco price supports have remained untouched in the Congress for decades because they were placed out of reach by the powerful Southern politicians who dominated the House of Representatives and the Senate for so many years. Unlike their Northern counterparts, they were re-elected for term after term, almost automatically. Some of them stayed in the Senate for over twenty years. Because seniority commanded power, this group of Southern politicians gained control of most of the key committees whose deliberations affected tobacco's continuing prosperity. They ensured that tobacco was given 'permanent authorisation': in other words, tobacco price supports, unlike those for other agricultural commodities, did not have to be renewed on a regular basis. For decades tobacco was safe from its political enemies.

The other reason for its survival is that it is a matter of political life and death for the forty tobacco state Congressmen who are sent to Washington to defend it. The tobacco lobby on Capitol Hill enjoys a power out of all proportion to its size. The crop is only grown in fifty-one of America's 531 congressional districts, and is a major factor in only twenty-seven of those.[21] But the forty politicians who represent a constituency which outnumbers the combined membership of the United Auto Workers and United Steelworkers of America, know that they will not get re-elected if they do not fight for tobacco until their last breath. John Merritt, the administrative assistant to North Carolina Congressman Charles Rose, explained the political dynamic. 'When you've got forty members of Congress acting like kamikaze pilots, they cannot be defeated. There is no tomorrow if there's no tobacco programme. The boys here in the capital like to stay here. I guess they like the restaurants. When you threaten their very existence, they can get very active. There's no better lobbyist than a member of Congress on the floor of the House, fighting for his life. It's the most effective lobby in the world.' It was no idle boast. In 1981, the tobacco lobby defeated the most concerted attack ever made on the tobacco price support programme, in a way which astonished even its own supporters.

The conservative tide which had swept Ronald Reagan into the White House in November 1980 had also carried many of his conservative supporters into the Congress. There they joined a handful of conservatives already in place, led by Senator Jesse Helms of North Carolina, whose political machine, the Congressional Club, had played an important role in Reagan's election victory (as later chapters show). Helms, who had been a commentator on the tobacco radio network in his home town of Raleigh before his election to the Senate in 1972, makes Britain's 'freedom' lobby look progressive. One of his political goals was to dismantle the federal spending programme which, from Roosevelt's 'New Deal' to Lyndon Johnson's 'Great Society', had been designed to help America's less fortunate citizens but which Helms believed rewarded the indolent and penalised the hard-working. Reinforced by his new allies in the Congress and supported by a President who shared many of his views, Helms launched his attack on federal spending. But his Achilles heel was the tobacco price support programme, which logically he ought to have targeted, but politically he had to defend. Other conservatives did not share Helms' dilemma. The price support programme was now especially vulnerable, as it faced ideological as well as ethical opposition. In 1981, its opponents took the offensive in both the Senate and the House of Representatives. Because of its 'permanent authorisation', the only way tobacco price supports could be attacked was by tabling an amendment to the 1981 Farm Bill. Although tobacco was under sentence in both the Senate and the House of Representatives, its survival in the Senate was more assured because of the Republican majority and Helms' authority over his colleagues.

On September 17th, Senator Mark Hatfield of Oregon introduced Amendment 524:

> Purpose: to repeal federal provisions of law establishing agricultural programs concerning the marketing of the price support for tobacco . . .

Introducing his Amendment, Senator Hatfield said:

> Let the tobacco farmer stand on his own feet as we are asking the welfare recipients and the poor and the needy and the minorities and all the others in America because we are prone to cut the programs upon which they depend. I suppose that many people, including myself, find it unconscionable to allow Americans to go hungry while supporting an inedible and unhealthy crop like tobacco . . . are we placing more

importance on a product that destroys life than we are on a
concern to support lives and the needs for nutrition and health?
. . . We spend billions to discourage smoking, and yet continue
to assist the growing of tobacco.[22]

Senator Jesse Helms told his critics they had got it all wrong:

There is no such thing as a tobacco subsidy. I wish we had a
hundred programs like the tobacco program, because we
would not have to collect any income tax from anyone . . . I will
say to my friend that if he really wants to see a lollapalooza of a
welfare program, let him be successful in destroying the
program then he will see people on welfare who are now
making a living productively; he will see young people not
going to college who are going to college now, thanks to the
incomes of their parents who operate small family farms . . .
    Do you realise that the tobacco industry provides two million
jobs? The tobacco industry produces $30 billion in wages and
earnings annually. $30 billion? Do you realise it represents
$15.5 billion in capital investment? Every year this much
maligned industry produces for this government and for state
governments and local governments $22 billion in taxes. So the
simple arithmetic . . . is who is doing what to whom when
efforts are made to destroy this program? . . . We would really
be having a tough time trying to make ends meet were it not for
the tobacco program.[23]

Senator George Mitchell from Maine supported Senator
Hatfield's Amendment:

. . . at a time when budget cuts are making our schoolchildren
to treat ketchup as a 'vegetable' in their school lunches, even
lower cost programs have to go. Tobacco allotments and price
supports are a luxury we can no longer afford . . . There is a
direct link between the use of tobacco and lung disease, birth
disease and forms of cancer not previously associated with
tobacco use. But there is no rational link between tobacco and
government support of its production . . . If we are truly
concerned about the health of our citizens, and if we are to have

the courage to strike down government support of a product which imperils that health, we must vote to eliminate the tobacco program.[24]

Senator Walter Huddleston of Kentucky (whose state has 124,000 tobacco farmers) supported Senator Helms of North Carolina and spoke of what tobacco had done for his state:

> We have initiated certain programs to help, for instance, youngsters go to college. I venture to say that more Kentuckians have received a college education because of the tobacco program and by no other reason than by all the federal programs we have in the state to help educate young people, and it has not cost the government a penny . . . for 276,000 farmers in 22 states is the principal cash crop . . . what happens if all these small farmers, or if very many of them have to leave the farm? Where is the city in the United States that has excess jobs available to take care of these farm families, the youngsters, the parents who cannot stay on the farm . . .?[25]

Senator Helms and tobacco won the day. Senator Hatfield's Amendment was defeated by fifty-three votes to forty-two.

But the real battle was fought in the House of Representatives, where there was a Democratic majority whose ethical opposition to the tobacco price support programme seemed bound to ensure its defeat. Few gave tobacco any chance of survival. But the tobacco state Congressmen had spent years buying political insurance for a time like this, and they were now ready to cash in their investment, to save tobacco and themselves. The way they did it is the most graphic illustration of how the politics of tobacco work on Capitol Hill.

The architect of this remarkable victory was Charles Rose, one of North Carolina's Democratic Congressmen (the other four were Republicans) and his administrative assistant John Merritt. The key to their strategy was to win the support of the House Democratic leadership and in particular of the House Majority Leader, Tip O'Neill, next to Edward Kennedy, Boston's most famous politician. Rose had astutely made his number with O'Neill when he first came to Washington as a freshman

Congressman in the early 1970s. Before the new Congress officially went into session, he had noticed in *Time* that three men were running for the most important job in the House of Representatives—House Majority Leader. Rose asked around to see who was the best bet and O'Neill emerged as the clear favourite. Just before the election was held, Rose walked into O'Neill's office and found him at his desk, studying six dozen photographs of the new freshman Democrats who were going to ensure his election or defeat. Rose walked over to the desk, picked up his own photograph and held it up before O'Neill. 'I wanna be the first one for you, Tip,' he announced. (Boston politicians always remember who is for them, but they have a special memory for those who are for them first.) Rose was the first freshman from the class of '73 to give O'Neill his support and he has reaped the benefit ever since. Tip O'Neill pulled the levers of the Democratic machine out of loyalty to Rose and his Democratic colleagues from North Carolina. In the bitter fight over Reagan's budget cuts, most of the Southern Democrats had defected and voted with the Republicans. North Carolina's Democratic delegation, although regarded as part of the South, had no part in what was seen as an act of betrayal. They stayed faithful to the party line and were duly rewarded. 'No matter what their philosophy,' said O'Neill, 'the bulk of the party appreciates loyalty to the leadership.'[26] The word went out from the leader and the votes for tobacco came in. All but one of the twenty-five Committee Chairmen voted to keep the tobacco programme. Even California's Democrats, hardly tobacco's most natural friends, fell into line and voted fifteen to six in favour after the leader of the delegation had appealed for their help at their weekly breakfast meeting.[27]

'We put together a real extraordinary coalition,' explained John Merritt. 'Tobacco politics at the grower level in the form of a member of Congress, is the most sophisticated level of give and take politics there is. We're always doing favours. They're indelible. It's not quite as dramatic as signing in blood, but it's pretty close to it.' He gave me some examples. Dale Kildee, a Congressman from Michigan who is known as 'the Good Samaritan' because he helps senior citizens mend their leaky roofs and has a special typewriter in his office to communicate with deaf callers,[28] asked Rose for his support for a special education programme for the mentally retarded. 'Kildee would come up to these guys from North Carolina and say, "I know philosophically you may not be in support of this but believe me, it's good for the country and I'd really like your help on it." "Sure Dale," comes the reply, "I'd be glad to help ya. The folks back home won't understand, but I'll help you anyway." It's a kind of profile in courage. They vote for Kildee and Kildee does not forget. Kildee remembers that. Three or four years later, they come back to Kildee and say, "Dale, I've gotta have it now, buddy. I've gotta have it now." And Dale comes through for you.'

Over the years the North Carolina Democrats had made sure they had voted the right way (right, that is, for tobacco) on all the key issues. In 1979, most of the delegations had voted to support loans to bail out the Chrysler Corporation. Calling in the favour, Rose went across the floor of the House to one of the Michigan Congressmen, James Blanchard. Blanchard, who represents Detroit, opened his wallet and took out a crinkled piece of paper on which was recorded the vote on the Chrysler loan two years earlier. He looked down the list which confirmed that most of the North Carolina delegation had voted his way.[29] Blanchard gave tobacco his vote. In 1978, seven of Rose's delegation voted to support federal loan guarantees for New York City. 'We were for New York City,' says Merritt. 'Our constituents were dead against it. I mean dead against it. People in North Carolina don't like New Yorkers. One, they beat us in the Civil War; two, they talk funny; three, they're not very genteel and courteous. It's worse than the Argentinians and the British. Rose tells his incredulous constituents, "You'll just have to trust me." ' The North Carolina Democrats also voted to support federal fare subsidies for the New York Metro—although it was another issue which found little popularity with their constituents. One of the architects of this urban–rural coalition was former Congressman and Mayor of New York, Ed Koch. 'In the old days,' says one who watched him in Congress, 'Ed was bellicose about farmers. He's supposed to have said one time, "Who needs farms when we've got grocery stores." But over the years he was educated in the course of several Farm Bills. Deals were done. "you support us on our price support programs and we'll support you

on your special urban needs!"' When the time came, nine of
New York City's Congressmen voted for tobacco. The North
Carolina Democrats had also voted for Earthquake and Dis-
aster Aid to California, and Special Brucellosis Protection for
Texas.

One of the most effective allies was Carl Perkins, the
sixty-year-old Congressman from West Kentucky. Many of his
constituents are poor tobacco farmers. Over the years as
Chairman of the House Education and Labor Committee
Perkins, who represents one of the nation's poorest Congressional
districts, ensured that his constituents reaped every benefit from
every social and economic programme on offer. (It used to be said
of Wendell Rivers, who chaired the House Armed Services
Committee, that if he put one more military installation in his
district, it would sink.[30] Carl Perkins is the Wendell Rivers of West
Kentucky.) The poor, the blacks, the labour unions and the
teachers all had reason to be thankful to Carl Perkins. 'They love
"Pappy" Perkins on that Committee,' said Merritt. 'They love
him to death. They can't imagine what life would be like without
him. So he turns to the teachers' unions and the labour unions and
says, "Guys, I may not return if the tobacco program goes down
the tubes." So, because all their programs before Congress are
served by him, they say to their constituents back home, "We've
got to help 'Pappy' Perkins on this one, we've got to do it." And
whereas they may think that smoking is the worst thing in the
world, they can understand the intellectual arguments as to why
they can support the tobacco program and they come through for
"Pappy" Perkins. It's straight one on one, old time politics. "You
do me a favour and I'll do you a favour. If you really love me,
you'll help me."' The labour unions all came out in support of
tobacco; the United Auto Workers, the United Mine Workers, the
Teamsters, the AFL-CIO, the United Food and Commercial
Workers, and the International Ladies Garment Workers even
put their lobbying machines at its disposal. Evelyn Dubrow, a
lobbyist for the Garment Workers, said the unions supported
tobacco out of loyalty to Perkins and because the North Carolina
Democrats had voted with them in opposition to the Reagan tax
cuts. 'These are people who have been our friends,' she said.[31]
Perkins also rang Clarence Mitchell, the President of the National

Association for the Advancement of Coloured Peoples, and asked blacks to support tobacco. Blacks did.[32]

No arm was left untwisted. But not everyone gave in. With the backing of the American Lung Association and the American Cancer Society, Thomas Petri, a Congressman from the agricultural state of Wisconsin, obtained the support of over sixty of his colleagues in the House of Representatives for a bill to abolish the tobacco programme. When the Farm Bill came before the House, Petri had his bill redrafted as an amendment to the farm legislation. He admits he came under pressure from the powerful dairy lobby back home in Wisconsin, but despite calls from his dairy farming constituents,[33] Congressman Petri stood by his amendment and voted to abolish tobacco price supports.

Even Jesse Helms himself (although in the Senate and not in the House of Representatives) was a factor in the fight. Helms had made many political enemies because of his uncompromising stand on right wing issues. He had also made enemies within his own party, especially amongst those liberal Republicans who saw his philosophy leading them to electoral disaster. In the Senate, some Republicans voted against tobacco as a way of getting their own back on Helms. In the House of Representatives, the argument was turned on its head: the North Carolina delegation went round telling their fellow Democrats that if they did not vote for tobacco, Helms' political organisation, the Congressional Club, would eat them alive at the polls as the party which had lost North Carolina its tobacco programme.

Tobacco's opponents, or what was left of them, did not stand a chance. Price supports were saved because Democrats voted two to one to keep them: 156 Democrats and seventy-five Republicans voted in favour; seventy-eight Democrats and 106 Republicans voted against.[34] Tobacco had cashed its insurance policies and no one had failed to pay up. After the victory, Congressman Rose rode the special subway that leads from the Capitol to the House building where he had organised his troops. The old man who drives the train shouted, 'Hey, Congressman, my wife asked me to tell you how much she appreciated you saving our tobacco allotment. She's got a little farm down in North Carolina that we rent out, and it's got an allotment on it.'[35] As a result of the fight, tobacco politicians were astute enough to recognise that modifications would have to be made to some aspects of the price support system. At the time of writing, allotments are under review and farmers are considering a self-imposed levy on their crop, to pay for the cost of the programme. But these compromises were overshadowed by a setback tobacco's supporters had not foreseen. In July 1982, Senator Helms voted in support of President Reagan's tax bill which, among other things, doubled the excise tax on cigarettes from eight to sixteen cents. Helms fought the increase but failed to win the day. He argued he had no alternative: his continued opposition would have meant redrafting the bill in a way hostile to conservative interests.

The golden leaf survived in 1981 against the odds because its political supporters and their predecessors had spent many years refining the political skills necessary to defend tobacco in the Congress. The next chapter will show how those skills have been exercised to head off the repeated political attacks made on tobacco since the Surgeon-General published his landmark Report in 1964.

10

Unfair and Deceptive Practices

Throughout the 1960s and 1970s, the drive to regulate cigarettes came not from the US Congress, which tobacco had well under control, but from the Federal Trade Commission (FTC), the government agency which had the power to take action against 'unfair and deceptive practices' in business. For nearly twenty years a running battle was fought between the FTC, which was determined to take effective action against cigarettes, and the industry's supporters in Congress, who were determined to ensure that any action was largely cosmetic. The fight often centred around the Senate Commerce Committee which exercised responsibility over the FTC and had the power to confirm or curb its authority. The leading figure throughout the period was Michael Pertschuk, who served as a staff member of the Commerce Committee in the 1960s, then became its Senior Counsel and finally, in the late 1970s, was appointed Chairman of the FTC. Michael Pertschuk saw the battle from all angles.

The FTC was established in 1914 in the anti-trust climate in which Buck Duke's tobacco empire had been taken apart. Its original purpose was to prevent 'unfair methods of competition in commerce',[1] but its powers were widened in 1938 when it was given authority to regulate 'unfair or deceptive acts or practices in commerce'.[2] This authority was reaffirmed by the US Supreme Court in 1972. The FTC consisted of five Commissioners who were appointed by the President for a seven-year term of office. Not more than three Commissioners could be members of the same party, in order to preserve the political independence which was its hallmark. The President also appointed the Chairman. The agency has a formidable array of powers at its disposal: it can hold hearings, conduct investigations, subpoena documents and make rules. It also has teeth: if one of its 'cease and desist' orders is violated, it can seek civil penalties in the Federal Court of up to $10,000 a day for each violation.[3] The FTC posed a threat to the tobacco industry because, unlike the Congress, its political independence made it difficult to control. Michael Pertschuk explained the basis on which the Commission had the authority to act against cigarettes: 'The FTC has always pleaded legally that cigarette advertising is both unfair and deceptive, so there's an argument that failure to disclose warnings is a form of deception. Nevertheless, the promotion of a hazardous product is an unfair practice, if anything is an unfair practice. That has been a strong underpinning for the Commission's authority.'

In 1964, the FTC acted with remarkable speed within a week of the publication of the Surgeon-General's Report. The Commission declared that the mounting evidence of the 'grave hazards to life and health', and the failure of cigarette manufacturers to warn consumers of the danger, constituted an unfair and deceptive practice. It announced that it proposed to issue a rule, mandating a warning on all packets and advertisements. On March 16th, 1964, the five Commissioners began three days of public hearings on the proposed rule. Four of the Commissioners favoured strong action, while the fifth, a native of North Carolina, favoured negotiation with the tobacco industry.[4] One incident during the hearings shows how sensitive the industry's legal nerves were in the wake of the Surgeon-General's Report. 'The cigarette companies were constantly terrified of making an admission [that cigarettes were harmful],' recalled Robert Wald, a Washington attorney who was then counsel for the Lorillard cigarette company and a member of the industry's legal team. Both he and Philip Elman, who was one of the FTC's Commissioners at the time, remain convinced to this day that during the course of the hearings, such an admission was made by the industry's senior counsel H. Thomas Austern. 'Tommy

Austern argued as a lawyer that the warning was not necessary, because the public was already aware of the dangers of smoking cigarettes,' said Philip Elman. 'I remember interrupting him saying, "Everybody knows that smoking cigarettes presents a danger to health" and asking, "Are you telling us that everybody knows cigarettes are dangerous to health?" and he replied, "I'm telling you that no warning is necessary to tell people what they already know." ' Robert Wald also remembers the scene vividly. 'The industry's representatives, who were everywhere in the hearing room, looked like they were in shock—or ready to commit mayhem against Tommy!' Mr Austern is equally insistent that he never made the admission. He remains confident that he stressed throughout the terms 'asserted', 'alleged' or 'claimed'. 'That thing was so sensitive, anybody in my position was walking on eggs,' he told me. (He regarded the incident as the kind of *ad hominem* attack which sometimes characterises American public controversies.) 'My briefing was that I could not admit on the data then available that cigarettes were indeed "toxic". But I did make the point that it would not achieve any purpose to put a warning statement on, when the whole public had been barraged about the hazard of cigarettes. I could not as a barrister go in there and admit that cigarettes would hurt you, because there were about $300 million in lawsuits pending. I was then careful to put the word "alleged" in. The damned reporter, because of all the confusion and noise, left the word "alleged" out. I raised hell with the Commission for distorting it.' Mr Austern does however agree that he filed a motion to correct the transcript of the hearing to include the word 'alleged'. Philip Elman remembers receiving the request to change the record. 'My fellow Commissioners looked at the motion and said, "Poor Tommy, he's in a terrible situation with the industry. There's no reason why we should be bastards about all this." So they agreed that the record should be altered to insert the word "alleged". I wrote a little dissent on the ground that "Truth has its claims". Austern's argument that there was no need for a warning made little sense if the public was aware only of *alleged* dangers.'

About two months after the hearing, the FTC proposed a rule that all cigarette packets and advertisements should carry the warning, 'Cigarette Smoking is Dangerous to Health and May

**WHY DO YOU THINK
EVERY PACKET CARRIES A GOVERNMENT HEALTH WARNING?**

Issued by the Scottish Health Education Unit

1. The final version of the Scottish
Health Education Unit's anti-smoking advertisement.

2. The Prime Minister, Margaret Thatcher, with her husband Denis, inspecting the John Player Special racing car at Norwich on August 5th, 1981.

3. Martina Navratilova in Kim colours at Wimbledon, 1982.

4. Peter Sanguinetti, formerly of Imperial Tobacco (right), at the Glyndebourne Festival Opera with George Christie, Chairman of Glyndebourne Productions Ltd., in the dressing room of singer Elizabeth Harwood.

5. The London Philharmonic's transporter at Glyndebourne.

6. John Williams conducting the Peter Stuyvesant Pops at the
Barbican Centre, London, in summer 1982.

SM<u>OKING</u>
SPOILS
YOUR
LOOKS.

AMERICAN ✚ LUNG ASSOCIATION

7. The Brooke Shields campaign originally commissioned by the US Government and then rejected by the Reagan Administration as 'not suitable'.

8. J. C. Galloway, the North Carolina tobacco farmer, with written assurance from Ronald Reagan that his Administration would not be 'proselytising against the dangers of cigarette smoking'.

9. Family photograph of Bob Julian, the brand inspector from 'Death in the West'. Died of lung cancer October 29th, 1976.

10. The only cowboy to survive from 'Death in the West'. John Holmes, emphysema victim, with portable oxygen supply on his ranch in New Mexico June 13th, 1982.

11 and 12. Marlboro versus Montecarlo:
fighting for Number One in the Dominican Republic.

13 and 14. Making the Dominican Republic
Marlboro Country.

15. A street vendor sets up his stand in Santo Domingo.

16. Cigarette advertisement in a remote village store in Brazil.

17. Aerosol protest in Australia by BUGA UP (Billboard Utilising Graffitists Against Unhealthy Promotions).

O prazer mais perto de você
SUDAN 85
85 mm FILTRO
Cr$ 13.50

THEIR GOLD YOUR LUNGS
When only the best will do.
BUGA UP

Cause Death from Cancer and Other Diseases'. It was a rule the industry could never accept: the inclusion of the words 'cancer' and 'death' risked triggering an even greater avalanche of product liability suits; and the obligation to include the warning in advertisements risked undermining all the seductive images designed to sell cigarettes. Clearly the industry had to pre-empt the FTC's potentially damaging warning. (It was also worried that individual states and municipalities might legislate on their own.) Throughout the FTC's hearings, the industry's case had been that only Congress and not the FTC had the authority to legislate: the FTC, it claimed, was seeking to exceed its authority. The industry looked to its friends in the Congress for help. Nearly a quarter of all Committees in the Senate, and a third of all those in the House of Representatives, were chaired by Senators and Congressmen from the main tobacco growing states. The industry indicated to its friends that it was prepared to go along with legislation which placed a mild health warning on packets (which offered some legal protection) but not on advertisements. Its strategy was to make these minimum concessions in order to circumvent the FTC and ensure it kept its hands off cigarettes for the foreseeable future. There was a sympathetic ear in the White House too. President Johnson, who had just been elected in 1964, was not anxious to face a political storm over tobacco. In his State of the Union message at the beginning of 1965, he announced a number of health proposals, but no mention was made of smoking and health. As a Southern politican from Texas, Johnson knew that tobacco spelled trouble. He owed his position in the White House to the fact that John F. Kennedy had chosen him as his running mate in 1960 because of his ability to carry the Southern states.[5] He was now about to introduce civil rights legislation, which was bound to alienate his own political base in the South, and was not keen to add to his problems by taking on tobacco. The industry chose one of Johnson's closest political friends, Earle Clements, to mastermind its strategy. Clements was a former Kentucky Senator who had joined the Tobacco Institute as a lobbyist in 1964, having spent most of the previous decade walking in Lyndon Johnson's political footsteps. He had been Senate Majority Whip when Johnson was Majority Leader (effectively his Number Two) and had stood in as Leader when

Johnson had a heart attack in 1955. He had also served as head of the party committee which distributed campaign funds. In 1960, when it became clear that Hubert Humphrey's bid for the presidential nomination was running into the sand, Clements went round whipping up support for Johnson. Clements also had strong personal ties with the Johnson White House through his daughter, Bess Abell, who was Lady Bird Johnson's social secretary. The industry also had further access to the White House through Abe Fortas, a partner in its law firm of Arnold, Fortas and Porter. Abe Fortas, whom Johnson described as 'the most experienced, compassionate and intelligent lawyer I know',[6] was one of the President's closest political advisers. He was also a member of the industry's legal team which helped Earle Clements formulate the industry's strategy and prepare its appeal to the courts in case it failed.[7] But no appeal was necessary. Cigarette Labelling Bills were drawn up in the Senate and the House of Representatives. Ironically, the man who drafted the Senate Bill which, in the first instance, gave the industry most of what it wanted, was Michael Pertschuk, who was then a twenty-nine-year-old staff aide to the Commerce Committee. Part of his job was building a legislative record on consumer protection for the Chairman of the Commerce Committee, Senator Warren Magnuson. Pertschuk spent many hours discussing the legislation with Clements. 'I got caught up in the game plan and did something for which I was not at all proud,' he told me. 'It was clear that the tobacco industry had decided strategically that they would have to vent some of the public steam by accepting the warning on the package—and doing it legislatively. In exchange for this, they hoped to gain legislative language which barred the FTC from requiring the warning in advertisements (which they truly feared) and states and municipalities from regulating advertising. I saw the opportunity for Magnuson to be the author of a Bill which would place cigarette warnings on all packages and, of course, which would sail through if it also had the pre-emption against the FTC and the states taking any further action. I knew that I was really participating in an effort which was in effect cutting off the potential for regulating cigarette advertising. As I recall my state of mind at the time, I simply felt that the tobacco industry was so powerful and had so many allies in the Senate and in the

House of Representatives, that it would be futile to stand in the way of this legislative juggernaut. So I thought I might as well go along with it and gain the credit for Magnuson as the author of the Bill putting the warning on the package.'

Pertschuk, who enjoyed great autonomy, conducted his negotiations with Clements entirely on his own. On January 12th, 1965, he circulated a draft copy of the Bill round the Commerce Committee for the first time. No one paid any attention to the fine print about the pre-emptions. There appeared to be no problems. He then circulated the draft among a few friends outside the Commerce Committee. One of them was Stanley Cohen, the Washington Editor of *Advertising Age*, who had been covering the nation's capital since 1947. Pertschuk asked Cohen what he thought of the Bill. Cohen said he thought it was 'shocking, shocking'. Pertschuk realised what he had done. 'Cohen knew it was the industry's Bill. I was naïve. I remember the terrible feeling of guilt. I remember going out to dinner with friends—it was my birthday—and having this terrible sense of guilt, and not being able to sleep all night. Clements had created a kind of conspiratorial atmosphere in which he included me, and I'd been drawn in, only half aware of it. I was young. I was twenty-nine. I was charmed and fascinated by power. Magnuson was due to introduce the Bill the next morning.' When Pertschuk went into the office he told his Staff Director how he felt. He was told that if he was worried he should take the pre-emption out. Perschuk did so, only to find that the House of Representatives put it back in again. Magnuson and Pertschuk fought the pre-emption and finally succeeded in getting it restricted to three years.

By this time Pertschuk admitted he had recovered his senses. But the Bill still gave the industry more or less what it wanted: a mild health warning 'Caution. Cigarette Smoking May be Hazardous to Your Health'; no warning on advertisements; and, most important of all, a pre-emption that neither the F T C nor the Federal Communications Commission (which was responsible for television advertising) would take any further action for the next three years.

President Johnson signed the Cigarette Labelling Bill without fanfare, in the privacy of the White House. The F T C was quietly seen off for the next three years. The *New York Times* called the law:

> A shocking piece of special-interest legislation . . . a Bill to protect the economic health of the tobacco industry by freeing it of proper regulation.[8]

The Bill became law on January 1st, 1966—the year Earle Clements was named President of the Tobacco Institute.

By 1977, Michael Pertschuk had risen from Chief Counsel to the Commerce Committee to become Chairman of the FTC. In 1970 he had seen the Congress strengthen the health warning to 'Warning—the Surgeon-General Has Determined that Cigarette Smoking is Dangerous to Your Health': in 1971 he had seen the Congress ban cigarette advertisements from television (as a result of a long and skilful campaign masterminded by John F. Banzhaf III, the founder of America's Action on Smoking and Health); and in 1972, he had seen the FTC complete at least some of its unfinished business from 1964, by getting the industry to agree to put health warnings on advertisements. Each of these small steps was a result of the continuing battle between the FTC, the industry and the Congress. Looking back, Michael Pertschuk has no doubt who won:

> That the cigarette industry strategy was sound can now be confirmed by its continued health and prosperity ten years later and by the absence from the public agenda of any serious threat of new regulatory action to curb cigarette advertising, despite the FTC's best efforts to the contrary. So when we reflect longingly on the 'high consumerism' of the Sixties, nostalgia is freighted by the knowledge that during that very period *no* government action was taken that seriously threatened the short-term market or profitability of the most lethal consumer product ever openly sold in this country. All it took was a little skilful corporate lobbying to deflect the pang of public outrage.[9]

An FTC lawyer of the time explained why the industry put its money on the Congress. 'I'm sure the industry thought, "The FTC we can't control, the Congress we can. If it's Congress that's acting we can be sure that what gets done will be, at worst, a compromise we can live with." When it came to the FTC, they probably thought, "Look at what these crazy people are doing. They want to tell everybody that smoking is killing people. They're trying to find an effective way of doing something rather than an ineffective way. We can't have that." That was their strategy. The FTC was the real threat and I think it has been perceived as the real threat to this date.'

If cigarette sales were any measure, the strategy was successful. Between 1970 and 1980 they increased by nearly 100 billion— from 521 billion to 611 billion.[10] Advertising expenditure shot up accordingly. Estimates (allowing for inflation) put the increase at over fifty per cent between 1967 and 1979.[11] By the end of the decade, the tobacco companies were spending an estimated $1 billion a year to make cigarettes the most heavily advertised product in America.

In 1976, the FTC fired the opening shots in its second great battle with the industry, again over cigarette advertising. The adversaries remained locked in combat for the next five years. The Commerce Committee only became involved at the end, when it moved to disarm the FTC. The origins of the conflict were unspectacular. One of the few benefits which the FTC had derived from the Cigarette Labelling Bill of 1965 was the obligation to present Congress with an annual report on cigarettes. In 1976, the FTC decided, as part of this obligation, to conduct a thorough investigation into cigarette advertising by using its power of subpoena to obtain all the advertising documents and memoranda kept by all the companies and their advertising agencies, going as far back as the 1960s. The statutory purpose of the subpoena, which was one of the FTC's most crucial powers, was:

> To determine whether persons, partnerships, or corporations engaged in the manufacture, advertising, promotion, offering for sale, sale or distribution of cigarettes may have been, or may be engaged in the use of unfair or deceptive acts or practices, in or affecting commerce, in the advertising, promotion, offering for sale, sale, or distribution of cigarettes in violation of Section 5 of the Federal Trade Commission Act.[12]

The subpoena was designed to leave no stone unturned. The word 'documents', as defined by the subpoena, meant:

> All written, recorded, transcribed, punched, taped, filmed or graphic matter. This includes books; records; schedules; correspondence; telegrams; memoranda; notes or tapes of interviews, conferences, telephone calls and other communications; raw data; tabulations; computer print-outs; data sheets; data processing cards; code books; surveys; strategies; marketing plans; research papers; reports or minutes of meetings; advertisements or other promotional material; intra-office memoranda; work papers; and preliminary drafts or versions of all of the above.[13]

The industry feared the FTC was out to kill. 'They want to seek the evidence they need to destroy all form of cigarette advertising,' said one cigarette executive.[14] The companies accused the FTC of going on a fishing expedition and went to court to fight the subpoena. 'There's a normal minuet in legal battles,' explained Michael Pertschuk. 'A law enforcement agency will not know how companies index and catalogue their documents, so that as a matter of strategy it will produce a blanket subpoena asking for everything. The companies usually fight it in court, but they never win.' The companies fought and lost. The minuet lasted over two years. In January 1979, US District Court Judge Barrington D. Parker ordered six cigarette companies and twenty advertising agencies to hand over the material to the FTC.[15] Judge Parker ruled that probing cigarette advertising was well within the FTC's power, and said the industry was using legal tactics 'to resist the FCT's investigative efforts'. He concluded that the subpoena unquestionably sought relevant material. FTC lawyers were elated. 'I don't know whether there's going to be a smoking gun in there or not,' said one of them. 'But we'll just take a look.'[16]

Eventually most of the cigarette companies agreed to a phased submission of documents as and when the Commission required them, having established exactly what the FTC wanted. They submitted most of the material in reasonable and digestible amounts, in one case four drawers, in another, a large file folder. But BAT's US subsidiary, Brown & Williamson, collected over

seven tons of documents, loaded them into a truck and
despatched it to the FTC. They were determined to make as much
mileage as possible out of what they called 'a prime example of
reckless bullying by a federal agency'.[17] They accused the FTC of
'throwing the dust in the eyes of the court'.[18] They said they had
spent 24,000 man-hours collecting 750,000 bits of paper going
back fourteen years, in an operation which cost them over
$800,000.[19] They showed a photograph of the heroine of the
Herculean task, Doris Ziebert, surrounded by piles of boxes
which she had spent three years collecting and co-ordinating with
'this cloud hanging over her'. They showed another photograph
of her dedicated team of helpers. 'We had them running around
the clock,' said Brown & Williamson's Vice-President and Senior
Counsel, Ernest Pepples. 'Their faces show the tension, the
weariness of performing such a worthless activity under an
unlawful and unreasonable subpoena.'[20] The fruit of Doris'
labours was loaded into the back of a truck and the driver ordered
to deliver the consignment to the FTC in Washington. 'They
could have rented a U-Haul one tenth the size, but that wouldn't
have been the public relations gimmick,' one of the FTC's
attorneys told me. 'They decided it was the great public relations
opportunity of a lifetime, and they decided to give the FTC the
whole kitchen sink, I think under the theory that if they gave the
Commission 6,000 documents, they wouldn't read any of them.'
Brown & Williamson tipped off the press with the truck's
ETA—nine thirty a.m. on Thursday, July 5th.[21] But the truck
arrived two days early. The driver, George Wright, rang Brown &
Williamson and said that he was not expected. The company told
him to drive away and come back again on Thursday at the same
time. 'I'm gonna have a good time for two days,' he said, coming
off the phone.[22] 'Brown & Williamson screwed it up,' said the
FTC attorney, 'and the benevolent bureaucracy enabled them to
get away with it. Instead of saying, "Fine, let's get the documents
inside," which would have wiped away the PR advantage they
were looking for, they sent the truck away and told it to come
back later in front of all the TV cameras! It's hard to believe that
when you're involved in such hard ball politics, you can be that
kind and benevolent. Brown & Williamson blew it and the FTC
gave it to them.'

The FTC's team hired computer programmers and catalogued all the documents under headings such as 'Children', 'Women' and 'Health', to narrow the focus of the investigation. Not every one of the thousands of documents was read, but hundreds of spot checks were made. If something looked interesting, a full analysis was made of its contents. One of the team came across a dry but interesting memorandum written in lawyer's language, and showed it to other members. When they looked up the back-up material there was much more to it. 'The irony was they never expected the staff to really go through all these documents,' said Michael Pertschuk. 'But indeed the staff did and the most incriminating documents which came out of the investigation were Brown & Williamson's. They got a PR black eye, partly I suppose because they didn't screen all those documents as well as they might have, if they weren't so preoccupied with embarrassing the Commission.' Not that all the other companies emerged unscathed. Among the mountain of documents, the Commission found R. J. Reynolds' 1977 'Salem Annual Marketing Plan', which made no secret of its target group:

> Through the association of Salem and its brand styles with emulatable personalities and situational elements that are compatible with the aspirations and lifestyles of contemporary young adults, this important target segment will be attracted to the brand.[23]

There was also a reference to Liggett and Myers' Eve cigarettes (a brand designed for women). They were intended to appeal to a 'sophisticated, up-to-date, youthful and active woman who seems to have distinct ideas about what she wants'.[24]

But Brown & Williamson's truckload of documents provided the most interesting material of all. Document AO 11345 showed that in March 1975, a market research company called Marketing & Research Counselors, Inc. was requested by Ted Bates, Brown & Williamson's advertising agency, to conduct research into discovering and creating the best possible image for Viceroy cigarettes — a brand the company had marketed for many years and which they now wished to update. Viceroy is a 'full-flavour' cigarette which is comparatively high in tar. (In 1978 Viceroy with eighteen milligrams ranked 111th out of 128 filter brands in the FTC's official tar league table.[25]) Eighteen 'Focus Group Interviews on the Subject of Smoking' were carried out by the market research company, and the results, 'A Conceptual Summarization', were sent to Ted Bates. One chapter in the Report is devoted to how 'young starters' can be introduced to Viceroy:

> For the young smoker, the cigarette is not yet an integral part of life, of day-to-day life, in spite of the fact that they try to project the image of a regular run-of-the-mill smoker. For them, a cigarette, and the whole smoking process, is part of the illicit pleasure category . . . In the young smoker's mind a cigarette falls into the same category with wine, beer, shaving, wearing a bra (or *purposely* not wearing one), declaration of independence and striving for self-identity. For the young starter, a cigarette is associated with introduction to sex life, with courtship, with smoking 'pot' and keeping late studying hours.[26]

The chapter then goes on to suggest how 'young starters' can be attracted to Viceroy:

> Thus, an attempt to reach young smokers, starters, should be based, among others, on the following major parameters:
> —Present the cigarette as one of a few initiations into the adult world.
> —Present the cigarette as part of the illicit pleasure category of products and activities.
> —In your ads create a situation taken from the day-to-day life of the young smoker but in an elegant manner have this situation touch on the basic symbols of the growing-up, maturity process.
> —To the best of your ability (considering some legal constraints) relate the cigarette to 'pot', wine, beer, sex, etc.
> —*Don't* communicate health or health-related points.[27]

The Report summarises the result of its research by asserting that many smokers perceive the habit as a 'dirty' and dangerous one engaged in only by 'very stupid people'. It concludes:

Thus, the smokers have to face the fact that they are illogical, irrational and stupid. People find it hard to go throughout life with such negative presentation and evaluation of self. The saviours are the *rationalization* and the *repression* that end up and result in a defense mechanism that, as many of the defense mechanisms we use, has its own 'logic', its own rationale. Thus, smokers don't like to be reminded of the fact that they are illogical and irrational. They don't want to be reminded by either *direct* or *indirect* manner.[28]

The way round the problem, the Report suggests, since there 'are not any real, absolute, positive qualities and attributes in a cigarette' is to 'reduce objections' to the product by presenting a picture or situation ambiguous enough to provide smokers with a rationale for their behaviour and a means of repressing their health concerns about smoking—i.e. that cigarettes provide the smoker with social acceptance, an acceptable means of rewarding himself/herself, a stimulant, a tranquilizer, or a better self image. As far as the health issue is concerned, it offers the advice: 'Start out from the basic assumption that cigarette smoking is dangerous to your health—try to go around it in an elegant manner but don't try to fight it—it's a losing war.'

The FTC's investigation states that Brown & Williamson adopted many of the ideas contained in this market research Report in developing its Viceroy campaign. Document AO 15538 entitled 'Viceroy Strategy' clearly picks up some of the themes outlined in the market research report carried out for Ted Bates. It is dated March 3rd, 1976 and is from V. C. Broach, Group Project Manager, Brown & Williamson. It notes repeatedly that Viceroy's advertising campaign must provide consumers with a rationalisation for smoking and a 'means of *repressing* their health concerns about smoking a full flavour Viceroy'.

> Full flavour smokers perceive cigarette smoking as dangerous to their health ... Given their awareness of the smoking and health situation, they are faced with the fact that they are acting illogically. They respond to this inconsistency by providing themselves with either a rationalisation for smoking, or, by repressing their perceptions of the possible dangers involved ...

The marketing efforts must cope with consumers' attitudes about smoking and health, either providing them a *rationale* for smoking a full flavour VICEROY or providing a means of *repressing* their concerns about smoking a full flavour VICEROY.

Advertising Objective To communicate effectively that VICEROY is a satisfying, flavourful cigarette which young adult smokers enjoy, by providing them a rationalization for smoking, or, a repression of the health concern they appear to need.[29]

Document AO 15486, a memorandum dated July 14th, 1976 from M. M. Matteson to V. C. Broach, Brown & Williamson's Group Project Manager, outlines three advertising strategies for Viceroy:

1. The 'satisfaction' campaign provides a rationalization: VICEROY is so satisfying that smokers can smoke fewer cigarettes and still receive the satisfaction they want . . .
2. The 'tension release' campaign provides a rationalization: VICEROY'S satisfying flavour can help the smoker in a tense situation . . .
3. The 'feels good' campaign appeals to the smoker by repressing the concerns he may have about smoking by justification: If it feels good, do it; if it feels good, smoke it . . .[30]

According to the FTC's investigators, these strategies were employed in a six-month media campaign conducted in three test cities in 1976. The advertising allotment for the campaign was approximately ten times the normal advertising dollar amount for a six-month period.

Viceroy was also designed to appeal to women and blacks. An advertisement in *Ms* magazine in November 1975 shows a pretty girl, Viceroy in hand, taking lap times at a race meeting. Above her is the quote, 'Why Viceroy Super Longs? Because I'd never smoke a boring cigarette.' Another ad in *Ebony* magazine in May 1976 shows a young black in a checked suit lighting up a Viceroy at the ringside while two boxers slog it out above. The slogan reads: 'He's the brains behind the next heavyweight champ. He'd never smoke a boring cigarette.' At the bottom, both ads carry the message, 'Viceroy. Where excitement is now a taste'. As far as the strategy designed to attract 'young starters' to Viceroy is concerned, the FTC's investigators stated categorically that the advice was translated into an advertising campaign featuring young adults in situations which the vast majority of young people would probably experience and in situations which demonstrated adherence to a 'free and easy, hedonistic lifestyle'. Brown & Williamson, however, denied the claim that they had carried out any campaign based on the market research company's report suggesting that cigarettes be linked with 'illicit' adult pleasures. They said their confidential marketing information had been taken totally out of context and that the advice of the market research company had been unsolicited and not acted upon.[31] In a statement the Company said:

> The real issue is what we do publish, not rejected advertising proposals. We reject many of the advertising suggestions made by our advertising agencies and consultants. However, we do stand by what we say to our consumers. We stand firmly behind the integrity of our advertising.
> The accusations made are totally false and gravely misleading. Brown & Williamson's published advertising is not deceptive nor misleading, nor is it geared to young people.[32]

But that was not the end of the story. Brown & Williamson is one of the most powerful constituents of Senator Wendell Ford of Kentucky who, when it comes to tobacco, is to Kentucky what Jesse Helms is to North Carolina. 'Brown & Williamson didn't have to go after Ford,' said Michael Pertschuk. 'They didn't have to lobby him. They're a corporate unity. Ford doesn't separate himself from the tobacco industry.' Senator Ford was the latest in a long line of Kentucky Senators who had sat on the Commerce Committee to make sure that the interests of their state and its main industry were fully represented. When Wendell Ford (a Democrat) defeated Marlow Cook (a Republican) in the Senate race in 1974 (the year Watergate produced a Democratic landslide), Cook became a legal counsel for the Tobacco Institute[33] and Ford took his place on the Commerce Committee.

Pertschuk, who by that time had become Chief Counsel to the Committee, received a call from Earle Clements, the President of the Tobacco Institute, who said that Ford was anxious for a seat on the Committee. Clements told Pertschuk that Ford was a keen consumer advocate as shown by his record as Governor of Kentucky: he was sure that Pertschuk would like him very much. 'I'm sure he's a fine man,' said Pertschuk, 'but there are no vacancies on the Committee.' At the time there were seventeen Senators on the Commerce Committee, two more than allowed by the rules of the Senate, because in the past exceptions had been made. At the beginning of the new session in 1975, both the Democratic Chairman of the Committee, and its senior Republican were determined to reduce the size from seventeen back to its original fifteen. 'So,' according to Pertschuk, 'there was no conceivable way that Wendell Ford would have a seat on the Senate Commerce Committee.' Clements told him not to worry: Ford was a very decent fellow and they would enjoy working together. When the Senate Steering Committee which appoints Senators to the various Committees met at the beginning of 1975, they did not reduce the size of the Commerce Committee by two but increased it by one to accommodate the new Senator from Kentucky. 'It was clear to me,' said Pertschuk, 'that Clements, who as a former member of the Senate had direct access to all these members, simply went and lobbied them to make sure that they would have their representative on the Committee. That investment was crucial to them.' The investment paid off very quickly. Senator Ford pre-empted an attempt to get tobacco brought under the control of the Product Safety Commission (for which the Commerce Committee was also responsible) by introducing an amendment which expressly exempted tobacco products from the Commission's jurisdiction. By 1979 Senator Ford had moved into a key position on the Commerce Committee, as Chairman of its Consumer Sub-committee. At the time the FTC under its Chairman Michael Pertschuk was upsetting not just tobacco, but a whole range of business interests, including insurance, automobiles, mobile homes, undertakers, doctors, drugs, opticians and, in particular, 'Kid-Vid'—children's television advertisers. Senator Ford, backed by many of the industries under attack, hit back by saying that his purpose was to return the FTC to the path of being 'a respected, responsive and responsible agency'.[34] Three months after Brown & Williamson dumped their documents on the FTC's doorstep, Senator Ford as Chairman of the Consumer Sub-committee held oversight hearings 'to examine the enforcement and administrative authority of the FTC to regulate unfair and deceptive practices'.[35] 'We don't want to take the teeth out of the tiger,' he said, 'but it is clear that the FTC has pushed its authority above and beyond the limits set by Congress.'[36] Ernest Pepples, Brown & Williamson's Vice-President and General Counsel, came to Washington to testify before Senator Ford's Sub-committee. In a lengthy statement he called on Congress to curb the FTC:

> If Congressionally granted independence has enabled an agency like the FTC gratuitously to position itself at the leading edge of legislative expansion and experimentation in the shaping and control of business practices and the censorship of advertising, then Congress ought to rein it in. Congress wrote the enabling laws delegating the overbroad authority which has allowed the FTC to wander off the reservation, and Congress can amend the law to set more precise standards governing the agency's exercise of its delegated powers.[37]

'You know there's an old adage about curiosity killing the cat,' Senator Ford reminded Mr Pepples. 'And curiosity here might kill an agency.'[38]

Senator Ford's FTC Bill, which the Senate passed by seventy-seven votes to thirteen on February 7th, 1980, did not kill the agency but cut back two of its sharpest claws. The new law deleted the word 'unfair' in all the FTC's future rulemaking proceedings involving 'unfair and deceptive practices' where commercial advertising was concerned, and it severely curtailed the FTC's crucial power of subpoena. In future the FTC had to indicate much more precisely than before the nature of the violation or the exact reason it was seeking the information. As Senator Ford explained, there would be no more fishing expeditions on grounds of 'official necessity'. Tobacco had finally neutralised its most dangerous opponent.

But Brown & Williamson's battles involving the FTC were not over. The Company was soon involved in another controversy, but this time the FTC's role was different. The complaint involved not Brown & Williamson's advertising, but the design of its new low tar cigarette, Barclay, and was made not by the FTC but by Brown & Williamson's commerical rivals. The Barclay case shows the companies fighting each other as ruthlessly in the marketplace as they fight their opponents on the smoking and health issue. This time the FTC was the referee. The reason for the action was the fierce competition in the latest and fastest-growing section of the US cigarette market, 'ultra' low tar cigarettes. According to the FTC, whose smoking machines officially register the tar content of all cigarettes, a 'low tar' cigarette produces between nine and fifteen milligrams of tar. In 1976, low tar cigarettes only accounted for less than seventeen per cent[39] of the total US market: five years later they accounted for more than sixty per cent.[40] In 1980 alone, a hundred new low tar brands were launched.[41] The phenomenal growth in the market was a clear indication of how concerned consumers were about the health risks. But by this time, the industry had also developed 'ultra' low tar cigarettes, most of them of six milligrams or less. Companies fought with each other to see how low they could get without losing the taste or 'kick' in cigarettes that is so important to smokers. The development was made possible by a series of technical improvements: growing 'milder' tobacco, designing better filters, making cigarette paper more porous and, above all, by developing chemical additives which gave cigarettes the flavour they automatically lost when the tar was reduced. These advances triggered the 'tar wars'. By 1982, the 'ultra' low tar sector held ten per cent of the total $13 billion US market. With each percentage point of its market share worth over $100 million,[42] no company could afford to stay out of the most rapidly growing section of a market whose overall growth was limited to around one per cent. Companies increased their profits at their rivals' expense, or watched them wither away. No company could merely stand on the sidelines and watch. Brown & Williamson was the last to enter the fray.

The key to success in the 'tar wars' was to design a cigarette which would give the smoker maximum satisfaction with minimum tar. In 1981, Brown & Williamson launched its late contender in the 'ultra' low tar stakes, Barclay, a cigarette claiming one milligram of tar and the largest promotional budget in cigarette advertising history—$150 million.[43] The advertisements claimed that Barclay was '99% tar-free', and showed a series of handsome men in the presence of elegant ladies in sophisticated settings. 'The pleasure is back', they declared. Brown & Williamson's rivals were worried by the latecomer's arrival, in particular R. J. Reynolds, which had captured the biggest slice of the low tar market, and Philip Morris, which had just spent $50 million launching a one-milligram cigarette, Cambridge, which had only succeeded in capturing three-tenths of one per cent of the market at the end of 1980.[44] What worried Brown & Williamson's rivals was not Barclay's record promotional budget, but the design of its special 'Actron' filter. They had conducted their own tests (as all companies do on their competitors' products) and found that when Barclay was smoked by a human smoker, it delivered more tar than officially recorded by the FTC's smoking machine. They discovered that smokers tended to block the ventilation system of Barclay's specially designed filter, with the result that air was excluded (air dilutes the smoke) and more tar was delivered. In the business this was known as 'cheating' the tar tables. R. J. Reynolds is said to have reported its findings to Brown & Williamson three times and asked them what they proposed to do. Brown & Williamson disagreed and apparently said they proposed to do nothing.[45] Reynolds, backed by Philip Morris, complained to the FTC. The Commission selected a panel of three respected independent scientists to review the evidence. They were Dr Michael Guerin, of the Analytical Chemistry division of Oak Ridge Laboratory; Dr Fred Bock, formerly Director of Orchard Park Laboratories; and Dr Lynn Kozlowski, of the Addiction Research Foundation in Toronto. All three scientists had tobacco expertise but no connection with any tobacco company.

Having taken submissions from all sides, the panel upheld Reynolds' complaint. (Philip Morris even submitted film taken inside a smoker's mouth, showing what happened to Barclay's filter once between the smoker's lips.) The three scientists were unanimous in their verdict. Dr Guerin said he was convinced that cigarettes which contained the Barclay type filter were inappropriately ranked by the FTC's current testing method. Dr Kozlowski said that in his opinion the research strongly supported the conclusion that Barclay delivered tar and nicotine out of proportion to the FTC rating. Dr Bock concluded that the preponderance of data indicated that the FTC's tar and nicotine yield values of Barclay were misleading, and that there was need for action. They all agreed that Barclay's tar rating should not be one milligram but somewhere between at least three and seven milligrams. Philip Morris and Reynolds urged the FTC to direct Brown & Williamson to recall all Barclay packets, cartons, posters and advertising material showing the one per cent tar representation; to disclose that Barclay's tar yield was significantly higher than that indicated by the FTC's method of testing; and to issue 'corrective' advertising, indicating that its past advertising had been misleading. Brown & Williamson, of course, which still protested its innocence, was going to do no such thing. Reflecting on the Barclay case, one top tobacco executive said:

> Hell, every company in the cigarette business knew how to make a product which would fool the FTC machine. None of us had the nerve to take the chance Brown & Williamson has taken.[46]

As a result of the investigation, Brown & Williamson was informed by the FTC that Barclay could not be accurately tested by the current FTC method and that continued 'tar' claims made by relying on that method would be disallowed. The Commission also announced its intention to conduct a thorough review of its tar testing system and warned smokers that, although Barclay's filter posed a unique problem, all cigarettes with ventilated filters were capable of delivering a higher tar yield if smokers blocked the holes in the filter when they put the cigarette between their lips. However, before the Commission could commence its review and adapt its testing method to the unique design of the 'ultra' low tar filter, Brown & Williamson obtained a court injunction to prevent the Commission from proceeding and from challenging as deceptive Barclay's one milligram tar claim based on the FTC test. The Commission appealed against the injunction, while

Barclay continued with its highly successful 'ultra' low tar campaign. On April 1st, 1983 the US Court of Appeals for the Sixth Circuit lifted the injunction, thereby leaving the FTC free to take action. The following month the Commission declared that Brown & Williamson could not use the FTC's current test results to substantiate claims for Barclay's tar content and announced its intention to re-examine its testing methods in order to cope with cigarettes like Barclay.[47]

Barclay seems to have caused the industry and the FTC more concern than many of its smokers. Although its sales fell in 1982 (as did the sales of most 'ultra' low tar cigarettes because the trend headed back to higher tar brands), Barclay, only a few years old, had risen to and remained America's twentieth best selling cigarette.[48] Despite the FTC's efforts over nearly twenty years to reverse the trend, overall cigarette sales continued to grow. In 1982, they reached an all-time record of 635 billion.[49] Throughout the 1970s the industry had successfully met every challenge, and made sure that most of its customers carried on smoking. It had done so by not only developing lower tar cigarettes but, as following chapters show, by using its influence with the White House and its own vast resources and wealth to beat off its political and public opponents as successfully as it had the FTC.

11

The Six Million Dollar Men

The consumer is a crucial link in the Smoke Ring. As long as his or her loyalty is assured (and addiction helps secure it) the Smoke Ring holds fast. If consumers defect, it breaks and the whole structure which protects the industry falls apart. If people stop smoking, the industry stops working. There is no revenue, no jobs, no exports, and therefore no binding connection between government and industry. The tobacco industry knows how vital and vulnerable the link is and will fight to protect it at all costs. When it came under attack in California in 1978 and 1980 from citizens' groups who tried to make smoking in public places illegal, the industry spent over $6 million to keep the link intact. The link is under strain in most Western countries because smoking is no longer generally considered socially acceptable. One of the industry's observers in Stockholm at the Fourth World Conference on Smoking and Health noted, '. . . the social acceptability issue will be the central battleground on which our case in the long run will be lost or won.'[1]

The trend, particularly in America, has been given added impetus by medical evidence showing that the health of some non-smokers can be affected by the smoke from other people's cigarettes. This 'second hand' smoke can endanger the health of smokers' children, cause respiratory disease in non-smokers and worsen the condition of those already affected by heart and lung disorders.[2] This is why 'passive smoking' has become a political issue in America. In 1970, there were ten Bills introduced at local level to restrict smoking in public places: by 1980, there were nearly 200.[3] Nevertheless by 1980, forty-six states (and Washington DC) had some form of state or local laws banning or restricting smoking; only eleven states had purely local laws or ordinances (including the tobacco growing states of North and South Carolina, Tennessee and Kentucky); and only four states had no legislation at all—Delaware, Mississippi, Vermont and West Virginia. Much of this legislation had been pioneered by the American Action on Smoking and Health (which has no connection with its British equivalent other than sharing the name and goal) under its founder and Executive Director, John F. Banzhaf III, who became the American champion of non-smokers' rights. (Minnesota's 'Clean Indoor Air Act', enacted on June 2nd, 1975 which provided no-smoking areas in all public buildings, became the model for other states across America.) The industry recognised that the battle was now being fought on a different and more dangerous front. The new non-smokers' rights movement posed a threat which had to be countered. In May 1980, Brown & Williamson's Manager of Corporate Affairs and Communications, Wilson W. Wyatt, Jnr, warned:

> Throughout the 1960s, the tobacco industry successfully confronted many adversaries in Washington. We ... had to establish ourselves with the best possible talent to participate in the numerous controversies which grew to surround our industry. We were successful then and we continue to be.
> Highly organised adversaries, however, have shifted their attacks from the industry to our consumers. Controversies spread from the traditional Washington centre to state and local governments.[4]

The industry's worst fears had been confirmed in 1978 when the Roper Organisation, which over the years had carried out a series of polls on public attitudes towards cigarette smoking, presented the Tobacco Institute with its sixth study.[5] Roper told its client that there were a certain number of 'silver linings' to the 'many clouds' on the horizon, but the results were 'mostly foreboding as regards the very future of the tobacco industry'. There were only eleven clouds and only seven silver linings. The silver linings included:

> . . . compared to crime, drugs, pollution . . . smoking is at the bottom of the list of personal concerns.

> There is little sentiment for a total ban on cigarette smoking in public places.

> The percentage of smokers in the 17–24 year old age group is up, and the amount smoked per day per young smoker is also up.

These were some of the clouds:

> More than nine out of ten Americans believe that smoking is hazardous to the smoker's health.

> A majority of Americans believe that it is probably hazardous to be around people who smoke even if they are not smoking themselves.

> There is majority sentiment for separate smoking sections in all public places we asked about.

> The percentage of people who smoke cigarettes is at the lowest level measured in the past ten years.

> A steadily increasing majority of Americans believes that the tobacco industry knows that the case against cigarettes is true.

> Favourable attitudes towards the tobacco industry are at their lowest ebb.

> Two-thirds of smokers would like to give up smoking.

And most ominous of all for the political battle,

> More people say they would vote for than against a political candidate who takes a position favouring a ban on smoking in public places.

Roper told the Tobacco Institute what its members had long
known: that the blows the industry had suffered in the 1960s and
early 1970s—health warnings on packets and advertisements
and the banning of cigarette ads on television—had been
successfully weathered because they had all been directed against
the smoker himself, and awareness of the health risk had 'not
persuaded very many smokers to give up smoking'. But now the
issue was different. Non-smokers' rights had become a powerful
political movement.

> What the smoker does to himself may be his business, but what
> the smoker does to the non-smoker is quite a different matter
> ... As the anti-smoking forces succeed in their efforts to
> convince non-smokers that their health is at stake too, the
> pressure for segregated facilities will change from a ripple to a
> tide as we see it.

Roper suggested some of the arguments the industry might use to
hold back the tide: the cost to the taxpayer; government intrusion
('Where will it all end'); and the portrayal of the anti-smoker as a
'fumaphobe'—'an irrational anti-smoking zealot'. The rise of
non-smokers' rights was, Roper concluded, 'the most dangerous
development to the viability of the tobacco industry which has yet
occurred'.

As long as tobacco's opponents worked through the traditional
political channels, their activities posed the industry little threat
because it knew how to handle the country's national and local
political representatives. But when the new non-smokers' rights
movement appealed directly to the people over the heads of their
politicians, the industry knew it was in trouble. As disillusion-
ment with the established political system grew in the shadow of
Watergate, many states and cities turned to the citizens' ballot as a
form of direct democracy which circumvented the traditional
political and economic power blocs. This made it possible for the
electorate rather than its representatives to enact legislation by
simply voting Yes or No to a 'proposition' placed before them on
the ballot paper at election time. Whatever its name—'proposition', 'initiative' or 'referendum'—the principle had been
established by the historic 'one man one vote' decision by the

Supreme Court in the Civil Rights battle of the 1960s.[6] By 1980, twenty-three states and over a hundred cities had incorporated the ballot initiative and used it 175 times through the decade.[7] Big business in general and the tobacco industry in particular viewed the development with alarm. Brown & Williamson's Wilson Wyatt described it as 'a threatening ballot box tool':

> The initiative, the referendum—the political extensions of 'I'm mad as hell and I'm not going to take it any more'—are perhaps the most far-reaching political and constitutional developments in our lifetime. Public unrest—faddish, negative in the extreme and always subject to the volatile and shifting emotions of the moment—has been unleashed in the political arena, not as a voice of debate, but as a fist ever poised to strike . . . Candidate politics, with which we are reasonably comfortable, at which we are reasonably adept, is essentially a percentage business where single wins or losses are only rarely crucial . . . But the loss of a single initiative can be devastating to the corporate interest and to the societal stability.[8]

To defend itself from the new threat, the industry needed to surround itself with all the political experts and computerised tools which had become indispensable to electoral success: political consultants, market researchers, direct mailers, census trackers, advertising agencies and specialist lawyers. But above all it needed organisation and money to develop its own political machine and buy the media time necessary to get its case across. Because the proponents of these ballot initiatives (which affected many other industries besides tobacco) were invariably grass roots, citizens' organisations, the industry under attack usually channelled its millions of dollars through front organisations of 'concerned citizens'. In California in 1980 when a proposition threatened to put a ten per cent surtax on energy profits to improve public transport, the oil industry channelled $5 million through 'Californians for Fair Taxation'.[9] Standard Oil contributed over $1 million, Shell, Atlantic Richfield and Union Oil over half a million dollars each, and Exxon and Mobil a quarter of a million. The proposition's supporters, 'Citizens to Tax Big Oil', raised $463,000. Oil won. In New York's Westchester County in

1979, the power companies spent $1.3 million channelled through 'Westchester Citizens Against Government Takeover' to fight a proposition which would have empowered the county to operate its own local distribution network for electricity.[10] The power industry outspent its opponents eighty-three to one. Consolidated Edison spent $16,000. Power won.

The tobacco industry was not unprepared for the attack. The Roper Report was not the first warning. In the mid 1970s, market researchers had advised the tobacco companies to set up their own 'legislative support units' in anticipation of the battles which lay ahead. In 1975 Philip Morris hired political consultant Ed Grefe, a veteran of thirty political and business campaigns, to set up their political—or 'public affairs'—unit. Grefe was no stranger to controversial industries. When he was hired by the nuclear power industry and asked what he knew about the business, he said he had seen the movie. (*The China Syndrome*, starring Jane Fonda.) 'They didn't appreciate that,' he told me. 'But as far as I was concerned, that's what everybody has seen. That's what the public thinks. I'm a political candidate manager. So, if someone says to me, "This is the situation: our product has been accused of killing people", I say, "So what else is new?" ' Ed Grefe served as Philip Morris' Vice-President, Public Affairs from 1975–79. His job was to build the company a political organisation. He clearly defined his purpose:

> Public affairs is political affairs. The goal or strategic mission of public affairs is the protection of future market availability for the corporation's products or services . . . It is essential to understand that public affairs is a discrete function . . .[11]

I asked him what was the difference between public affairs and public relations. 'If the town's on fire,' he said, 'you hire a public relations guy to convince everybody it's urban renewal: you hire a public or political affairs person ideally in advance to set up a fire prevention service.' Grefe's strategy was to build up political support within the company by convincing each one of its tens of thousands of employees, from board room to factory floor, that they had a vital interest in Philip Morris' political success. 'It's politicising the corporation in a way that the corporation

becomes the candidate for office,' he said. 'The Chairman of the
Board walks down to his employees and says, "I'm in a political
battle and I need your help. I need your votes and I need your
support. Man the barricades with me!" ' Why did Philip Morris
and the other tobacco companies feel that they needed a public
affairs unit? 'Otherwise they don't have any votes. If you don't
mobilise your own people, who else have you got? What you're
trying to demonstrate is that there's a community support for you
as an industry: that people really give a damn about you. When
you have morale at an all-time low because your product's being
attacked, you have an obligation to the people who work for you
and even to the people who use your product. For example, if the
saleswoman who works for you is being asked by her girlfriends,
"How can you sell cigarettes, when it kills unborn children?" and
she wants to continue working for you, she wants to know the
answer. You'd better answer to her satisfaction or you lose an
employee. You reinforce the employee's sense that all the
questions have not been answered and build morale within your
own employee workforce. I want a workforce that believes in me
and believes in my product. I can win the political battles after
that.'

The politicisation of the workforce also acted as an early
warning system. Built into the sales reports of Philip Morris'
thousands of salesmen, first across America and then across the
world, was a section in whch they could notify the company of
any political development which might be harmful to the interests
of Philip Morris or the tobacco industry. 'Company employees
are not only the richest resource but they're your most active alert
system,' said Grefe. 'They'll tell you what's going on in their
community.' At one meeting early in 1979, a member of Grefe's
team turned up a salesman's report from Zehpyrhills, Florida,
which warned of a proposed city ordinance banning smoking in
public places and segregating restaurants into smoking and
non-smoking sections. 'Where the hell is Zephyrhills, Florida?'
asked one. 'It doesn't make any difference,' he was told, as Grefe's
lieutenants scurried to pore over a map. The ordinance was the
result of a one-man crusade by a fifty-five-year-old second-hand
bookseller, Don Kossuth. Kossuth had quit smoking in the 1950s
and has since plastered 'No Smoking' signs in many languages

amongst the Zane Grey Westerns in his book store. Customers often came in for the argument, not the books. Zephyrhills—population 60,000 in the winter sunshine, 20,000 for the rest of the year—didn't take kindly to Kossuth's campaign. Its senior citizens—who comprised most of the population living in the city's 125 Mobile Home parks—called him a Communist and accused him of interfering with their pleasures and their freedoms. A group of local businessmen and restaurant owners formed 'The Committee for Reasonable Government' to oppose Kossuth's crusade.[12] The city fathers were less than enthusiastic when he handed in the thousand signatures he needed to qualify for the citizens' ballot in the April election. They ruled his petition invalid as it did not include addresses with the names. Kossuth asked for his petition back so he could fill them in. He was told the photocopies would cost him fifty cents a sheet as the petition was now city property. He started again from scratch and drew up another petition with nearly a thousand signatures, complete with addresses, each one of them a registered voter in the city. This time the Zephyrhills city council could not refuse him.

Ed Grefe sent one of his lieutenants down to Zephyrhills. 'He did a complete profile of the community. Fortunately for us, the person proposing it was seen as somewhat of a crackpot and we were told not to worry about it. We just ran a few ads.' In the April election 735 Zephyrhills citizens voted on Don Kossuth's ordinance—200 for it and 513 against (the balance presumably being spoiled ballots).[13] Armageddon was postponed. But, as Grefe acknowledged, Zephyrhills showed 'we were prepared to do anything in any community'.

California was not Zephyrhills, but the industry's richest and most important national market, consuming nearly ten per cent of all the cigarettes smoked in America with sales worth $1.6 billion[14] a year. If anti-smoking legislation was passed in California and smoking was outlawed in public places, it was estimated that sales would drop by ten or fifteen per cent and lose the industry millions of dollars. But that was not the industry's only worry. California was the nation's weathervane state. 'In this country, everything happens first in California. Every consumer and cuckoo idea starts in California,' said Grefe. 'If we lost in California, we were finished, absolutely finished.' The industry's opponents in California could not be dismissed as 'crackpots'. They included lawyers, doctors, academics and professional men and women, many of whom had been schooled in radical politics on the California campuses of the 1960s and early 1970s. They now seized the direct weapon of the citizens' ballot to put into practice what they long had preached. Among them was Paul Loveday, a six-foot-seven-inch San Francisco attorney, who had once played basketball for the University of California and the Baltimore Bullets. Loveday was allergic to cigarette smoke and along with two other graduates of the University of California, Peter Hanauer and Tim Moder, founded the local chapter of GASP—Group Against Smoking Pollution. 'We had no support,' Loveday told me. 'We were a core of about twenty people. We weren't regarded at all—we were ignored. Some people thought we were a religious organisation opposed to smoking on moral grounds: in fact we were concerned about the effect of other people's cigarette smoke on us. We only had $200 in the bank, but we had big plans: to get a local law passed in the Berkeley City Council—which would give us political experience; to put together a state-wide political organisation; and then to get state-wide legislation.' Loveday, Hanauer and Moder did get the local legislation passed, having sat in the City Council Chamber for fifteen weeks in a row. 'We weren't surprised we won,' said Loveday, 'we were just surprised it took so long. We were very cocky.' It proved more difficult to unify the diverse anti-smoking groups throughout California. In 1976 GASP joined forces with a group in Southern California, Californians for Clean Indoor Air, headed by another lawyer, Edward Tabash, who had already tried to get a measure on the ballot. 'They were even more naïve than we were,' remembers Loveday. 'They had no money at all. They asked if they could mail us the ballot petitions collect as they couldn't afford the postage.' Together they formed the group which drafted Proposition 5—known as the 'The Clean Indoor Air Act'—which they planned to place on the California state ballot in the November 1978 election. In order to do so, they first had to collect around 600,000 signatures, twice the legal number required, in order to be on the safe side. They started collecting the signatures in September 1977, and qualified for the ballot in March the following year. But they only just met the deadline. At one stage they thought they were not going to make it as, with two weeks to go to the deadline, they were still around 200,000 signatures short. Suddenly, the papers started to flood in at the rate of 20,000 a day, and Proposition 5 narrowly squeezed on to the November ballot. The Clean Indoor Air Act proposed that smoking should be made illegal in all public places unless exempted by law (rock concerts were exempted, jazz concerts were not); that those who broke the law should be subject to a $50 fine (on the parking ticket principle); and that partitions should be erected in offices and public buildings to segregate smokers and non-smokers. The Act was to be enforced on the grounds that 'smoking in enclosed areas is detrimental to non-smokers' health, welfare, comfort and environment'. 'It took ages to hammer the words out,' said Paul Loveday. 'Some members of our coalition said that smokers had no rights, but cooler minds prevailed.'

The way Proposition 5 was framed, with its levying of fines and building of walls gave the industry a field day. Posters appeared depicting its proponents as Carrie Nation, the lady who smashed up saloon bars with an axe in the days of Prohibition. 'The industry wins because the anti-tobacco people invariably trip themselves up,' said Grefe. 'The more vociferous the opposition, the happier I am. When you become strident, I win.' Grefe had first heard what was in the wind in California in March 1977, six months before signatures were collected for the ballot, when he was in Las Vegas at a conference of the California Association of Tobacco and Candy Dealers.[15] The Association's Director, Jack Kelly, had first heard that moves were afoot to draft an anti-tobacco initiative in the late winter of 1976. Grefe, who had been asked to draw up a 'legislative support programme' for the tobacco and candy men, was now asked to map out a 'game plan' in case the threatened initiative ever got beyond the starting blocks. The tobacco industry did not need salesmens' reports to get the message this time. 'The industry had decided this was their Rubicon,' one of their public affairs executives told me. 'The money spent and the amount of management and executive time were extraordinary.' Ed Grefe became one of the tobacco industry's regular passengers on the 'Red Eye Special', the flight that leaves New York at midnight and arrives in Los Angeles at two a.m., leaving no working hour unused. Grefe's first problem was to persuade the industry to act together, as some companies were suspicious of Philip Morris' motives. 'Initially we were out on a limb,' he said. 'We were distrusted because there was a market consideration. They suspected we were trying to get a bigger share of the market and that we'd end up the victors. Certainly that was R. J. Reynolds' feeling, but in time we broke that down. But it took time. It's almost impossible to get industry accord. There's always distrust, always suspicion that the company who's proposing the strategy is proposing it because it's to their advantage.' Grefe told me he had other strategic problems too, in particular on the health question. 'In fact the biggest argument I had internally throughout the entire campaign was to convince the other companies to keep their mouths shut about the health issue. They would say, "Shouldn't we put out a little brochure?" I said, "Forget it, we want no goddam brochure on the health question. We can't win on the health question. We'll lose." Legally they could fight and win on the health issue, they'd been doing it for years, but politically they couldn't. It's no use bucking public opinion. It's like trying to convince the American public that you can trust the Russians.'

Grefe insisted that the campaign should be fought on the issue of freedom and civil liberties, not health (part of the strategy now adopted by the cigarette companies in Britain). Another former public affairs executive told me, 'The idea was you never talked about the health issue. You talked about all the side issues, like individual privacy, government interference, Big Brother, and all that. The whole campaign was run on the idea that this violates the individual's right to do what he wants to. I remember one ad in particular which had scenes of crime, buildings burning, horrific scenes of chaos, which said, "The police won't have time to deal with this any more: they'll be too busy enforcing anti-smoking laws". Then they'd show someone smoking in a restaurant and the police grabbing the guy and dragging him out. It worked.' Grefe believed in attack not defence, or, in public affairs jargon, to be 'proactive' not 'reactive'. 'I don't care what my opponent's perspective is,' he said. 'If I run my campaign upon the basis *you* think I should run my campaign, I lose because I'm playing the game according to the rules you've established. I establish the rules around which you play. I wanna force you to play it my way. I don't care what you think at the moment, what I really care about is what will get you to change your mind. So in California we said, "Okay, let them go against us. I can anticipate what their arguments are going to be. We'll ignore their arguments." ' The way voters' minds were changed was by identifying their 'soft' spots and then asking key 'conversion' or 'what if' questions to win them over. The architect of this 'conversion' technique was one of America's leading political pollsters, V. Lance Tarrance. Grefe attributes the industry's victory in California to Tarrance's research and identification of these key questions.[16]

The industry took the first step in the campaign in the autumn of 1977 when the Tobacco Institute hired the San Francisco-based campaign management firm of Woodward & McDowell. By the beginning of March 1978, they had received $27,000 in fees.[17] Woodward & McDowell expanded the 'game plan' which Grefe had outlined for California's Tobacco and Candy Dealers in Las Vegas in July 1977. The initial polls showed that the industry was in for a three to one defeat and, according to Grefe, many industry leaders believed there was no way they could win. V. Lance Tarrance was consulted early, thus enabling Woodward & McDowell to plot what Grefe called 'a true course'. The polls seemed to indicate that only one issue could turn the tide; the cost of enforcement to government and the taxpayer; if it cost half a million dollars, over seventy per cent would vote for Proposition 5; if it cost $5 million, there would still be a majority; but if it cost $20 million, barely forty per cent would vote in favour. This was the key 'what if' question, and $20 million was the key 'what if' figure. Early on in the operation, a citizens' group was established to oppose Proposition 5. It was called 'Californians for Common Sense'. Ed Grefe says that Californians for Common Sense was nourished by the industry.

We decided to create a full blown campaign, involving a large number of citizens, some of note, some not, in an organisation called Californians for Common Sense. It was this coalition that would seek political and editorial support for our position and reach out to as many voters as possible, inviting their active and financial participation.[18]

Besides retaining the campaign management firm of Woodward & McDowell, the Tobacco Institute also hired the San Francisco law firm of Dobbs & Nielsen. By the beginning of March 1978, they had paid them $24,400 for work in relation to Proposition 5 and nearly $5,000 in legal fees.[19] Californians for Common Sense also retained Woodward & McDowell and Dobbs & Nielsen. By March 1978, when the *New York Times* reported 'The Tobacco Institute . . . professed to have no direct knowledge or part in the anti-initiative effort',[20] the Tobacco Institute had already spent $61,668 with Woodward & McDowell and Dobbs & Nielsen for work in connection with Proposition 5. The question of who was behind Californians for Common Sense tended to produce evasive answers. When Vigo Nielsen, one of the law firm's senior partners was asked in court how Californians for Common Sense had started, his memory appeared to fail him.[21] How did they come into being? 'I am not sure I am aware.' Did he participate in the drafting of their articles of incorporation? 'Yes, I drafted them.' Who retained him to draft the articles? 'The organisation I was about to form.' Who contacted his office? 'I don't remember.' Did they represent or were they associated in any way with the tobacco industry? 'I don't know.' And who contacted you? 'I do not remember.'

Part of the work which Dobbs & Nielsen did for its client the Tobacco Institute in the early days of the campaign was to commission a survey by Economic Research Associates[22] which estimated that the cost to the taxpayer of Proposition 5 (for 'No Smoking' signs, etc.) would be the magic figure of $20 million plus an additional $20 million to enforce it. The industry now had the $20 million figure to answer the key 'conversion' question — how much Proposition 5 would cost. As Grefe had predicted, the opponents hit back on the industry's chosen ground. They obtained a copy of the ERA Report which their mathematical wizard, Dr Stanton Glantz, an Associate Professor of Medicine at the University of California, went through with a toothcomb and calculator. (Dr Glantz was the academic who later received a copy of 'Death in the West' in the post and promoted the programme across America.) He discovered a mathematical error which made the real cost $20,000, not $20 million. He explained the mistake: the square root of 4 million had been calculated at 2 million instead of 2,000. 'You try explaining all this at a press conference,' he lamented. Dr Glantz tried, armed with his pocket calculator. 'The story got picked up and then stonewalled,' he said. 'Who cares about square roots anyway?' By this time a barrage of commercials had fixed the figure of $40 million firmly in the public's mind, which Dr Glantz's maths lesson had done little to dislodge. Coming home on the bus from their press conference, Dr Glantz and Paul Loveday felt well satisfied that they had successfully punctured the $40 million myth until they heard a radio commercial ridiculing the lower estimate with gales of laughter. 'It was very effective,' said Dr Glantz, 'in the end even my friends believed it.' Ed Grefe was amused by the exposure of the mathematical error. 'All that square root stuff? The error is irrelevant. The whole strategy is to put the other person on the defensive. If I say, "It'll cost a billion dollars" and you say, "No, it'll only cost a million", you've lost, you're dead.'

Proposition 5's opponents saturated the media with their messages about freedom, Big Brother, crime in the streets, the cost to the taxpayer and the cost to California business: but, as Ed Grefe recognised, the media did not do the job on its own. 'Everybody knows the industry spent $6 million on advertising and on television, but what's not remembered is that 1.8 million pieces of literature were delivered door to door by 12,000 volunteers.' Many of them were the industry's own employees. The industry had become the candidate as Grefe had forecast, and its employees had become its campaign workers, just as Grefe had planned. But in the end it was not the devotion of the industry's employees that won the day, but the $6 million which it channelled through Californians for Common Sense. And the money was not just used to buy media time. As the campaign progressed, voters' mailboxes must have groaned under the weight of campaign literature which the direct mailers sent out from their computers. One such newsheet, called *The United Democrat*, was circulated amongst the one million people of Alameda County, the fifth largest county in the state, which contains the cities of Berkeley and Oakland. Edition One of *The United Democrat* made no mention of Proposition 5. But two issues later, things had changed. Edition Three contained a fierce attack on Proposition 5. It warned voters:

When you vote on Proposition 5, you will not be voting *for* or *against smoking*. You will be voting on whether you want to increase California's taxpayer burden with new local and state spending. The proposed new law would require installation of signs containing about 20 words at every entrance of every facility of every state and local governmental entity. This includes everything from mosquito abatement district offices to school houses and the State Capitol! Peace officers, under general law, would be required to arrest anyone they see violating the new smoking prohibitions. A study by a national economics research firm estimates the signs, enforcement, prosecution and court time would cost California taxpayers $43 million in the first year![23]

Campaign returns later showed that Californians for Common Sense gave $5,000 to the group (through its Treasurer) which produced that particular edition of *The United Democrat* for the purpose of producing slate cards. In fact, the official recommendation of the California Democratic Party was to vote Yes on Proposition 5.

'Common Sense' and the industry won the day. The successful execution of Ed Grefe's game plan swung the initial prediction of a three to one defeat to a fifty-four per cent to forty-six per cent victory. The victory cost the industry overall $6,390,607—99.7 per cent of all the money raised to defeat Proposition 5. It set a new record for spending in a California campaign, and exceeded the total amount spent by both candidates for Governor in the same election. According to Dr Glantz's calculations, each tobacco company contributed an amount roughly in proportion to its market share in California.[24]

Company	Total Contribution	Percentage Contribution	Percentage Market Share
R. J. Reynolds	$2,351,786	39.9	37.7
Philip Morris	1,760,000	29.8	30.3
Brown & Williamson	1,170,000	19.8	18.0
Lorillard	587,845	10.0	10.0
Liggett & Myers	28,025	0.5	4.0

The battle in California was won in November 1978, but the war was not over. Six months later, in May 1979, the industry faced another attack, this time in Dade County, Miami, Florida, where an anti-smoking initiative had made it on to the ballot. Dade County, many of whose citizens are exiled New Yorkers, is another patch on the political weather map of America. The initiative was opposed by the Dade Voters for a Free Choice, through whom the industry channelled nearly $1 million—ninety per cent of all the contributions which the group received. The supporters of the initiative—the Miami chapter of GASP—raised $9,000. The industry won by only a handful of votes; 95,700 voted Yes, 96,500 voted No.[25]

Encouraged by its near victory, GASP drew breath again in the election of November 1980 with a further initiative on the ballot. This time GASP were opposed by Floridans Against Increased Regulation—FAIR—through whom the industry channelled nearly $600,000 (non-industry contributions amounted to $185). Supporters of the initiative raised $7,500.[26] FAIR fought the campaign by concentrating on the law and order issue. One of its ads featured a cartoon showing a couple of crooks loaded with loot walking past an 'All-Nite' Bowling Alley with an empty police car parked outside. 'Geez, the cops!' says one. 'Relax, Louie,' says the other. 'Dem cops is inside enforcin' da no-smoking law.' The Dade County Police Benevolent Association (the PBA, the police officers' trade union) came out in unanimous opposition to the initiative by twenty-six votes to nil.[27] There was some embarrassment when it was reported that the President of the PBA had received a $1,000 consultancy fee from FAIR and was due to receive a further $1,000 for his services. (He denied it had anything to do with the Association's stand on the issue and returned the money.) The industry won again in November 1980, this time by a slightly less hair-raising margin: 248,613 voted No (51.7 per cent) and 232,655 voted Yes (48.3 per cent).[28]

The industry faced a pincer movement in November 1980. On the other side of the country the California non-smokers' rights coalition which had drafted Proposition 5 in 1978 returned to the attack with a more carefully worded ballot, Proposition 10 (called the Smoking and No Smoking Sections Initiative). It was designed to give less offence and afford less opportunity for ridicule. There were to be no arrests, no partitions and no differentiation between jazz and rock concerts. By this time, Ed Grefe had left Philip Morris to run his own political and public affairs consultancy, International Civics Inc. There had been differences over strategy. Grefe believed that Philip Morris should take an 'up front' position: others thought the company should stay within the shelter of the industry's collective umbrella. Grefe's view did not prevail. Grefe had also advocated keeping the grass roots in California well watered in case they were needed again—as indeed they were in 1980. Not everyone agreed. The industry was sensitive to the charge of having bought the last election with its $6 million, and was reluctant to be seen to be still spending. Reflecting on the Proposition 5 fight, one of California's leading political pollsters, Mervin Field, commented that if the industry had spent 'a couple more million dollars, it might have lost the election'.[29] Now, faced with Proposition 10, the industry was more cautious about how it was seen to be spending its money. Grefe had argued that it did not matter as the companies would only be criticised by their critics. When battle was joined again in California in November 1980, the industry channelled its money through an organisation called CARE—Californians Against Regulatory Excess. By the end of September 1980, with polling day only six weeks away, the industry had only spent $372,000, a fraction of the $2.4 million it had spent at the same point during the Proposition 5 campaign two years earlier. It was not even as much as the proponents themselves had raised ($410,787— although most of it had been used in qualifying for the ballot). The opposition was suspicious. At the time Peter Hanauer, the Treasurer of the 'Yes on 10' Committee, was quoted as saying that the only way to turn the election round would be a 'major blitz in the last few days in the campaign'. He said, 'It seems logical the tobacco companies will withhold their contributions until it is too late for the public to realise what they are doing.'[30]

With six weeks to go, the polls were showing the supporters of Proposition 10 leading by two to one.[31] Peter Hanauer's prophecy was fulfilled. In the weeks that followed, tobacco money poured in. R. J. Reynolds and Philip Morris each put in over $600,000; Brown & Williamson, $300,000; and Lorillard over $200,000.[32] This influx of over $1 million enabled Californians Against

Regulatory Excess to saturate the media in the closing stages of the campaign. Between September 24th and October 20th, CARE made 537 payments totalling $710,784 to California's radio and TV stations.[33] Once again, the industry's money snatched victory. Proposition 10 was lost by fifty-three per cent to forty-seven per cent. This time the industry only had to spend $2.5 million to ensure the enemy's defeat.

The non-smokers' rights movement had to wait three years to take a sip of revenge. This time the Proposition was a letter not a number and applied only to San Fancisco, not the whole state of California. Proposition P required all employers to adopt a written policy to accommodate smokers and non-smokers in the workplace. It was placed on the ballot in the San Francisco Municipal Election of November 8th, 1983. The campaign was a replay of Propositions 5 and 10.

Californians for Non-Smokers Rights mailed an advertisement which asked, 'Why would these 6 people want to vote YES on P on November 8?' Beneath the caption were photographs of Humphrey Bogart, Betty Grable, Buster Keaton, Jack Benny, Nat 'King' Cole and John Wayne. The answer was supplied. 'Because they would know about the dangers of smoking if they were alive. They all died of lung cancer.' The coalition opposed to Proposition P, No on P, argued in its direct mailing that the ordinance would 'drive people apart and set friend against friend'; it warned that it would 'breed conflict, promote discrimination and harassment'; and it complained of 'too much government' with the reminder that 'our city faces real problems such as increased crime, serious traffic congestion, and control of contagious disease'.

Again as in Propositions 5 and 10, the tobacco industry heavily outspent its opponents. By polling day, the cigarette companies had contributed just over one million dollars to the No on P campaign — around ten times the amount raised by the other side. But this time the money made no difference. The voters of San Francisco voted in favour of the Proposition by 50.4 per cent to 49.6 per cent.

The non-smokers rights movement had waited five years to savour its victory, albeit limited to San Francisco. Converting California, as the battles over Propositions 5 and 10 had shown, was a far more difficult task, although after the 1983 victory it might seem less formidable. The two previous statewide campaigns in 1978 and 1980 were ones the tobacco industry had to win (and it spent $10 million in order to do so), not just because of what was at stake in California but because it was under heavy attack nationally from President Carter's Secretary for Health, Education and Welfare, Joe Califano.

12

Tobacco and the White House

The tobacco industry had an added incentive to defeat Proposition 5 in 1978. For the first time it faced in government an opponent as committed to the anti-smoking cause as the enemies it met on the hustings in California. Joe Califano, President Carter's Secretary for Health, Education and Welfare (HEW), repeatedly warned America that smoking was 'slow motion suicide'. To the industry, Joe Califano was a 'fumaphobe' in the White House. But, for two and a half turbulent years, he posed a greater threat to the political health of the President and his party than he did to the tobacco industry. This above all was due to the politics of one state and one man: Jesse Helms, the US Senator for North Carolina.

Jesse Helms was North Carolina's first Republican Senator since Reconstruction. Throughout the 1960s he had been a commentator on the Tobacco Radio Network which emanated from station WRAL in his home town of Raleigh, North Carolina. Twice every weekday for over a decade his five-minute spot, 'Viewpoints',[1] was fed over the airwaves to the sixty stations to the east which covered tobacco country, a diet of anti-Communism, anti-liberalism and flag-waving patriotism. Helms is against welfare, abortion, food stamps (welfare coupons given to the poor to buy food), federal spending (except on tobacco price supports), foreign aid, busing, detente, holding hands with the Russians (or Red Chinese), and sin. 'What have we reaped as a nation from our personal and collective delinquencies?' he asks. 'Atheistic schools, rampaging crime, Godforsaken homes, drugs, abortion, pornography, permissiveness and a sense of cynicism and spiritual desolation unprecedented in our country's history.'[2] In 1970, Jesse Helms left the Democratic Party and joined the Republicans, at a time when Richard Nixon's brand of conservatism offered many of North Carolina's Democrats the natural home which their own party no longer afforded as it moved 'left' under Hubert Humphrey and George McGovern. Two years later Helms was persuaded to run for the Senate on the slogan 'Richard Nixon needs Jesse Helms', by a shrewd Raleigh attorney and campaign manager, Tom Ellis. Helms' opponent was against the Vietnam war. Helms won and John Wayne joined the 'Friends for Jesse Club'.[3] To pay off $200,000 worth of campaign debts and to build an organisation which would spread the Helms gospel, Tom Ellis and a small group of Helms' supporters set up the Congressional Club, with its headquarters in Raleigh, the new Senator's home town. Membership was $100 a year. The campaign debt was wiped out in just over twelve months. The Congressional Club kept on growing and became the richest and most effective private political machine in American political history. Helms' Congressional Club laid the ideological and financial foundation for the victories of the New Right and Moral Majority when Ronald Reagan swept into the White House eight years later. 'The fact that Reagan is President and the Senate is Republican is, we believe, directly attributable to the fact that Jesse Helms was elected to the US Senate in 1972,' George Dunlop told me, who helped elect the Senator in 1972 and is now Staff Director of the Senate Agriculture Committee which Senator Helms chairs. 'America's concerned about social issues, the family, the neighbourhood. These folk know the difference between right and wrong. They see the issues in moral terms. These are the issues that the conventional wisdom in American politics refused to discuss for twenty to thirty years. The issues of the day were what the sophisticated liberal establishment wanted them to be. They didn't want these "instinctive" issues on the agenda. Jesse Helms came to Washington to put them there. They laughed at him at first but they're not laughing now. Helms has redefined the agenda for the nation and he's done it virtually singlehandedly.'

Jesse Helms would never have got to Washington and stayed there were it not for his support of tobacco and tobacco's support of him. In his office on Capitol Hill crossed tobacco leaves are displayed over the mantelpiece (next to a quote that says, 'Communist with knife and fork would like to meet Capitalist with steak and kidney pudding'). Leaflets abound: 'Cigarettes— America's Most Overtaxed Commodity'; 'Tobacco and the Economy'; 'Tobacco—From Seed to Smoke amid Controversy'; 'Cigarette Plant Free Guided Tours'; 'The Golden Leaf'; and 'North Carolina and Tobacco'. Tobacco and Jesse Helms depend on each other. Helms' political base is in the eastern part of North Carolina where Democrats outnumber Republicans by seven to one. The only way any North Carolina Republican can be elected to national office (overall Democrats outnumber Republicans in the state by three to one) is to win the support of Democrats, in particular in tobacco country where they are most heavily concentrated. Throughout the 1970s, thousands of North Carolina Democrats, more concerned with a candidate's conservative credentials than the party label attached to his name, voted for Jesse Helms. They became known as the 'Jessecrats'. History has taught politicians the lessons of tobacco politics in North Carolina. The state can be divided roughly into three sections: the mountains and the west, traditionally Republican since the Civil War; the central area between Winston-Salem and Raleigh, where most of the state's urban and industrial centres are located; and tobacco country in the east. In national elections, voting has tended to follow the same pattern: Republicans start well in the west and are swamped by the Democrats in the east. In the presidential election of 1956, fought between the Republican Dwight D. Eisenhower and the Democrat Adlai E. Stevenson, Eisenhower lost North Carolina by forty-nine per cent to fifty-one per cent. General Eisenhower started well in the west of the state and was ahead with fifty-nine per cent of the vote by the time he got to Winston-Salem; by Raleigh his vote had dropped by one per cent; by the time he had crossed the east of the state, it had plunged five per cent. Eisenhower lost North Carolina in tobacco country. A similar pattern was repeated in 1960 in the race between Richard Nixon and John F. Kennedy (Nixon won forty-eight per cent of the vote and Kennedy fifty-two per cent). Again in 1964, when Lyndon Johnson beat Barry Goldwater by fifty-six per cent to forty-four per cent (that year there was a Democratic landslide: Goldwater did not even win in the West, he just lost by less). Again in 1968 when Richard Nixon beat Hubert Humphrey by thirty-nine and a half per cent to twenty-nine per cent because the intervention of the third party candidate, George Wallace (a Conservative populist) split the Democratic vote in tobacco country. And again in 1972, in the battle between Richard Nixon and George McGovern, when Nixon swept the state in a stunning victory—seventy per cent to twenty-nine per cent—because his Democratic opponent was too 'liberal' for the political stomachs of Democrats in the east of the state. The political lesson is clear: any Republican who hopes to win national office has to win over Democrats in tobacco country; and any Democrat who hopes to stay in Washington has to hold on to tobacco. President Carter, as a Southern politician himself, knew the lesson as well as anybody. North Carolina was vital to his plans for re-election. Although the state was geographically part of the South, where the President had his political base, its relatively liberal traditions also gave it close associations with the North. North Carolina gave Carter a foot in both camps. But his political advisers in the White House, especially those around Hamilton Jordan, who ran his political office, repeatedly warned him against alienating his tobacco constituency and playing directly into Jesse Helms' hands. They not only feared for the President's political health but also for that of North Carolina's second senator, the Democrat Robert Morgan who, like the President, was up for re-election in 1980. Helms intended to defeat Morgan and give North Carolina its second Republican Senator. The potential for political disaster if the President lost tobacco was also of great concern to the state's popular Democratic governor, James B. Hunt, Jnr, who was one of the party's rising young stars.

When President Carter asked Joe Califano to be his Secretary for Health, Education and Welfare, he had no idea he was handing Jesse Helms one of his greatest political assets. Nor had Califano (who had once served under Lyndon Johnson)[4] any idea of the trouble which lay ahead. He had been a two pack a day man until he quit in 1975 when his son asked him to give it up as an eleventh birthday present. Nor, with $15,000 of stock in Philip Morris,* did he appear to have any ethical objections to cigarette companies. Between his election and inauguration, President Carter invited Califano to his vacation retreat, the estate of the heir to the R. J. Reynolds tobacco fortune, Smith Bagley, on St Simons Island off the coast of Georgia.⁵ The President told his new Health Secretary that he wanted him to move forcefully into the area of preventive health.⁶ He did not single out smoking, although his father, who had smoked four packs a day, had died of lung cancer.⁷ It was only when Califano interviewed doctors for a hundred jobs in the Health Department that he became aware that smoking was such a problem. 'Every doctor I talked to,' he told me, 'every doctor I interviewed for a job at HEW said that we couldn't have a serious disease prevention programme unless we had an anti-smoking programme. It was that serious. I wasn't aware of that before. I hadn't thought twice about it.' Califano was converted. He called for the facts and figures and was particularly struck by two things: that ninety per cent of adult smokers had tried to quit within the last twelve months; and that seventy-five per cent of smokers were hooked before they were twenty-one. 'This is what really sets me off,' he said. 'Heroin mimics cigarette smoking in terms of when people get hooked. The overwhelming majority of heroin addicts are hooked before they're twenty-one. Virtually no one gets hooked after they're twenty-five. It's the same with cigarettes.' Within months, Califano went on the attack. His first target was the tobacco price support programme, until he realised his mistake. 'It was quixotic to go after that,' he said. 'It was politically undoable. You'd be surprised at the kinds of Congressmen who speak out in favour of it.' Instead, Califano decided to launch a heavily publicised, high profile anti-smoking campaign to alert the American public to the danger of cigarettes.

But the President's advisers feared that Califano's campaign would endanger the President's political health. The evening

* This was subsequently transferred into a blind trust administered by Lehman Brothers of New York City. The Philip Morris stock was sold, according to US Office of Government Ethics, prior to 30 March 1979.

before Califano was due to launch his anti-smoking programme, he received a phone call from Dr Peter Bourne, who had been Jimmy Carter's health adviser since his days as Governor of Georgia. 'I'd worked for Carter for six or seven years,' Dr Bourne told me when I met him in Washington to discuss those turbulent days for tobacco. 'Most of his health positions were positions I'd developed for him anyway. I knew how Carter's mind worked.' Dr Bourne, somewhat late in the day, advised the Secretary not to mount a major anti-smoking campaign. Bourne had already angered Califano a few months earlier when he had told a meeting of the American Cancer Society that smokers should not be treated as 'outcasts',[8] using what Califano regarded as Tobacco Institute language. The phone call from Dr Bourne on the eve of the launch of the anti-smoking campaign was Califano's first hint of trouble. 'Either he was doing what the President was telling him to do, or what Hamilton Jordan was telling him to do, or, on his own, he was just going with the tobacco industry,' Califano told me. Dr Bourne explained his side of the story to me. 'The sole thing dictating what I did was what was in Carter's interest in maintaining his political base,' he said. 'As Carter's health adviser, I was constantly caught in the middle of these issues. I was there to look after Carter's interests. Every time Joe went out on some tangent, I was the person who had to bring him back, and Joe is not the sort of guy you bring back very easily.' It was clear that there was little love lost between the President's health adviser and his Health Secretary. 'Joe seized the tobacco issue as one on which he himself could come out looking extremely good and make it very difficult for us in the White House to oppose him, without getting into difficulty with a significant part of our constituency in the health field,' said Dr Bourne. Nor, it seemed, were relations between Joe Califano and the President much warmer. 'He was picked as Secretary for HEW at the suggestion and pressure of Vice-President Mondale, with whom he'd had a long-standing personal relationship,' Dr Bourne continued. 'Califano was somebody who was picked without Carter having any great enthusiasm for him, but more as a favour to Mondale. Right up to the day of the election Califano had been a less than enthusiastic supporter of Carter around this town. Anyway, Joe ended up with the job. He owed Carter absolutely nothing because he'd never been particularly loyal to him. In the job he was a sort of model of disloyalty and quite uncontrollable.'

President Roosevelt once said he wanted people working for him who had 'a passion for anonymity'. Joe Califano had no such passion. He ignored Dr Bourne's advice to go easy. The President never relayed him the message direct. The anti-smoking programme was launched in a blaze of publicity, heightened by the Tobacco Institute's advanced denunciation of a programme it had not been allowed to see. Califano condemned cigarette smoking as 'Public Health Enemy Number One'.[9] He answered the Tobacco Institute's charge that his actions were those of a zealous, reformed smoker by reminding the nation that cigarettes killed 320,000 Americans every year—220,000 from heart disease, 78,000 from lung cancer and 22,000 from respiratory diseases. He also emphasised the huge public and private cost of smoking: $7 billion in health care costs and $18 billion in absenteeism, lost wages and lower productivity. He announced the foundation of an Office on Smoking and Health, with a budget of $12 million for public education. Its Director was to be John Pinney, who had previously headed the National Council on Alcoholism.[10] He persuaded Congress to almost treble the research and education budget for HEW's anti-smoking programme during his time in office, from $19 million to over $50 million.[11] But Joe Califano's particular concern was to stop young people from starting to smoke. He commissioned a survey of teenage smoking, which showed that four million teenagers were regular smokers and that children and teenagers smoked the most heavily advertised brand, Marlboro, three times more than adults.[12] He wrote to the Chief Executive Officers of all the major cigarette companies and suggested that they devote ten per cent of their advertising budget to a special campaign to discourage smoking amongst children and teenagers, on the basis that the companies repeatedly said they did not wish to encourage children to smoke as it was an 'adult' custom. All refused. George Weissman, the Chairman of Philip Morris, said he did not think 'advertising is effective in altering the behaviour of teenagers in regard to the use of cigarettes'. William Hobbs, the Chief Executive Officer of R. J. Reynolds, claimed that advertising played no part in encouraging teenagers to smoke, therefore he had no responsibility to urge them not to smoke. The most 'fatuous' reply Joe Califano said he received was from Raymond J. Mulligan, President of the Liggett Group, who declined on the grounds 'the mothers and fathers of this nation, whether smokers or non-smokers, should continue to have freedom of choice in the education and training of their children'.[13]

Califano was convinced that the young were being seduced into smoking and was particularly angry when the House Appropriations Sub-committee on Health, Education and Welfare (which had to approve HEW's budget) knocked out $2 million to fund a programme informing young people in schools about the dangers of smoking.[14] The Sub-committee was chaired by Congressman William Natcher of Kentucky, who held the final 'mark up' session of the Committee in private. ('Mark up' is where the decisions are finally made on what is left in and what is cut out of the budget.) One of Califano's staff, whose job it was to steer HEW's budget through Natcher's Committee, told me it was 'decimated' when it came out of the final session. 'Everyone knew Natcher was hurting back home,' he said. Califano, who had given evidence before the Sub-committee, along with the Director of the new Office on Smoking and Health, John Pinney, regarded the $2 million allocation for anti-smoking education in schools as an important part of his budget request because it targeted young people. He had no doubts why it was killed. 'The industry really lobbied to knock that out of the budget. They lobbied the Appropriations Sub-committee, Congressman by Congressman. Natcher of Kentucky is a very strong tobacco supporter. It confirmed my suspicions—and now I know—that they really go after the kids: that's who they're after in their advertising; and that's who they're after in trying to sell cigarettes.'

The repercussions of Califano's campaign in tobacco country were instantaneous. No sooner had it got off the ground than the state legislature of Kentucky voted to impeach him.[15] In North Carolina, motorists drove around with bumper stickers warning, 'Califano is Dangerous to My Health'. But the Secretary for Health, Education and Welfare was doubly unpopular in North Carolina because at the same time he was trying to enforce a long-standing court order desegregating the state's higher education system. Califano was tackling head on two of the

South's most sensitive issues, tobacco and race. President Carter knew he was in trouble within weeks of the launch of Califano's campaign. In February 1978, the year of the mid-term Congressional elections, with Jesse Helms running for another term in the Senate, an anxious Governor Hunt and Senator Robert Morgan of North Carolina met with the President. They urged him to get Califano to 'cool the rhetoric'[16] on the anti-smoking campaign: they said it was devastating politically: that it could kill any chance they had of beating Jesse Helms, and could even cost them seats in the forthcoming mid-term elections. They told the President that Jesse Helms and the Republicans were running against Califano, not the Democratic candidates. They also warned that if Califano pushed the desegregation issue, it could cost Carter the state in the 1980 presidential election. Inside the White House, Dr Peter Bourne watched the President caught between tobacco and the Secretary for HEW. 'The President faced a very real political problem, in that his real political base was the south-east of the United States, which was economically dependent on tobacco cultivation,' he said. 'He couldn't afford to overtly antagonise that base, but Joe Califano successfully did that for him, to a point where Governor Hunt of North Carolina eventually called Carter early in 1978 and said, "If you don't do something about Joe Califano, North Carolina is totally lost to you for the re-election." Hunt had said this to me periodically all along from when Joe first started talking about the tobacco issue. But it grew stronger and stronger until it was almost—in fact it was—an ultimatum from Hunt to Carter.'

The President visited North Carolina three times in 1978 to try to mend the fences. A few weeks after the warnings from Governor Hunt and Senator Morgan, he made his first trip to deliver a speech on Defence in Winston-Salem, which began with the words:

> As someone who comes from a great tobacco producing state, it is an honour for me to be here in the capital of the greatest tobacco producing state in the world.[17]

He went on to assure the people of North Carolina that he committed his administration to 'a balanced campaign to protect the health of the tobacco industry'. He also made an appearance with his Commerce Secretary, Juanita Kreps, who was in North Carolina to dedicate R. J. Reynolds' new world headquarters in Winston-Salem.

President Carter never told Califano to his face to ease off. The nearest he came to it was at a meeting in the Oval Office in May 1978 when he told Califano to keep the anti-smoking programme off his desk. But the President told Dr Bourne what he never told Califano directly. 'Early on, we'd talked about it at some length. Carter said to me repeatedly what a problem Califano was creating for him. He was angry about it. A lot of people in the White House who weren't particularly involved in health but were involved in the political area, Hamilton Jordan for one, were also extremely upset. They felt that Califano was wilfully making problems for the President and carving out a separate position for himself. Califano wasn't a team player. If he'd ever worked for Margaret Thatcher, he'd have been gone a helluva lot quicker.'

Shortly after the meeting in the Oval Office, Califano went off to Geneva for the Thirty-First Annual World Health Assembly to deliver a major speech on health promotion and disease prevention in the Third World. It was the first time any HEW Secretary had attended the Assembly, and the President was particularly anxious that Califano should go. Dr Bourne had spent months working on the speech. The trip passed off without incident, and the speech with zero attention. Tobacco was not on the agenda while Joe Califano was in Geneva. But it came up just after he had gone. The Saudi Arabian delegation introduced a tough anti-smoking resolution co-sponsored by the delegations of Cyprus, Finland, Greece, Italy, Jordan, Kuwait, Netherlands, New Zealand, Poland, Romania, Sweden and the United Kingdom. It noted:

> . . . the alarming increase in the production and consumption of cigarettes during the last two decades in some of the countries, particularly developing countries, in which it was previously not widespread, and . . . the extensive promotional drive for the sale of cigarettes being carried out on radio and television, in newspapers and other news media, and through association with sporting and cultural events, often inducing young people to smoke tobacco.[18]

The resolution recommended, among other things, strengthening health education programmes, increasing taxation on cigarettes; restricting 'as far as possible' all forms of advertising and promotion; and protecting the right of non-smokers to enjoy 'an atmosphere unpolluted by tobacco smoke'.[19] Califano was anxious to give America's support to the resolution, not only because he personally believed in it, but because he thought it would also underline the administration's commitment to Third World health issues. The head of the US delegation in Geneva was Dr John Bryant, the author of a famous study on health in developing countries. Dr Bryant felt there was widespread support for the Saudi resolution, but had to check with the US State Department in Washington (which was responsible for international conferences such as this) before he cast his delegation's vote. The State Department's instinctive view was that there were precious few Saudi resolutions in the international arena with which America could agree, and that when a reasonable one such as this came up, America should give it her support. Saudi Arabia was, after all, one of America's few friends in the Arab world.

But the White House did not share Califano's enthusiasm, Dr Bryant's commitment, or the State Department's political reasoning. 'I remember being very upset that this issue had distracted people's attention from what we thought was a much more important issue,' Dr Bourne recalled. 'We just thought that it was going to create disastrous political problems here for Carter if we were supporting a resolution that says we're against the sale of tobacco overseas, when there is a significant sale of tobacco overseas from North Carolina.' He took a second opinion, consulting Anne Wexler, the White House political aide who was responsible for the President's various 'constituencies'. 'It was her job to be on top of who was going to get sensitive about what,' said Dr Bourne. 'I talked to her about how she thought our support of the Saudi resolution would affect the President's perception domestically. We were pretty much in agreement. If we could get this thing killed quietly, that was fine.' Dr Bourne then telephoned the State Department and instructed them not to support the Saudi resolution. Califano's staff came under pressure too. Anne Wexler contacted Peter Bell, HEW's Deputy Under-

Secretary for International Affairs, and, according to Califano, pressed him to substitute 'Tobacco Institute language' about the 'possible' harmful effects of cigarette smoking. Califano noted:

> Wexler was concerned about the impact of supporting the resolution on US tobacco interests, the re-election of Jesse Helms, and the already low standing of the administration in North Carolina.[20]

Having been directed by the State Department not to support the Saudi resolution, Dr John Bryant in Geneva telephoned Peter Bell in Washington. 'As I recall,' Peter Bell told me, 'he expressed considerable consternation that he had been instructed to vote against the resolution. He was just terribly concerned. He's a public health professional. He asked me what he should do, as he did not feel that in good conscience he could obey State's instructions. He realised that there were political criteria that were being brought to bear and this disturbed him very much.' Bell was angry and told his boss, Joe Califano, that he thought it was an incredible political intrusion. Califano was furious and said he would go to Cyrus Vance, the US Secretary of State, if necessary. He ordered Peter Bell to disregard the directive and to call the State Department and tell them to ease the White House pressure. 'Bourne's a doctor,' he told Bell. 'He can't stand such public exposure of such blatant support of tobacco interests.'[21]

Peter Bell spent the weekend on the telephone, trying to get the decision reversed. The State Department was sympathetic, but said they were under instructions from the White House. 'We had an ally there,' said Bell, 'even though the order had come from State, the opposition hadn't come from State.' Bell then rang the White House. He was told that the Saudi resolution was in violation of the First Amendment (which guarantees the right to free speech) because it proposed restrictions on advertising. Bell was not convinced. 'Of course the real reason was the importance of the Southern strategy to the President,' he said, 'and the fact that North Carolina was viewed as a key state within that strategy. It was a leader among the Southern states. It was felt that if the President couldn't get the support of North Carolina, he wasn't likely to get very far in the South.'

Dr Bourne was out of Washington over that crucial weekend before the vote was due to be taken in Geneva, sitting on a Commission in Maryland to select academics who would become White House 'Fellows' for a year. 'There must have been fifty phone calls over that period of time,' recalls Dr Bourne. 'It was just backwards and forwards all weekend long. I just remember being called out of meetings constantly for a blow-by-blow account from Geneva.' After a weekend on the telephone, Peter Bell happened to meet Dr Bourne at a ceremony marking the twenty-fifth anniversary of HEW. Dr Bourne was about to take his seat in the VIP section when Bell rushed up to him and took him by the lapel. 'I don't think he had a chance to sit down,' he remembers. 'It was one minute to midnight. I emphasised how shortsighted the White House position was, and how dangerous it would be if it ever really came to light that what they were doing was making a political issue out of something which otherwise wouldn't have been. Who would have noticed a unanimous vote at the World Health Assembly in favour of a Saudi resolution? It wouldn't have got an inch of space in an American newspaper. However, if the US cast the only vote against the Saudi resolution, that would have been a story, because of the political motivation in the vote. I insisted Peter go to the phone and call the White House.' With the ceremony about to begin, Bell accompanied Dr Bourne to the nearest telephone inside the HEW building. 'I stood there while Peter placed his call to the White House switchboard,' said Bell. 'I did not, out of deference, stand there and listen.' The pressure was called off; the State Department withdrew its instruction to vote against the Saudi resolution. There was no earthquake in North Carolina.

Two months later, in August 1978, President Carter made a second trip to the state. The mid-term elections were only weeks away, and Jesse Helms' political machine was busy generating over $7 million for the Senator's re-election, more than any Senate candidate has ever raised in US history. Helms' opponent, a populist and conservative Democrat, John Ingrams, only raised just over $250,000. The President spoke at a Democratic rally, and visited a tobacco warehouse in Wilson, in the heart of tobacco country, forty miles east of Raleigh. The President joked with the crowds:

I had planned today to bring Joe Califano with me, but he decided not to come. He discovered that not only is North Carolina the Number One tobacco-producing state, but that you produce more bricks than anyone in the nation as well.[22]

He then made jokes about rumours of pot smoking in the White House:

Joe Califano did encourage me to come though. He said it was time for the White House staff to start smoking something regular.

But Helms' staff thought the President was playing right into their hands. 'Carter simply drew attention to his predicament,' said Helms' political adviser, George Dunlop. 'He'd have been better off staying away. He went down there for Jimmy Carter, not for Senator Robert Morgan. All he did was give his opponents an opportunity to point out what a mess Carter had made of things in terms of the tobacco situation. He went down there and made some mealy-mouthed flapjaw on how they were going to look into some of these problems. People didn't want it "looked into". They wanted it resolved. So he actually brought upon himself further wrath.'

Still Califano pressed on. He had commissioned a special Surgeon-General's Report to mark the fifteenth anniversary of the First Report in 1964. In his introduction Secretary Califano wrote:

It demolishes the claims made by cigarette manufacturers and a few others fifteen years ago and today: that the scientific evidence was sketchy; that no link between smoking and cancer was 'proven'. Those claims, empty then, are utterly vacuous now . . .[23]

The new Surgeon-General's Report devoted a section to children and smoking:

The percentage of girls who smoke has increased eightfold since

1968. Among the age group 13–19 there are now 6 million regular smokers. One hundred thousand children under 13 are regular smokers.

Indeed, it is children who are the main focus of our efforts to inform and persuade. It is nothing short of a national tragedy that so much death and disease are wrought by a powerful habit often taken up by unsuspecting children, lured by seductive multimillion dollar cigarette advertising campaigns.[24]

The Report was scheduled for release on January 11th, 1979. The day before, Califano received a phone call from Jody Powell, one of the President's closest political advisers. He was calling from Washington National Airport, on his way to North Carolina, oblivious to the imminent publication of the three-inch-thick Report. Powell told Califano where he was headed and asked if there was anything he should know. Califano broke the news, but could not offer him any advice. 'I'll just smoke like hell when I'm down there!' said Powell.[25]

The Report received massive media coverage. All three networks covered its contents, and then showed the President among the tobacco leaves in Wilson, North Carolina. 'Jeez,' said Vice-President Mondale to his friend Califano, 'those guys in the White House really have it positioned—the President's for cancer and you're for health!'[26] In the fortnight after publication, more Americans tried to quit smoking than in any other two-week period since the release of the First Surgeon-General's Report in 1964. By this time Califano knew he was in trouble. 'You're driving these tobacco people crazy,' warned the Speaker of the House of Representatives, Tip O'Neill. 'These guys are vicious. They're out to destroy you.' Senator Edward Kennedy's message was the same. 'You've got to get out of the Cabinet before the election. The President can't run in North Carolina with you at HEW. He's going to have to get rid of you.'[27]

In June 1979, Joe Califano packed his bags for Stockholm (as did Britain's junior Health Minister, Sir George Young) to attend the Fourth World Conference on Smoking and Health. The foyer of the conference hall was full of cartons of complimentary copies of the huge Surgeon-General's Report. Califano told the delegates that it summarised:

... the decisive and devastating evidence added in the past fifteen years [which convicts] cigarette smoking beyond a reasonable doubt of crimes against the public health.

He warned of 'the formidable economic and persuasive power of the cigarette industry' and concluded:

We can expect that the tobacco industry will do everything in its power to counteract our public health efforts.[28]

At the same conference the British junior Health Minister, Sir George Young, made his first major public speech on smoking and health. Joe Califano made his last. Shortly after he got home, he was fired. He had been President Carter's Health Secretary for two-and-a-half years. Sir George Young lasted for roughly the same time. Tobacco beat them both. Califano, visibly shattered, told television viewers:

The President told me yesterday afternoon that I had done a superb job as ... Secretary for HEW. But that the same qualities of leadership and drive that made a good Secretary, created friction with certain members of the White House staff. They were telling reporters ... they are kind of concerned about the tobacco and smoking issue and that he had to change the Cabinet around to get ready for the 1980 elections.[29]

But it was too late to repair the political damage. Jesse Helms was re-elected to the Senate in 1978. Senator Robert Morgan lost his seat in November 1980. 'That's what we beat over Jimmy Carter's head,' Jim Cain of Helms' Congressional Club told me. 'Califano was killing tobacco and Califano was Jimmy Carter's right-hand man. We used that issue more than any other in the state to kill Carter—and we used it against Robert Morgan.'

In the presidential election of November 1980, Jimmy Carter lost tobacco, North Carolina and the presidency. Jesse Helms gave Ronald Reagan the state, and with $5.5 million raised by his political machine, helped put Reagan and tobacco in the White House.

13

Tobacco in the White House

In March 1976, Ronald Reagan looked set to ride into the political sunset. His campaign to challenge Gerald Ford for the Republican nomination had been a disaster. His campaign managers had originally concluded that their only chance of victory was to persuade the Republican party that their man was not an electoral liability, a right-wing fanatic with his finger on the nuclear trigger. They had not forgotten the electoral ruin which the ultra-conservative Senator Barry Goldwater had brought on his party in the presidential campaign of 1964 by injudiciously speaking his mind on the issues. Ronald Reagan was not to be allowed to make the same political mistake. His campaign manager, John Sears, had mapped out the strategy at the beginning of the presidential primaries of 1976: exuding reasonableness and moderation, Reagan was to beat Ford in the first primary in New Hampshire on February 23rd, confirm his ascendancy in Florida on March 9th and be hailed as the Republican party's champion in his own original home state of Illinois on March 16th.[1] From there, so the Sears blueprint went, Reagan would sweep all before him and win the nomination at the Republican Convention: by then Gerald Ford would have retired gracefully from the race. But it did not work out like that. Reagan the 'moderate' failed to set the world alight, a fact which came as no surprise to Jesse Helms and his supporters in North Carolina.

Before the primary battles began, Tom Ellis, the Chairman of the Congressional Club who had been responsible for electing Helms to the Senate in 1972, had met John Sears in Washington and warned that Reagan was heading for disaster if he was portrayed as something he was not. Ellis attacked Reagan's bland television commercials. The Congressional Club wanted Reagan to come out with guns blazing, not with a water pistol. Sears brushed off Ellis' attack and said his strategy would be vindicated by Reagan's victory in New Hampshire.[2]

But the first primary vindicated Ellis, not Sears. Reagan lost New Hampshire. He was then badly beaten by Ford in Florida and Illinois. On the eve of the North Carolina primary, March 23rd, Reagan looked set for political oblivion. Without Reagan's knowledge, Sears had already met Ford's campaign manager to discuss terms of surrender in anticipation of defeat in North Carolina.[3] Four defeats in a row would mean Reagan was finished. But Jesse Helms and the Congressional Club gave Ronald Reagan the kiss of life. 'Senator Helms was the principal supporter that Governor Reagan had in Washington,' said George Dunlop, Jesse Helm's political acolyte since the early days. 'He was the first member of Congress, as far as I am aware, to endorse Reagan's candidacy. Everybody else was for Gerald Ford. In the 1976 campaign, Reagan wasn't hard-hitting enough, so Jesse Helms and his political allies down there in North Carolina threw out the political operatives who were working for Reagan. They told them to get out of the state and they'd manage their own affairs. Senator Helms worked with Nancy Reagan to obtain a copy of a film of Governor Reagan. We then raised the money and put it on TV all across the state [it was shown on fifteen of North Carolina's seventeen stations]. Reagan came across hard-hitting, talking about the Soviets, the Panama Canal and Henry Kissinger dilly-dallying with the Russians. The real Reagan. We swept the state. He went on and came within an eye-tooth of being nominated in Kansas City.' Reagan devastated Gerald Ford in North Carolina by fifty-two per cent to forty-six per cent. At the Republican Convention in Kansas City, Reagan shared the spotlight with Ford. 'North Carolina gave us momentum,' said Jim Cain of the Congressional Club. 'Most people thought Reagan was too old to look to 1980, but Jesse

Helms and some of the faithful realised they had a man who was so vivacious he could hang on for another four years. That relationship between Reagan and Helms was solidified.'

'They think alike,' said George Dunlop. 'They both have the same instinctive understanding of the feelings that the American people have—for "Joe and Sally Lunch-bucket" out there. Jesse Helms and Ronald Reagan know-how-they-think,' he said, stressing each syllable.

Reagan's regeneration in the tobacco fields of North Carolina put the Congressional Club on the national political map. It hired the direct mailing expert, Richard Viguerie, to help raise funds. Nearly $8 million were harvested for Jesse Helms' re-election to the Senate in 1978, almost three times the amount ever raised for a US Senator before.[4] The Congressional Club's next step was to get Ronald Reagan into the White House in 1980 and to get rid of North Carolina's Democratic Senator, Robert Morgan, who was up for re-election the same year. The candidate the Congressional Club chose to oppose Senator Morgan, and whose campaign it ran, was John East, a conservative political science professor from Greenville, Pitt County, in the heart of tobacco country. Helms' protégé, who was largely unknown and confined to a wheelchair with polio, was not thought to stand a chance against the incumbent Democratic Senator Morgan. The Congressional Club's problem in the election of 1980 was not raising money, but spending it. The Club was registered as a Political Action Committee, and under federal election law no PAC may give more than $5,000 to any candidate in an election. But ways were found round the restriction. 'We cranked up a national campaign for Reagan which was independent of what the official campaign did,' said Jim Cain. 'We created an independent expenditure organisation which meant that, without any co-ordination or collaboration with the Reagan national campaign committee, we could raise and spend our money in any way we chose to. It was called 'Americans for Reagan'. We raised money through direct mail—$5.5 million. It couldn't go to him directly, but we could spend it for him—most of it on national television. We created our own Reagan commercials. We did some anti-Jimmy Carter stuff which aired all around the country. We couldn't give more than $5,000 to the official Reagan campaign, but we could do the project as a subordinate group of the Congressional Club. That took up a lot of our fund raising and staff resources in 1980.' John East's campaign for the Senate was run along similar lines and financed through a subsidiary company called Jefferson Marketing, which the Congressional Club set up in the same building. The new company used the Congressional Club's staff and resources. In November 1980, John East defeated Senator Morgan and Ronald Reagan swept North Carolina and rode on to the White House. 'Conservatives sweep to victory. Mission accomplished', proclaimed the headlines in the Congressional Club's newsletter, above a list of of eighteen conservative Republican Congressmen and Senators who had been elected with the help of the Congressional Club. The editorial declared:

> Ronald Reagan has made it clear that 1981 marks a new beginning for America. The Congressional Club has rededicated itself to furthering Ronald Reagan's dream to make America 'a shining city on a hill'. With the continued support of thousands of principled Americans, the Congressional Club and Ronald Reagan will be successful.[5]

Ronald Reagan's election also marked a new beginning for tobacco. 'The context of the Reagan commitment to tobacco can only really be fully understood in the context of the full-scale, anti-tobacco assault emanating from every pore and fibre of the Carter Administration,' said George Dunlop. 'It's like night and day in terms of the way tobacco's being treated now. We've a sympathetic administration instead of a hostile one.'

J. C. Galloway, the tobacco farmer from Greenville, was one of Pitt County's most fervent 'Jessecrats'. There's a photograph of Jesse Helms on his study wall, with an inset of Ronald Reagan and the inscription, 'To J. C. Galloway, with grateful appreciation of your friendship. Kindest regards, Jesse Helms.' Hanging next to it is a photograph of Senator John East (who also comes from Greenville) with the message, 'To J.C. —a great friend and supporter and my favourite tobacco farmer. John P. East'. J. C. Galloway has been a political ally of Jesse Helms for over a decade, although he is not a Republican. 'I worked real hard for Helms when he was elected in 1972,' he told me. 'I was just about thrown out of the county, being the only Democrat that was supporting Jesse Helms. But I'm conservative and Jesse's conservative. A big bunch of us Democrats jumped in and we donated and we politicked and we worked for John East and Ronald Reagan. I still am a registered Democrat, but I voted for East and Reagan because of their support for tobacco.' And so did thousands of others. J. C. Galloway had the commitment in writing. During the campaign he had sent a letter to Reagan. 'A bunch of us were dissatisfied with the ways things were going,' he said. 'We sat down and wrote to Candidate Reagan and asked him what his position would be on tobacco if elected President. We wanted to know what his position would be on the health issue, towards the tobacco industry in general and farmers in particular.' Galloway and half a dozen other tobacco farmers who wrote similar letters received the same reply:

REAGAN/BUSH COMMITTEE

Dear Mr Galloway,

I would like to take this opportunity to write to you and several other well-known North Carolina tobacco farmers to spell out my views on federal tobacco programs.

First, I want to assure you that I fully support this nation's tobacco price support program. Tobacco price supports have helped to sustain more than a quarter-of-a-million family farms in 16 states, and have proven to be an unqualified success. The Secretary of Agriculture in a Reagan/Bush administration will represent my feelings in this regard, as will all officials and agencies which play a role in tobacco programs.

I also want to assure you that my Administration will end what has become an increasingly antagonistic relationship between the federal government and the tobacco industry. The Carter administration has all too often singled out the tobacco industry for selective criticism and damaging restrictions. Tobacco—no less than corn, wheat, or soyabeans—should be viewed as a valuable cash crop with an important role to play in restoring America's balance of trade. I can guarantee that my own Cabinet members will be far too busy with substantive matters to waste their time proselytising against the dangers of cigarette smoking. I can also guarantee you that I will seek

Senator Helms' views on any decision my administration makes concerning federal tobacco policies.

I hope that you consider these matters in deciding which candidate to vote for this November.

> Sincerely
> (Signed)
> Ronald Reagan

J. C. Galloway sent copies of the letter to Jesse Helms and John East. He also placed it in several newspapers as a full-page political advertisement, with the message, 'This is what Ronald Reagan says he'll do for tobacco.' A man of his word, Ronald Reagan carried the commitment into the White House.

But health officials in Reagan's administration did not share the President's obligation to tobacco. They believed that a statement on preventive health which had been written into the 'strong families' platform at the Republican Convention gave them the licence to act against smoking:

Health professionals, as well as individuals, have long recognised that preventing illness or injury is much less expensive than treating it. Therefore, preventive medicine combined with good personal health habits and health education can make a major impact on the cost of health care.[6]

President Reagan's new health team at the Department of Health and Human Services (HEW had been renamed), consisted of the Secretary for HHS, Richard Schweiker; the Assistant Secretary for Health, Dr Edward Brandt; and the Surgeon-General, Dr Everett Koop. One of the team's first acts was to commission a new Surgeon-General's Report on 'Cancer'. The Report was published in 1982 as part of the continuing series 'The Health Consequences of Smoking' which the Congress had mandated after the first Surgeon-General's Report in 1964. Dr Koop (whose appointment had been strongly supported by Jesse Helms because of his strong anti-abortion views) wrote in his Introduction:

Cigarette smoking, as this Report again makes clear, is the chief, single, avoidable cause of death in our society and the most important public health issue of our time.[7]

In his Foreword, Dr Brandt focused on the rising incidence of lung cancer amongst women:

> The American Cancer Society estimates there will be 111,000 lung cancer related deaths in 1982, of which 80,000 will be in men, and 31,000 in women . . .'
>
> The lung cancer death rate for women is currently rising faster than the lung cancer death rate for men, a fact that reflects the later adoption of smoking by large numbers of women. The lung cancer death rate for women will soon surpass that of breast cancer (perhaps as early as next year), currently the leading cause of cancer mortality in women . . .
>
> This Department is committed to continuing the programs of education and information for all our citizenry regarding the adverse health consequences of smoking. There is no more important aspect of this than the health education of our young, to convince them not to start smoking, or to quit the habit before it becomes difficult to break.[8]

When Dr Brandt became Assistant Secretary for Health at the beginning of 1981, he inherited a campaign designed to dissuade young girls from smoking. (Surveys showed that teenage girls were smoking more than teenage boys.) It had been approved by Dr Brandt's predecessors, but had not yet been launched. The star of the campaign was Brooke Shields, the sixteen-year-old actress and model who had played a child prostitute in Louis Malle's film *Pretty Baby*, and advertised Calvin Klein's jeans. (She had made 'family' films too, but they had failed to attract the same attention.) Brooke Shields' picture no doubt adorned the bedroom walls of millions of young teenage girls whom the campaign was designed to reach. 'She was the hottest property in the world at that time for that age group,' said John Pinney, the Director of the Office on Smoking and Health, who was in charge of the campaign. Furthermore, the star's services had been obtained at virtually next to nothing. She was against smoking and said that both her grandfathers had died because of it. She only asked to be paid a nominal $1 for the photographs, and the union minimum of $500 for the television commercials, for which she would normally command anything up to a million dollars. At

$65,000, the Brooke Shields campaign was a bargain.[9] John Pinney made a presentation of the material to Dr Brandt and his officials. According to Pinney, the Assistant Secretary for Health thought it was 'wonderful'. But not all the HSS officials shared his enthusiasm. No decision was made. Dr Brandt had to leave for Geneva for a meeting of the World Health Assembly, and said he needed the matter resolved. While he was away, a group met to review the campaign: it included a former assistant to Jesse Helms, a member of the Campus Crusade for Christ International, and an anti-abortionist from American Citizens Concerned for Life. The Moral Majority sat in judgment. The campaign was killed on the grounds that Brooke Shields was not 'a suitable role model'. Mort Lebow, Dr Brandt's Public Affairs Director, asked for the decision not to be made public until Dr Brandt returned from Geneva. His request was refused. Dr Brandt was presented with a *fait accompli*. Mort Lebow was disgusted at the decision. 'I really feel that nobody in the tobacco lobby felt the need to call the White House, Secretary Schweiker or anybody to kill the Brooke Shields campaign,' he told me. 'They had no need to do it because the people who represented them, felt the same way that they did, were inside government. Outside was in. They could sit back and be sure that this very effective campaign would never get off the ground.'

But the campaign was not buried. The Department handed it over to the American Lung Association 'to prevent any waste of taxpayers' money'.[10] Mort Lebow later resigned. He went to see Dr Brandt and told him he was leaving. 'I'm glad I don't have to work with them any longer,' he said. 'I'm just sad that you do.' (According to James A. Swomley, the Managing Director of the American Lung Association, the campaign was 'highly successful'. Ironically, eighteen months after the Department of Health and Human Services had turned their backs on Brooke Shields, she was Vice-President George Bush's guest at the White House, as a representative of the American Lung Association.)

But the Brooke Shields campaign was only the beginning of Dr Brandt's embarrassment on the issue of smoking and health. In May 1981, the FTC published the result of its five-year investigation into cigarette advertising. It concluded:

1. Cigarette smoking is far more dangerous to health than was thought in 1964.

2. With the exception of the health warning, cigarette advertising contains no health information.

3. While the number of Americans who are generally aware that smoking is in some way hazardous to health has grown steadily, some, especially smokers, still do not know this basic fact. More significantly, a much larger number know too little about the specific health hazards of smoking to be able to assess accurately how dangerous smoking is and whether the health risks of smoking have any personal relevance or application to themselves.

4. The current health warning is rarely noticed and is not effective in alerting consumers to the health hazards of smoking.

Based upon these findings, staff is concerned that current cigarette advertising practices may be deceptive. Staff has also concluded that additional action designed to provide consumers with more information about the health consequences of smoking may be necessary. An effective remedy should be noticed by consumers, should maintain its noticeability over time, and should effectively convey sufficient information to prevent any possible deception.[11]

The FTC Report recommended a new system of health warnings, changing the size, the shape and, above all, the words. It suggested that the word 'death' should feature prominently. Health Secretary Richard Schweiker wrote to the new Chairman of the FTC, James C. Miller III, to congratulate him on his staff's 'thorough and scholarly' Report and to offer his support for the necessary action. He concluded:

The Report calls upon the Commission to proceed further in developing a new system of cigarette warnings and we encourage you to proceed. If the Public Health Service can be of assistance in this effort, we will be pleased to work with you. Smoking is the chief preventable cause of death in our society,

and I am personally and as Secretary of Health and Human
Services committed to effective action to reduce cigarette-
related disease and death.[12]

James Miller was a Reagan conservative and a Reagan appointee
and not a chairman in the mould of his energetic predecessor,
Michael Pertschuk. Nor had his previous utterances on smoking
and health given his staff much encouragement. At a press
conference a few months earlier, he had admitted he had not read
the FTC Staff Report and said:

> I wouldn't want to speak too much about smoking. I tend to be
> fairly libertarian about such matters. If people want to smoke,
> that's their business.[13]

Nevertheless, Miller thanked Schweiker for his encouragement
and offer of assistance. He said he found the issue of smoking and
health a 'subject of deep concern' and looked forward to the
'possibility of co-operation'. Word of the exchange of letters
leaked out and alarm bells rang again in North Carolina. One of
the politicians particularly worried by the threat of more action
against cigarettes was Republican Congressman Eugene Johnston, who had been swept to Washington in November 1980 on
the votes of North Carolina Democrats who had deserted their
party because of Joe Califano. In the Sixth District which he
represented, Democrats outnumbered Republican by three to
one. The District was also heavily dependent on the tobacco
industry. Johnston feared that if the Reagan administration now
joined the battle against smoking, his first term in Washington
might be his last. He wrote to Secretary Schweiker and reminded
him of the commitment the President had made to J. C. Galloway
during the campaign:

> I can guarantee that my own Cabinet members will be far too
> busy with substantive matters to waste their time proselytising
> against the dangers of cigarette smoking.

Johnston informed the Secretary that he was extremely concerned
about the Reagan administration developing a Joe Califano

image, and warned him against appearing to antagonise an industry that had supported the administration thereby pleasing a few zealots who would like to see him replaced with Joe Califano. Johnston sent copies of his letter to President Reagan, and Senators John East and Jesse Helms. Secretary Schweiker also received other reminders from North Carolina's politicians (including the Democrats) about the President's commitment to tobacco.

As soon as Jesse Helms received Eugene Johnston's letter, he issued his own sharp reminder to Secretary Schweiker in which he said he was worried about 'incipient Califanoism' in his Department:

> If the written commitment by the President himself, and prior assurance by Jim Miller and others, are to mean anything, this sort of thing should not continue. Otherwise the impact could be substantial in my state and others. It's hard enough to elect Republicans without this kind of trouble.[14]

But the FTC had prepared its ground carefully. It knew it had to proceed with caution after the legal battles with the industry over its cigarette advertising Report and the subsequent limitation of its power by Senator Wendell Ford's FTC Bill. 'The Commission had been fighting for its life,' one of its staff told me. 'The last thing it could afford to do was to totally irritate Congress at that point in time.' The FTC distributed its Report to every member of Congress and called for a public debate prior to announcing any action of its own. 'Politically it was a very astute move, even though it would slow down the process of accomplishing anything,' he continued. 'We were saying to Congress, "We're only really going to act if you want us to. In that way if we go forward, we can be sure we're going forward with your blessing, not without it." ' Although the FTC is not supposed to engage in lobbying, some of its staff thought it advisable to have a word in a few ears on Capitol Hill prior to publication. They briefed Senator Robert Packwood, the Chairman of the Senate Commerce Committee, and Congressman Henry Waxman, the Chairman of the House of Representatives Commerce Subcommittee on Health. Their staff members were also put in the picture.

The groundwork paid off. Congressman Waxman introduced a Bill, sponsored by the American Heart Association and other voluntary agencies, forcing cigarette companies to put a series of strong health warnings on packets. They included: 'Warning: Cigarette smoking is the number one cause of Emphysema and Lung Cancer'; 'Warning: Cigarette smoking by pregnant women may result in Birth Defects or Spontaneous Abortion'. The Bill also put the Office on Smoking and Health (which had never been institutionalised as a government body) beyond the reach of attack by its enemies by making it permanently part of the Department of Health and Human Services. Introducing his Bill, Congressman Waxman said:

> For years now the cigarette industry has sponsored advertising campaigns which attribute positive lifestyle values to smoking. These efforts have been all too effective and have served to blunt and undercut both Federal and private sector smoking education activities. It's time to take a new look at developing more effective anti-smoking activities.[15]

Senator Packwood introduced a similar Bill in the Senate, which also obliged the cigarette companies to report the chemical additives they placed in cigarettes. The Senate Bill was supported by the American Cancer Society, the American Heart Association, the American Lung Association, the American Public Health Association, the American College of Preventive Medicine and the American Academy of Paediatrics. For the first time, these organisations came together to lobby as one. Introducing the Bill, Senator Packwood said

> Over 30 per cent of the public is unaware of the relationship between smoking and heart disease. Nearly 50 per cent of all women do not know that smoking during pregnancy increases the risk of stillbirth and miscarriage. About 30 per cent of those polled do not know about the relationship between smoking, birth control pills and the risk of heart attack. The legislation we are introducing today is designed to fill the information gap.[16]

To the consternation of the tobacco industry, Senator Packwood's

Bill was jointly sponsored by Senator Orrin Hatch of Utah, the Chairman of the Committee on Labor and Human Resources which had jurisdiction over many federal health programmes. Senator Hatch was a conservative Republican from Utah and many of his Mormon constituents around Salt Lake City were strongly opposed to smoking (lung cancer is rarely seen amongst Mormons). Despite this, the industry was surprised to see him co-sponsor Packwood's Bill, as he was a Reaganite conservative who had spent much of the previous year deregulating or 'getting government off the people's backs'. Senator Packwood, a liberal Republican from Oregon, was no friend of the Reagan administration, but Senator Hatch was. 'The Tobacco Institute got rather nervous,' said an aide. 'Here was the wrong person doing this kind of thing. He was the kind of Senator they could always count on. He was de-regulatory and ideologically sound.' The Tobacco Institute had a meeting with Senator Hatch. They were courteous, polite and charming. They argued that the Bill was far too regulatory: that the Senator had been misled by his staff; that it was not the simple Bill he had been led to believe; that it would have grave implications for the tobacco industry. 'The Senator was a bit shaken at that time,' recalled the aide. 'He felt that maybe he hadn't understood what an imposition the federal government would place on the industry, not that he had any sympathy for the industry, it's just that he'd de-regulated everything else and was having a hard time justifying this.' But Senator Hatch's health advisers won the day and convinced him that the public health issue was important enough to warrant the exception.

Not all members of the two Senate Committees which were now responsible for the Bill agreed. Senator John East of North Carolina was a member of Senator Hatch's Committee on Labour and Human Resources; and Senator Wendell Ford of Kentucky was a member of Senator Packwood's Commerce Committee. Within a week of the Bill's introduction, Senator Ford wrote to all his colleagues in the Senate, urging them not to give it their support. He warned it would 'damage the economic viability of an industry which contributes each year more than $57 billion to the gross national product and a net favourable trade balance of $2 billion'. He warned:

. . . the legislation would establish the Secretary of HHS as a czar of personal behavior to co-ordinate a multitude of government programs, research projects, and behavioral studies to tell people what's good for them. Smoking happens to be today's targeted behavior, but who knows what tomorrow may bring?

You may agree that the American people do not need or want Congress to return government to its former position astride their backs.

At the hearings on the Bill, the Chairman of R. J. Reynolds, Edward A. Horrigan, gave evidence for the industry in his capacity as Chairman of the Tobacco Institute. Mr Horrigan raised the industry's now familiar flag of freedom:

. . . this Bill is bad legislation because it seriously erodes the principle of free choice. It implies that those who do not conform are uninformed—that they cannot be allowed to reject opposing views regarding the use of tobacco products. This reflects a prohibitionist mentality which the citizens of this nation have already rejected, and which we strongly doubt they would accept now.

This Bill is an unwarranted intervention by the federal government into the lives of private citizens, and represents a thinly veiled effort to further harass an industry which is already heavily burdened by regulations.[17]

Dr Edward Brandt, the Assistant Secretary for Health, was due to give testimony on behalf of the Administration in support of the Bills of both Congressman Waxman and Senators Hatch and Packwood. Because the issue was so politically sensitive, Dr Brandt's officials wanted to make sure that the way was clear for him to do so. When the testimony was drafted, they sent it off to the Office of Management and Budget (OMB) for clearance. OMB's function was to co-ordinate policy to ensure that all government Departments marched in step with the White House. Once testimony on an issue was received, it was circulated around all Departments with any interest in the subject, amended and then returned to the Department which had sent it. Dr Brandt's testimony was sent to OMB about a week ahead of the first hearing on Congressman Waxman's Bill, Thursday, March 11th, 1982. Dr Brandt's testimony was cleared by OMB and the White House. It arrived back at HHS, with a few minor amendments, the evening before Dr Brandt was due to appear before Congressman Waxman's Committee. Dr Brandt concluded his testimony by reading the last page, which began:

> We support the Bill's requirements for strong health warnings because we believe they would increase the public's knowledge of the hazards of smoking and make it possible for smokers and potential smokers to make better informed judgments as to whether to continue smoking or begin smoking.[18]

Dr Brandt was scheduled to give essentially the same testimony five days later before Senator Packwood's Committee, on Tuesday, March 16th, 1982. Again, to make sure nothing went amiss, HHS officials sent Dr Brandt's second testimony to OMB for clearance, on the day he appeared before Congressman Waxman's Committee. They also called OMB to make sure that Dr Brandt's second testimony had been cleared with the White House. Nothing was left to chance.

But the White House was already well aware of it. Over the weekend between the two testimonies, North Carolina's politicians went to work. They regarded Dr Brandt's testimony before the Waxman Committee on the Thursday as a clear breach of the commitment which the President had made to J. C. Galloway. They were determined to make sure the breach of faith did not happen again at the Senate hearing the following Tuesday. Jesse Helms, whom Reagan had promised to consult on any 'decision my Administration makes concerning federal tobacco policies', contacted the White House. According to his staff, Senator Helms had 'instantaneous' access to the President. On this particular occasion he may not have spoken directly to the President himself, but he got the reply he wanted. Helms was assured that 'the situation would be better', and quoted a White House aide who informed him, 'I believe you'll be reasonably satisfied with the administration's posture.'[19]

On the Monday, the President's Assistant for Political Affairs,

Ed Rollins, contacted Congressman Eugene Johnston who'd also expressed concern and told him that 'the administration would ease off a bit', and 'nobody would be embarrassed'.[20] Rollins assured Johnston that the White House was aware of his 'concerns' and that he would not 'have a problem'.[21]

Tobacco might not have been embarrassed, but health officials were. They remained oblivious to the backstage lobbying. 'We'd no idea there were problems, although we knew Brandt's testimony was being reviewed much more than it had been before, particularly at the White House,' one HHS official told me. On the Monday, copies of Dr Brandt's testimony had been run off in anticipation of official clearance, and were ready to be sent up to Capitol Hill for the Tuesday hearing. About six o'clock on Monday evening, the official who was going to take them ran into one of his colleagues who said, 'Hold it. We've got a problem on our hands.' He said he had just received a telephone call from OMB saying that Dr Brandt's testimony was not being cleared. He had reminded his caller that the Assistant Secretary was due to testify the next day and had been told he would 'need to go higher to sort this one out'. The officials made a flurry of telephone calls to try to reverse the decision to save embarrassment the next day. They told Dr Brandt and Secretary Schweiker what had happened. The Secretary rang the White House and a compromise was reached. 'By Monday night, it looked like Dr Brandt could go up and say that he supported stronger warning labels for cigarettes, but *not* mention any specific Bill,' said one of the officials. The administration was now only supporting the principle but not the actual Bill. To accommodate the hasty compromise, the officials tore off the back page of Dr Brandt's typed testimony—which contained the endorsement of the Bill. The incomplete testimony was then sent up to Capitol Hill.

At eight o'clock on Tuesday morning, one of Senator Packwood's staff read through the testimony as a matter of course before the hearing. He was surprised to find that the last page was missing. He rang his opposite number on Senator Hatch's staff. He too had a page missing. But by this time, HHS had even more problems. At seven thirty a. m. that morning, Dr Brandt received a call from OMB saying that, despite the compromise reached late the previous evening, he would not be allowed to support even the principle of the Bill: he could not say 'we support stronger warnings'. 'At this point things really got very, very touchy,' said one of his officials, 'because he wasn't going to go up and do that.' Dr Brandt contacted Secretary Schweiker and told him that he was not prepared to testify on that basis. Schweiker told him to go ahead and say what he felt he had to say and 'they'd take it from there'.

Half an hour before the hearing began, Dr Brandt and the Surgeon-General met Senator Hatch in his private office in the Dirksen Building. Dr Brandt was clearly disturbed. 'I've never seen a man more uncomfortable. He looked tired and nervous,' said one of those present. 'He was respected by all and had a long, genuine interest in preventive medicine and he personally endorsed the Bill. He suggested to Senator Hatch that it might be helpful if he were not asked questions about his actual endorsement of the Bill, because the administration had changed its position.' But Senator Packwood, who was no friend of the White House, was not as sympathetic, and wanted to place the administration's capitulation to tobacco on the record. At the hearing, the embarrassed Dr Brandt, perspiring heavily, was only able to say that he endorsed the 'concept' of stronger health warnings. Senator Packwood, searching for the last page, noted, 'The typewriter seems to have run out of ribbon before you finished your testimony here.' He ended by saying what Dr Brandt could not say publicly:

You are a very honest man. You strongly support the labelling . . . that was in your testimony last week. Between that time and this time, somebody has indirectly talked to someone in your Department and said to tone the testimony down and you are a good soldier and have done so . . . But it appears to me that the things which you personally believe and support, which are reflected in your testimony last week, touched a sensitive nerve someplace in the administration, and the testimony today does not reflect quite the staunch support that we saw five days ago.[22]

The ordeal was over. Dr Brandt told one of his officials that the worst thing was being made to look a fool and not be able to do anything about it. Subsequently both Bills died the death. No one was prepared to push them through in the teeth of such powerful opposition. The President had been true to his word and kept faith with North Carolina and tobacco. The White House had become an integral part of the Smoke Ring.*

---

* Renewed efforts were made in 1983 to institute stronger health warnings. Senator Hatch's Labor and Human Resources Committee approved a Bill on June 22nd requiring a warning which stated: 'Warning! Cigarette smoking causes CANCER, EMPHYSEMA, HEART DISEASE; may complicate PREGNANCY, and is ADDICTIVE.'[23] Congressman Waxman also tried to re-introduce a similar measure. At the time of writing, their fate is unknown.

14

The Third World
A Growing Problem

In the Third World a new Smoke Ring is being forged which is even stronger than the one in the West. It is made up of the same political and economic links—employment, revenue, trade, advertising and promotion—but it is stronger because the governments of many developing countries are even more dependent on tobacco. Few believe they have the luxury of choice. They face huge balance of payments deficits; astronomical energy costs; chronic shortages of food; lack of hard currency for imports; enormous debts; soaring food prices; runaway inflation; rising expectations on the part of their people; and the threat of political unrest which all these problems bring. To many Third World governments, tobacco offers a lifebelt. It provides jobs, revenue, exports, foreign exchange, education, training and prosperity. It creates wealth and aids development—assuming of course that 'development' is the creation of a consumer society which offers the West a market for its goods and services. Tobacco is a cash crop which, unlike cotton, cocoa, coffee, tea, sugar and groundnuts, is not subject to the fluctuations of world commodity prices: that is why for years international organisations such as the United Nations Food and Agriculture Organisation (FAO) and the World Bank (whose criterion for development is return on investment) have supported tobacco as a cash crop in Third World countries. In October 1982, in response to a series of World Health Assembly resolutions urging the FAO to study crop substitution in tobacco growing countries, the FAO Commodities and Trade Division compiled a report on the Economic Significance of Tobacco. It pointed out that tobacco was 'an important source of employment and cash income' and gave some telling examples:

> Zimbabwe's tobacco industry is the nation's largest employer of labour, supporting 17,000 tobacco farmers who are also able to supply 35 per cent of the maize, 30 per cent of the peanuts, 21 per cent of the beef and 17 per cent of the winter wheat produced in the country. In Malawi, 100,000 families rely on cash income from tobacco, and in Tanzania, tobacco cultivation generates the income of about 370,000 people, or 2 per cent of the population. In the south of Brazil tobacco farmers number about 115,000 and a further 650,000 are directly dependent on tobacco; in the Indian state of Andhra Pradesh, tobacco provides a living for 75,000 farmers and about 2 million other workers engaged in curing, packing and processing.

The report stressed that it made no attempt to quantify the economic and social damage caused by cigarette smoking. That, it said, was to be evaluated by its sister United Nations body, the World Health Organisation (WHO). It marked the beginning of an exercise in which the Secretariats of FAO and WHO were to attempt to weigh the social and economic costs of smoking against the economic and social gains derived from tobacco production, manufacturing and trade. There was no doubt about the FAO's findings:

> In conclusion, the cultivation and manufacture of tobacco result in a number of immediate and tangible social and economic benefits, particularly in the poorer producing countries. Tobacco-growing generates large-scale rural employment in over-populated areas and provides a ready source of cash for smallholders who would otherwise be dependent on less remunerative crops or on subsistence farming. In nearly every producing country, tobacco is one of

the most valuable crops grown, and its contribution to total agricultural income is almost invariably significant, reaching 25 per cent in the case of Zimbabwe. Tobacco is also one of the most remunerative cash crops, yielding net returns per unit of land which may be several times higher than those obtained from industrial crops or staple foodstuffs. In addition, tobacco leaf is an important source of foreign exchange for exporting countries. The value of world exports in 1979–81 averaged US $4,000 million, of which about US $1,600 million accrued to developing countries, and tobacco makes a substantial contribution to the agricultural export earnings of many individual countries, especially in Africa and Asia.

Tobacco manufacturing creates extensive employment opportunities, particularly in developing countries where manual methods of production are still the rule, so that the labour force may run into hundreds of thousands. The wages and salaries paid by tobacco factories compare favourably with those paid by other industries employing workers with similar skills.

Finally, tobacco products are a very important and easily tapped source of tax revenue for governments in both developing and developed countries . . .

In view of these factors, farmers continue to have strong incentives to produce tobacco, and governments to encourage its cultivation and manufacture.[1]

Thus the FAO drew the Smoke Ring around the Third World. The World Bank reached similar conclusions:

. . . tobacco is an important and unique agricultural commodity. It is an attractive cash crop and a valuable source of foreign exchange in many countries. It has, in fact, the highest cash return per area of any major crop. It is a crop of growing importance to developing countries, which, because of their lower labor costs, are capturing an increasing share of world trade.[2]

Between 1974 and 1982, the World Bank and its subsidiary, the International Development Association, made loans of over $600 million for rural development projects which included tobacco: in Malawi ($30m); Swaziland ($4m); Tanzania ($14m); Brazil ($68m); Paraguay ($53m); Philippines ($50m); Pakistan ($60m); Tunisia ($24m); Yemen ($10m); Greece ($30m); and Yugoslavia ($267m). The Bank notes that tobacco consumption over the current decade is likely to increase at one per cent a year in industrialised countries, and nearly four per cent in developing countries, with the result:

> Thus with developing countries consuming an increasing share of world tobacco output, there is considerable scope for increased production for this group.[3]

Nor does the World Bank, any more than the FAO, concern itself with the health issue:

> ... where governments and individuals have information on the consequences of smoking, it is up to the individual country to formulate a policy which it judges to be suited to it.[4]

Government aid agencies also help Third World countries with growing tobacco. Britain's Commonwealth Development Corporation (CDC) has loaned £3.9 million to the Malawi government to assist a thousand small farmers under the Kasungu Flue-Cured Tobacco Authority. (By 1983, £3.2 million of the loan had to be repaid.) The CDC has also loaned the Zambia government over £250,000 to help small farmers produce flue-cured tobacco, using only family labour — a project in which the World Bank is also involved.

The Golden Leaf is just as profitable and recession-proof in Malawi, Zimbabwe, Kenya, the Dominican Republic and Brazil as it is in North Carolina. No other crop offers the farmer in Pitt County or the peasant in Brazil the same, guaranteed return on his investment. Other crops may, on paper, be just as profitable, but the market always has to be right. I asked the North Carolina tobacco farmer J. C. Galloway why he did not grow tomatoes instead of tobacco, when figures showed that they were three times as profitable in terms of net return per acre. 'Pitt County could grow enough tomatoes to supply the whole of the United

States,' he told me. 'If tomatoes are so good, how come most of our tomatoes come from Mexico? People are losing money growing tomatoes. Why should we?' The only alternative cash crops whose returns are as attractive as tobacco's are poppies for heroin, coca shrubs for cocaine and marijuana. (Marijuana is now believed to be American's third most valuable cash crop, worth more than $10 billion a year.)[5]

It is clear why tobacco has become an even greater part of the political and economic infrastructure of developing countries than it has in the West. Few Third World governments are going to throw away the lifebelt when there are precious few others around. There is no eagerness to restrict the promotional activities of those they see as their benefactors and friends, despite the warnings of the World Health Organisation:

> The international tobacco industry's irresponsible behavior and its massive advertising and promotional campaigns, are . . . direct causes of a substantial number of unnecessary deaths.[6]

Warnings of epidemics still to come tend to fall on deaf ears as governments struggle to survive in the present. Few are disposed to bite the hand that feeds them. This is why the Third World not only affords the international tobacco companies the new soil and markets they need, but the political and economic climate in which to make the most of their opportunities.

Nowhere is this more so than in Brazil, a nation of 120 million people, the world's fourth biggest tobacco producer and one of the world's fastest growing cigarette markets. Seventy million Brazilians are under the age of twenty-five; forty million of them between ten and twenty. Cigarette consumption has been growing at over six per cent a year—six times faster than growth in most Western countries.[7] Rio de Janeiro's Ipanema beach on a weekend is the biggest and most glamorous cigarette advertisement in Latin America: wall to wall teenagers, stunningly beautiful girls and cigarettes everywhere. Brazil is a tobacco man's dream.

British-American Tobacco has dominated the Brazilian tobacco market since the 1920s. By 1980, its seventy-five per cent owned subsidiary, Souza Cruz, controlled a staggering eighty per cent of the cigarette market. Hollywood, its leading brand, is one of the world's best-selling top twenty cigarettes. Arizona, its Number Two, was launched to keep the Marlboro cowboy off the range, which it has successfully done to date. But BAT's dominance has not deterred its rivals from trying to elbow their way in, albeit at great expense. First to try was Rothman's in 1969, only to retire shortly afterwards, badly bruised.[8] In 1974, the giants, Philip Morris and R. J. Reynolds, started to move in. They are still recovering from the shock. By the end of the 1970s their losses were running at $15 million a year, while Souza Cruz's profit was running at $100 million and its market share holding fast at around eighty per cent. But both of BAT's rivals are convinced that the riches in store in Brazil far outweigh the losses they have had to sustain to get in. They intend to hang on and carve out a bigger slice of the market. In 1981, R. J. Reynolds declared:

> Brazil is the fifth largest cigarette market in the world with unit sales this year of 141 billion. It is also one of the fastest growing markets anywhere, and we have a deep commitment to building our position in this country over the long term. For RJR we see daylight at the end of a very long and dark tunnel . . .[10]

Philip Morris' view was much the same:

> While we are still experiencing considerable start-up losses in this market, we consider it a long term investment in much the same way Germany presented itself ten* years ago and we are confident of the long-term profit potential for us in Brazil.[11]

I asked one of Souza Cruz's British executives why BAT had managed to keep ahead in the face of such fierce and experienced competition. 'Because we're better than they are,' he said. Driving in from the airport in São Paulo, I saw none of the cigarette

---

* In 1982, Marlboro was West Germany's second biggest selling cigarette with 14.1 per cent of the market. Number One was BAT's HB, with 18.1 per cent.

hoardings which usually wallpaper most highways leading from airport to city. I thought perhaps I had come to the wrong place—until I turned on the television in my hotel room. A sun-tanned beauty leapt on to a surfboard and plunged into the waves. Another surfer swept into the shore to the beat of the music. Another beautiful girl drew a packet of cigarettes from the side of the briefest of bikinis. Another slid a cigarette from her boyfriend's lips. '*Ao successo con Hollywood*' — 'To success with Hollywood', was the message. It was as if the Surgeon-General had never put pen to paper. There were more Hollywood ads to come, all in the same vein and style: more beautiful young people riding dune buggies over the sand, driving sleek Porsches, and riding more waves on their surfboards. (The last commercial contained a memorable shot of the carpenter making the surf board wearing a mask across his face to keep the dust out of his lungs.) The same slogan, 'To success with Hollywood', appeared in huge letters on the base line of the Davis Cup tennis match between Brazil and Argentina which was being sponsored by Hollywood and carried over the nation's television screens. Having seen it on the screen, I went along to the event. Again, there were cigarettes everywhere. More beautiful girls, now wearing mini-skirts and blouses emblazoned with 'Hollywood', moved among the audience giving away free cigarettes and lighting them between the lips. Children gazed open-eyed at the performance.

All over the Third World, cigarettes are advertised and promoted in ways which would never be permitted in most developed countries, despite the assurances of British-American Tobacco's Chairman and Managing Director, C. H. Stewart Lockhart:

> Where promotion is concerned, our managers in developing countries are aware that local practice should not be incompatible with promotional standards in the industrialised nations . . .[13]

In Kenya, where BAT has held the monopoly (and also grows much of its tobacco), an advertisement in a glossy magazine shows a smooth black executive in black velvet jacket and bow tie, an elegant black lady at his side—both cigarettes in hand—at a gaming table in a Playboy type club with a Playboy type Bunny about to serve the drinks. 'Smooth International Embassy' reads the caption. 'The smooth way to go places.' There is no health warning in sight. In India—the world's third largest tobacco producer—an advertisement for 'Red & White' cigarettes (manufactured by Godfrey Phillips—an affiliate of Philip Morris since 1968 when the American company took it over)[14] appeared in the form of a cartoon in the romantic style of popular teenage comics. A train hurtles through the night. Suddenly someone shouts 'Fire'. There is panic among the passengers. One screams they're going to die. The alarm doesn't work. Suddenly a young man climbs through the door of the moving train and inches his way along the carriages to warn the driver of the fire. 'You've saved hundreds of lives,' says the driver back at the station. 'But the young man stood aside as if nothing had happened,' reads the caption. 'He coolly took out a R E D & W H I T E and lit it casually . . .' The young man sang, 'We Red & White smokers are one of a kind.' At the bottom of the page is a tiny health warning saying, 'Cigarette Smoking is Injurious to Health.'

But Brazil still takes some beating as far as cigarette advertisements are concerned. I asked Alan Long, the President of B A T's subsidiary, Souza Cruz, why Hollywood was associated with glamour and success. He said glamour was a very subjective word and 'success' referred to the 'success' of the brand. Were not fast cars, surfing and dune buggies with beautiful people smoking cigarettes, glamorous? He said he could not subjectively measure 'glamour', but the commercials were effective and that is what they were trying to achieve. When I asked him if he thought smoking was harmful to health, he said, 'The medical evidence as far as I am aware is of a statistical nature. It is, as you know, the industry's view that no evidence has been produced to establish a causal relationship between smoking and any of the diseases with which it has been associated.' I asked him whether he was saying he did not know. 'That's exactly what I'm saying,' he replied.[15] In Brazil there are no health warnings on cigarette packets or advertisements.

There is little pressure from the Brazilian government on Souza Cruz or any of the other cigarette companies. The government needs all the friends it can get, especially when they have plenty of money. Brazil is going broke. By 1982 its foreign debt had reached nearly $80 billion.[16] Like Poland and Mexico, Brazil borrowed on a huge scale in the rush for development and then found that it could not meet the repayments. With a trade deficit running at $10 million a year and inflation at eighty per cent, no Brazilian government is going to upset an industry that provides $300 million worth of exports, nearly $1 billion of tax revenue (nearly ten per cent of total federal revenue) and direct and indirect jobs for up to three million people.[17] The only conflict which does arise between the government and the tobacco industry in Brazil is over wealth not health—between company profits and government revenue. As inflation soared, the government refused to allow the companies to increase the price of their cigarettes: in 1980 when inflation was running at seventy per cent, cigarettes were still twenty pence for twenty. A price increase would have been politically unpopular and the government had enough problems without antagonising Brazil's twenty-two million smokers. The price increase would also have meant a drop in revenue as consumption was bound to fall. In 1981, the government gave in and agreed to an increase, although it was considerably less than the rate of inflation. Consumption dropped by six per cent. Cigarette sales plummeted by 10 billion from 141 billion in 1980 to 131 billion in 1981.[18] BAT didn't complain. In its 1981 Annual Report it declared:

> Brazil: Profit was much higher because of better price increases obtained during the year . . . Souza Cruz's market share was reduced slightly but was still over 80 per cent and its trading profit increased by 164 per cent in sterling terms, restoring it closer to levels achieved in earlier years.[19]

The main reason for the bond between the international cigarette companies and the Brazilian government lies nearly a thousand miles away from the great cities of São Paulo and Rio de Janeiro, in the country's most southern province of Rio Grande Do Sul, where seventy per cent of Brazil's tobacco is produced. From here over 80,000 tons[20] of Virginia tobacco are exported every year, much of it to Europe and America, to the chagrin of the tobacco farmers of North Carolina, who see their own crop being undercut by cheaper imports of high quality. Brazilian tobacco flourishes at North Carolina's expense, bringing prosperity to the once-poor regions in the south of the country, and especially to the town of Santa Cruz where the companies have set up their leaf-buying operations. Santa Cruz now calls itself 'the Tobacco Capital of the World'—a title that does not go down too well in North Carolina. I visited Santa Cruz in February when most of the tobacco harvest had been gathered in, and the town was full of many of the region's 100,000 tobacco farmers who had just brought their season's crop to market. Souza Cruz buys over fifty per cent of all the tobacco grown in the area. Its factory was working round the clock, employing 1,800 people in three shifts, most of them on the national minimum wage, which was then around £25 a week. The hours are long and the work is hard. There are no tea and coffee breaks. Each section is identified by the colour of its T-shirt. The 'loaders' and 'feeders' wear orange; the 'strippers' and 'sorters' wear blue. The 'strippers' are on piecework and make twenty to thirty per cent above the national minimum wage. Most of the workers are women. There was standing room only in the cash office crowded with farmers collecting their money within two hours of selling their crop, the greatest attraction of growing tobacco to a peasant farmer anywhere in the world. Growing tobacco has other attractions too. The companies arrange loans to set the farmer up in business, enabling him to buy equipment and build a curing barn; they provide him with free tobacco seed; they sell him fertiliser and insecticide at cost price, as well as lending him the money to buy it; and they see he is visited regularly by an agricultural instructor (Souza Cruz employs around 700 in the south of Brazil).[21] The company guarantees the loans, usually through the Bank of Brazil's rural credit scheme, as few farmers are well enough off to meet the standard of collateral required by the government. When the farmer sells his tobacco to the company, the money he owes is deducted from the payment he receives. Loans for fertiliser and pesticides are usually made over the growing season and repaid at the end of the year: bigger loans to buy a tractor or build another curing barn may often stretch over five years. The farmers have to grow tobacco to pay off their debts, as no other crop will bring in enough money to meet the repayments. In turn, they too become dependent on tobacco.

Perhaps the only way that Third World farmers can be weaned from tobacco is for governments to provide the same level of financial and technical assistance for the production of much-needed food crops as B A T provides for tobacco. But few Third World governments have the resources of B A T. Not only would they have to provide the same inputs and services, they would also have to subsidise the price the farmer would be paid for his alternative crop, to give him an incentive to grow it. Again, few governments could afford such subsidies. I heard few voices raised against tobacco during my visit to Rio Grande Do Sul; surprisingly one of them came from a leader of the Food and Tobacco Growers Union, Maurino Muller. He clearly placed food before tobacco. He told me that Santa Cruz imported most of its fresh vegetables from over a hundred miles away. 'We're called the "Capital of Tobacco". We've other alternatives—pigs, vegetables, dairy products—but it's hard to convince the farmers. In time, no doubt, we will persuade them that tobacco is not the only thing in life.'[22]

I talked with Mr Muller on a small tobacco farm in the hills above Santa Cruz. The 'sickness' he referred to affects the land as well as its people. In a corner of the farmyard, a young boy was feeding a huge pile of wood into a blazing furnace which was curing a recently harvested crop of tobacco hanging inside the barn. Great clouds of black smoke drifted across the bare horizon. I asked where the wood came from as there were not many trees around. I was told the farmer bought it at cost price from the company, as all the wood in the area had been used up long ago. There were once forests around the farms, but they had been cut down for fuel, mainly to cure tobacco. The leaf is cured by exposing it to a constant temperature of 160° for about a week.[23] It has been estimated that around 150 large trees are needed to cure just over one acre of tobacco.[24] (It has been said—although challenged on the grounds that no such calculation is possible—that 300 cigarettes consume one Third World tree.)[25] A quick calculation shows why the horizons are bare: the average size of a tobacco allotment in Rio Grande Do Sul is about four acres. Therefore, in one year, the area's 100,000 tobacco farmers need the wood of 60 million trees—or nearly 1.5 million acres of forest.* The problem is not unique to Brazil. Huge areas of the Third World where tobacco is grown have been stripped of their forests and woods to provide energy to cure tobacco. Eighty per cent of the energy is wasted. The effect on the ecological balance, especially in drier areas, can be disastrous: water tables are lowered, springs dry up, and wells are drained. Deserts may be created where forests once stood. BAT is well aware of the problems caused by tobacco's insatiable appetite for an increasingly scarce and valuable resource. In Kenya the company has already planted nearly ten million trees and now encourages each of its growers to plant 1,000 fast-growing eucalyptus trees for three consecutive years so that he becomes self sufficient in energy— although not all farmers have enough land to plant 3,000 trees, grow tobacco and produce sufficient food to eat. In Brazil, BAT has planted over 120 million trees over the past twenty years but this only represents ten per cent of the annual energy requirements of Rio Grande Do Sul's 100,000 tobacco farmers. The Economist Intelligence Unit, which has made a special study of tobacco growing in Brazil, recognised the scale of the problem:

> . . . the problems of energy conservation are considerable. The curing barns are fuelled by wood and the necessary timber . . . is now a scarce commodity despite the fact that local climatic conditions favour timber growth. Fast maturing eucalypts have been introduced as a substitute . . . but farmers are reluctant to tie up their land for ten years or more to provide fuel which, even now, is still obtainable—albeit with increasing difficulty —from outside the farm. There is also the making of a vicious circle in that increasing net incomes from tobacco will permit farmers to bear the cost of ever scarcer fuel.[28]

Most of the harvest was over when I visited Rio Grande Do Sul, and I had to travel into the mountains above Santa Cruz to find farmers who were still picking tobacco. The journey to the high

---

* The calculation is based on the statistic that one ton of tobacco needs the wood from between four and seven acres of forest.[26] On average each farmer in the south of Brazil produces 2.47 tons of tobacco. I include the figures merely as a guide to the scale of the problem.[27]

plateau was spectacular. Deep, green valleys plunged away from the road, their slopes dotted with orange brick curing barns with red slate roofs. Here I found Joao Homero da Silva out in the fields with his family, their arms full of freshly picked tobacco leaves which they were loading on to a bullock cart. He took me back to his house, a simple wooden shack with fading pink paint, the centrepiece of which was an incongruous Tyrolean stove painted with red and blue flowers, whose chimney shot up through the roof. Outside two girls were earning £1 a day in their school holidays tying the 'hands' of freshly picked tobacco leaves and hanging them over a pole ready for curing in one of Joao's three barns. He told me had had been growing tobacco for five years, after a man from R. J. Reynolds had paid him a visit and asked him if he wanted to make some money. He said he did and Reynolds set him up in business with all the necessary equipment, inputs, advice and loans. He said his agricultural advisers visited him once every fifteen days. He was now growing about fifteen acres of tobacco (considerably more than the average) on about a third of his farm. On the rest of the land he grew beans, corn, rice and potatoes. He also raised cattle and pigs. Tobacco, he told me, brought him twice as much as any other crop he grew. When he had paid off his loans ($2,000 a season) he still had $4,000 left over. With the money he has made over five years, he has bought another ten acres of land. He said he would have liked to have grown more tobacco on it, but could not get enough labour, so instead he grew corn. As I left, I asked him if he thought smoking was dangerous. 'We can't say that,' he said with a smile. 'We need people to smoke more so we can make more money.'

But many doctors in the Third World do not share such enthusiasm for tobacco. They are concerned that as the traditional killer diseases of developing countries (smallpox, yellow fever, malaria, etc.) are gradually brought under control and people live longer because of vaccination, better nutrition and medical services, millions of Third World smokers are beginning to incubate lung cancer, bronchitis and heart disease. (Because at the moment each smoker only consumes an average of 300 cigarettes a year—his Western counterpart smokes around 2,500—the World Health Organisation believes that there is still time to take avoiding action, to prevent the new epidemic. The tobacco companies however see the figures differently: they are a great opportunity to increase sales.) In some clinics and hospitals doctors are now seeing the signs of the smoking-related diseases which have swept the West. In Brazil I visited one of Latin America's largest cancer hospitals. Professor Jose Rosemberg, Professor of Medicine at the University of São Paulo, told me that over the past forty years, lung cancer deaths in the state of São Paulo had nearly trebled amongst men aged forty to forty-nine; increased nearly seven times in men aged fifty to fifty-nine; and nearly nine times in men aged sixty to sixty-nine.[30] He said that young people were starting to smoke earlier than they were ten years ago, and blamed 'the massive advertising on television which associated cigarettes with glamour and success in life. Young people from twelve to nineteen are very receptive to this kind of advertising. Forty per cent of our population is between ten and twenty years old. It's a huge market in which to introduce cigarettes.' Why was it so difficult to get anti-smoking programmes off the ground? 'Because the companies are involved in the tobacco business here. Cigarette taxes are very high (around sixty-seven per cent) and the government makes a lot of money from them. But we have to explain to the government that the public health problem is more important than the revenue.' Professor Rosemberg took me round the hospital. One patient was propped up in bed with breathing tubes up his nose and a packet of cigarettes by his side, which he hid when the doctors came into the room. He was crippled with emphysema. He was fifty-nine and said he had been smoking twenty a day since he was fifteen. I watched a lung cancer operation. The patient was forty-nine and had started smoking when he was ten. He was now having an extensive tumour removed, which was covering four of his ribs. If he was lucky, the surgeon told me, he might live five years: if not, he would be dead within six months. He told me that lung cancer was the third most common cancer amongst men in Brazil, but he expected it to be Number One by the mid 1980s. I asked Professor Rosemberg what would happen if no action was taken. He shook his head and sighed. 'Then we may pay in future the same price in mortality and disability that developed countries have paid—like North America and England.'[31]

Brazil is a microcosm of the dilemma which tobacco now poses for many governments throughout the Third World. The words and warnings of Professor Rosemberg in Latin America are echoed by doctors and public health officials in Asia and Africa.

PAKISTAN: Dr Abdul Aziz Choudri, Deputy Director-General, Public Health:

> Tobacco growing is one of Pakistan's most important cash crops and an important source of government revenue which shows a substantial annual increase. Approximately 120,000 acres of Pakistan's most fertile land is under tobacco cultivation.
>
> The cigarette industry is expanding. Cigarette consumption has been increasing at 8 per cent a year. Lung cancer is now the most common form of tumour found in men.[32]

THE PHILIPPINES: Dr T. Elicano, Director, National Cancer Control Centre:

> More women are beginning to smoke, especially college and university students. Lung cancer is now the most common form of cancer in men and is slowly increasing in women. Tar and nicotine contents are high. The Philippines is one of the main target areas for the tobacco companies. They use all the advertising and marketing techniques at their disposal. Thousands rely on tobacco production for their incomes. It's the government's second largest source of revenue after petrol. In 1980, the country imported over $100 million of Virginia tobacco for local cigarette production. Cigarette sales are on the increase.[33]

SRI LANKA: Dr T. Munasinghe, Assistant Director, Health Education Bureau:

> Cigarette consumption has been increasing by nearly 8 per cent a year. Government revenue from tobacco has trebled in the past 5 years. In the nation's capital, Colombo, 12 per cent of schoolchildren between the ages of 15 and 20 are regular smokers.[34]

THAILAND: Dr S. Puribhat, Director, Department of Radiation Oncology, National Cancer Institute:

Twenty per cent of the total population aged 10 years and over are smokers—mainly of cigarettes. One hundred million cigarettes are produced locally a day. Twenty per cent of individual income is spent on smoking. Smoking-related diseases are on the increase.[35]

INDIA: Mrs K. Jayant, Scientific Officer, Cancer Research Institute, Bombay:

India is the world's third largest tobacco producer—most of it consumed in 'bidis' (a traditional form of rolled cigarette). Eighty billion cigarettes are produced locally every year. Cigarette smoking is more prevalent amongst urban white collar workers and young blue collar workers. Major obstacles to anti-smoking programmes are the employment potential of the tobacco industry, agricultural considerations and government revenue.[36]

The same warnings came from Africa.

GHANA: Dr R. Amonoo Lartson, Deputy Director of Medical Services, Ministry of Health, Accra:

Smoking as a social and eventually a health problem is on the increase. The headmasters of almost all the schools in the Greater Accra region noted that cigarette smoking was a major problem amongst their pupils. The recent boom in cigarettes was probably the result of the government of the day wanting to raise more revenue. Ways have to be found of de-emphasising the role of tobacco as a major revenue earner and source of employment. Farmers should be provided with more extension services and facilities for increasing food production as the growth of the tobacco industry has been due to attractive services and prompt payment for crops produced by the tobacco companies.[37]

[257]

TANZANIA: Dr Konrad A. Mmuni, Specialist Physician, Kili-manjaro Christian Medical Centre, Moshi:

Tobacco is the Number Three cash crop after cotton and coffee. Tobacco remains a powerful revenue collector. The Ministry of Agriculture has not hidden its intentions of continued promotion of the crop. The tobacco industry enjoys unlimited advertising and promotion of cigarettes. There are no health warnings on packets. Other cash crops—tea, coffee and groundnuts—could replace tobacco in some areas. Smoking is on the increase.[38]

SWAZILAND: Dr Ruth Tshabalala, Public Health Unit, Mba-bane:

Amongst the young, smoking is a sign of maturity, sophistica-tion and freedom. Tobacco growing is on the increase assisted by the Ministry of Agriculture. There are 2,500 tobacco farmers. Most of the crop is for export. Cigarettes are massively promoted through press and radio. There are the first signs of tobacco related health problems, in particular amongst men in the 15–44 age group.[39]

BENIN: Dr Bruno Monteiro, Professor of Internal Medicine, National University Hospital Centre, Cotonou:

Between 1980–81, cigarette and tobacco imports rose by 167 per cent. Consumption is on the increase. Young people in the cities, imitating film heroes or advertising posters, have begun to smoke on a large scale. There is no counter-information to warn them of the dangers. The government is encouraging tobacco production to supply a new cigarette factory which is being built with the aid of the People's Republic of China and expected to produce 900 million cigarettes a year. To think of transferring arable land now growing tobacco to other more useful crops remains a pious hope. The priorities of those responsible for watching over the health of the masses are not always the same as the priorities of those who govern us. This is the dilemma of impoverished countries.[40]

All these statements were made in 1981 and 1982 at conferences organised by the World Health Organisation. They cause the industry concern not just because of what they say, but because of the international forum in which they are said. The tobacco companies fear that these criticisms may affect the policies of international organisations like the UN Food and Agriculture Organisation (FAO), who, as its 1982 report clearly shows, support their arguments and give institutional respectability to their cause. Already they have noticed the FAO shifting its position as a result of pressure from the World Health Organisation. In the mid 1970s, the FAO was involved in up to eight tobacco projects in a year. By 1980, it was only helping with two.[41] The United Nations Conference on Trade and Development (UNCTAD) has also shown signs of defection, with the publication of Dr Frederick Clairmonte's uncompromising attack on the marketing and distribution of tobacco.[42] But the industry has shown no intention of taking the attacks lying down. The tobacco companies monitor the enemy very carefully. In 1979, they set up a special Task Force to cover the Fourth World Conference on Smoking and Health in Stockholm. One of its observers, Dr Ernst Bruckner of the German cigarette industry, warned in a memorandum to the Conference:

> By introducing the emotional and political powers of Third World countries, the anti-smoking forces have given the fight about the smoking issue a new dimension . . . We must try to stop the development towards a Third World commitment against tobacco . . . We must try to get all Third World countries committed to our cause.[43]

Dr Bruckner noted that the industry's natural ally, the UN Food and Agriculture Organisation, was showing signs of switching sides: that efforts must be made to influence official Food and Agriculture Organisation and United Nations Conference on Trade and Development policy to take a pro tobacco stand; and that the industry must try to mitigate the impact of the World Health Organisation by pushing the organisation into a more objective and neutral position. Dr Bruckner then recommended action on the basis that anti-tobacco measures posed a long-term threat to the economies of many developing countries:

> It is a fact that tobacco is a Third World cash crop which cannot be replaced by any other commodity ... Target countries should be made aware of this fact ... Then it is possible to encourage the growers' countries to form alliances under the silent responsibility of the one of them which is affected the most. For example, Africa—Malawi; South-East Asia—Indonesia; Latin America—Brazil.[44]

Dr Bruckner's memorandum was written in 1979. Three years later there were signs that the World Health Organisation, whose activities the industry feared because of their possible effect on friendly governments, might be beginning to conserve its energies on smoking and health. In 1982, Dr Roberto Masironi, who co-ordinates WHO policy on smoking and health, mentioned that he had been told he had been working too hard on smoking and should therefore give it only half his time. A WHO memorandum outlining programme budget proposals for 1984–85, appeared to carry the same message: it said that after lengthy discussion on the subject of a programme of smoking and health, the consensus was to maintain activities at a low level; WHO's global work could be undertaken on a part-time basis, thereby freeing the responsible officer for other duties in the cardio-vascular disease programme. Perhaps these were indications that after all its attacks on tobacco, the WHO was beginning to adopt the more objective neutral position which the tobacco industry wanted. If the WHO could not be drawn into the Smoke Ring like many of the Third World countries whose health it was trying to protect, at least its attacks on it might now be blunted.

15

The Third World
The Natives Prefer Blond

It is no accident that developing nations have become dependent on tobacco. The dependency has been encouraged not only by the tobacco industry, but by the American government, which has seen the Third World as a valuable export market for its crop and a useful outlet for the surplus production generated by the price support system. These exports have also ensured that developing countries have acquired the taste for American 'blond' tobacco, which is milder than the locally produced 'dark' variety. The taste transfer was often further encouraged, as in the Dominican Republic, by developing local tobacco industries which grew their own 'blond' tobacco. The US government has helped to expand the opportunities for its tobacco industry by widening the market for American cigarettes.

America now exports nearly half the tobacco it produces. In 1981, nearly $600 million of mainly Virginia 'blond' tobacco was sold overseas.[1] These exports of tobacco leaf and tobacco products were worth over $2.7 billion.[2] But in recent years, the pattern of US tobacco exports has changed. The United Kingdom and West Germany are no longer its main customers, due to falling consumption, E E C tariffs and the high price of American leaf. The new markets for American tobacco, like the new markets for cigarettes, are now in the Third World. In 1981, Asian countries attracted nearly fifty per cent of all US tobacco exports, among them the developing countries of Thailand (18 million pounds), Korea (10 million pounds) Malaysia (7 million pounds), the Philippines (11 million pounts), and Taiwan (22 million pounds).[3] The soil has been well prepared. For nearly twenty-five years the US federal government helped tobacco exports to Third World countries by including the crop in the 'Food for Peace' programme— commonly known as P.L. 480 'the Agricultural Trade, Development and Food Assistance Act'. The priorities of 'Food for Peace' lie in the order its official title suggests. Its main purpose was not to combat hunger and malnutrition, but to develop new markets for US farm products, to dispose of surplus agricultural commodities, and to promote American foreign policy.[4] It is no coincidence that many of these markets are now in South-east Asia—Thailand, the Philippines, Malaysia, Korea and Taiwan. Under the 'Food for Peace' programme, developing countries could purchase American tobacco on federally guaranteed long term dollar loans (up to forty years) at low rates of interest (two to three per cent). If their governments resold the tobacco locally and used the money to finance approved development projects, they could then be exempted of the debt obligation.[5] Although tobacco only represented two per cent of the overall programme, by 1980 nearly $1 billion worth of tobacco exports had been financed under 'Food for Peace'.[6] In the 1960s this represented nearly twenty per cent of total US tobacco exports, although it fell to five per cent in the 1970s. Like the price support system, the 'Food for Peace' programme has come under repeated attack in the US Congress. In 1977, a concerted effort was made to have tobacco excluded from its list of commodities. The House of Representatives voted by 229 votes to 178 in favour of the exclusion.[7] But tobacco was saved in the Senate. The lines were drawn as they were in the debate over price supports. Senator Jesse Helms argued, 'Historically, these sales have developed new markets for American tobacco.'[8] Senator Mark Hatfield of Oregon maintained there was no justification for promoting the export of a commodity which was harmful to public health, and said that the Third World needed food, not tobacco.[9] Ironically, tobacco was rescued by the intervention of the liberal Democrat, Hubert Humphrey, who supported it out of loyalty to his Minnesota farming constituents. (They traditionally supported tobacco because tobacco supported them.)[10] The Senate reversed the House of Representatives' decision by fifty-six votes to thirty-seven.[11] The following year, a further $62 million worth of tobacco exports were promoted by 'Food for Peace'.[12] In 1980, tobacco's contribution to 'Food for Peace' amounted to $2.7 million.[13]*

The American tobacco industry has also been involved in more 'questionable' methods of extending its influence overseas. This is what the UNCTAD Report on the marketing and distribution of tobacco calls 'global corporate bribery or the "pay-off complex"'. Dr Frederick Clairmonte's Report states that the sums involved run into millions of dollars and that only a small fraction of the 'pay-offs' has been uncovered. It states:

> Invariably, all the tobacco conglomerates, as most other corporations, have received a bonus from the 'pay-off complex' by computing their profits on the basis of total costs, which are simply inflated to include bribes. The mode of conduct of the TTCs [tobacco transnational conglomerates] has not been dissimilar to other corporate entities to whom the pay-off complex has become the conventional medium for the marketing and distribution mechanisms, joined to the enveloping secrecy and non-accountability that govern corporate practices.[14]

R. J. Reynolds has admitted in evidence to the Federal Securities and Exchange Commission (SEC)—whose function is to protect the public and investors against malpractices in the security and financial markets—that its international tobacco subsidiaries have made 'questionable' payments of over $5 million to lower- and middle-ranking officials of foreign governments and the companies they controlled. (Twenty per cent of Reynolds' overseas business was conducted through state-owned monopolies of one kind or another.) Most of these payments were recorded as 'commissions to customers on the company's books', but the commission arrangements were seldom put in writing and

---

* In 1978, under renewed pressure, the Congress mandated that food commodities be given highest priority. Since then, very little tobacco has been shipped under the programme.

were made either in cash or by interbank transfer to a numbered account. Reynolds said it knew nothing of their 'questionable' nature at the time. No receipts were received. The company also paid nearly $400,000 to employees and agents of foreign governments to gain information on marketing conditions and to 'maximise distribution of the company's products'. Reynolds subsequently announced plans to establish 'specifice controls' to prevent any recurrence of these practices.[15]

Philip Morris also admitted making 'questionable' payments of nearly $2.4 million in the early 1970s.[16] The company said it may have made such payments, which were 'questionable but not necessarily illegal' in certain foreign countries, along with certain of its subsidiaries. It said that in at least seven foreign countries 'facilitating' payments (totalling around $5,000) may have been made to minor government employees 'for the purpose of expediting administrative action or obtaining procedural assistance in connection with governmental services'. Another foreign subsidiary made 'questionable' payments of $278,500 (most of them in cash) for 'what may have been legal political and lobbying expenses'. The company noted that 'such payments are customary in the countries involved and apparently condoned by local authorities'. In all cases, Philip Morris explained that the payments were made 'in order to further what were perceived to be the best interests of Philip Morris'.[17] Like Reynolds, Philip Morris promised it would not happen again.

These activities of two of the biggest tobacco multinationals only came to light in 1976 when, in the wake of the Lockheed bribery scandal, the Federal Securities and Exchange Commission offered what was tantamount to 'an amnesty' to US companies if they made a voluntary disclosure of 'questionable' payments made in pursuit of their business abroad. R. J. Reynolds filed its report in September 1976, the result of a massive investigation involving fifteen lawyers, up to seventy-five accountants and 400 interviews conducted in America and thirty foreign countries. Philip Morris' report, submitted in December 1976, was no less thorough. The company conducted a special audit of its own worldwide activities and the activities of its many subsidiary companies. (In 1976, Philip Morris sold more than 160 brands in about 160 countries and territories; it had manufacturing affiliates in twenty-two countries and licensees in seventeen nations and territories.[18] There were detailed field investigations. In their reports to the Securities and Exchange Commission, neither company mentioned the names of any country, company or individual involved. But within days of Philip Morris' submission, the *Wall Street Journal* lifted the edge of the curtain, having obtained a copy of the company's special audit of its forty-three per cent owned subsidiary in the Dominican Republic, Eduardo Leon Jimenes (ELJ). The audit named names and detailed specific figures for specific services rendered in the Caribbean island which, since 1966, had been ruled by President Joaquin Balaguer. According to the Philip Morris internal document quoted in the *Wall Street Journal* article:

> . . . there were monthly payments of . . . $1,000 throughout the year of 1973 on (ELJ) company checks (sic) to 'Presidente partido Reformista'. Several of them even show the official stamp of the central headquarters of the 'Partido Reformista' located in the National Palace of the Dominican Republic.[19]

The documents also reported, although no time frame was given, that 'Contributions to the President's political campaign amounted to $200,000 approximately.'[20] The *Wall Street Journal* pointed out that corporate contributions to political campaigns were legal in the Dominican Republic* and that these payments to President Balaguer may have been part of ELJ's acknowledged contributions to political parties. The *Journal* also pointed out that the documents 'disclosed that $16,000 was paid to a Dominican Republic tax officer in 1975 for a favourable ruling'[21] and '$120,000 was spent some time during the past few years to have a significant law enacted by the legislature.'[22] According to the document, Eduardo Leon told the Philip Morris auditors that

---

* Article 70, the law governing political contributions in the Dominican Republic, signed by President Balaguer, states that political contributions are illegal if they are specifically made to obtain political favours. If the contributions are made 'for the benefit of any organisation, its owners, members, activists, beneficiaries, directors or representatives' this constitutes an 'irrefutable breach of confidence with the parties and their candidates'.

such payments were necessary for corporate survival and profitability.[23] The *Journal*'s writers outlined the legislation referred to:

> The auditors also reported that E L J believed pay-offs were essential to get favourable legislation enacted. About six years ago, Mr Leon said in the telephone interview, Philip Morris helped E L J cultivate so-called blond or Virginia tobacco. E L J wanted legislation passed that would ensure that its competitor, Compania Anonyma [sic] Tabacalera S.A. [C A T] which has a 75 per cent market share compared with E L J's 25 per cent, would be required to purchase this tobacco from E L J. The memo recounting the June 21st interview with Mr Leon stated that 'the amount contributed to various legislators for this purpose [passage of the Bill] was $120,000'.

The following investigation into Philip Morris' legitimate lobbying activities in the Dominican Republic provides a rare insight into the political and economic relationship between a tobacco multinational and the government of a poor Third World country. For the past twenty years and more, the island has been an economic and political prisoner of its geography, sitting at the northern end of the Caribbean, an hour's flight from Miami, and next door to Cuba. When the thirty-year reign of its notorious dictator, Raphael Trujillo was terminated in a hail of bullets in 1961, the young President John F. Kennedy took a Reaganite view of his options:

> There are three possibilities in descending order of preference: a decent democratic regime, a continuation of the Trujillo regime or a Castro regime. We ought to aim at the first, but we really can't renounce the second until we are sure we can avoid the third.[24]

Kennedy's successor, Lyndon Johnson, agreed with the analysis and in 1965 sent in the US Marines to 'stabilise' the situation in the violence which erupted in the battle for the succession between left and right. Johnson warned Castro to keep his hands off the island. America settled for Kennedy's second option. In

1966, Joaquin Balaguer, who had served under Trujillo when he was assassinated, returned in triumph from his exile in New York[25] and was elected President, with the American seal of approval. To many, Balaguer picked up where Trujillo left off. Political dissent was ruthlessly suppressed. Two thousand of his political opponents are said to have 'disappeared'. Many of them were murdered.[26] But however repressive the regime, the Dominican Republic was safe from the Communist threat and secure for American business once again. The US companies like Gulf and Western (which owns one seventh of all cultivated land and whose sugar plantations account for nearly fifty per cent of the island's exports)[27] heaved a sigh of relief.

The gap between rich and poor in the Dominican Republic remains as pronounced as in most Third World countries. The supermarkets in Santo Domingo, the island's capital, are bursting with goods for the few who can afford them. A small tin of Del Monte pineapples (the R. J. Reynolds subsidiary) imported from the Philippines costs $1.39. Outside, street boys sell fresh pineapples at three for $1. The island's second biggest export (after sugar) is people. New York has become its 'second' city[28] where over a million Dominicans do the menial work which is the lot of those currently at the bottom of the ethnic pile. Back home, seventy-five per cent[29] of peasants are landless. Half the children are malnourished. Half the people suffer from calorie deficiency. Nearly half have no access to clean water. Thousands have now flooded into Santo Domingo, where they live in shacks made of cardboard, plywood and corrugated iron in the shanty towns along the river. Just outside the airport is what must be one of the biggest Marlboro billboards in the world, dwarfing the two small boys trying to earn a few cents cleaning shoes. The Marlboro cowboy is everywhere in the Dominican Republic: he is outside the huge new government office block, '*El Huacal*' (local slang for a crate of empty bottles); on buildings high above the traffic; outside the bars and shops; on news-stands; above the bus shelters; in the newspapers; in the cinema; and on the television. (One mother told me that her little girl thought that 'Marlboro' was the word for 'horse'.) And he rides all over the island. The road from Santo Domingo to Santiago is a Marlboro trail nearly a hundred miles long. Marlboro is on the kilometre posts, on the street signs, on the side of wooden shacks, and even in the front garden. I stopped outside one house with a twenty-foot Marlboro billboard towering above its tiny plot. I asked the lady who was watching the men play cards, how it got there. She said someone called four years ago and gave her $250 to put it up. Every night she pulls a lever behind the sign to light up the cowboy.

The Dominican Republic has not always been Marlboro Country. Traditionally it was the preserve of the state-owned tobacco company, Compañía Anónima Tabacalera (CAT) which, like Souza Cruz in Brazil, had a dominant eighty per cent of the market. For years its rival, Eduardo Leon Jimenes (ELJ), a small family business dating back to the beginning of the century, stood in its shadow. ELJ had been taken over by Trujillo and released after his assassination. In the 1960s both CAT and ELJ realised that with the increasing popularity of imported American cigarettes made of 'blond' tobacco, tastes were changing from the 'dark' tobacco which Dominicans had traditionally favoured. The change in taste was also the result of a change in the population. 'Dark' tobacco was smoked by the peasants in the countryside, but as more and more moved to the towns (by 1981, fifty-two per cent of the population was urban) they left their old tastes behind and exchanged 'dark' tobacco for 'blond'. Seeing the potential of this new market, the Dominican Tobacco Institute (no relation to its Washington counterpart) and the Department of Agriculture began experiments growing local 'blond' tobacco—'tabaco rubio'.[30] If local 'blond' tobacco could be successfully grown in the Dominican Republic, they reasoned, there would be more jobs, more revenue and savings on the balance of payments. Despite the obvious attractions, the state-owned company, CAT, was unable to take the experiment further, due to lack of resources. But ELJ was more fortunate. As a private company it had access to funds which the state company was denied. In the late 1960s, ELJ was reported to have been made three loans—of $600,000, $400,000 and $700,000[31]—by the Fund for Economic Development (FIDE). The loans were financed by the American government's development agency, USAID, the inter-American Development Bank and the Central Bank of the Dominican Republic.[32] The loan channelled through FIDE came from the First National City Bank of America.

Potentially the development of a local 'blond' tobacco industry would give ELJ a considerable market advantage over its much larger state rival, CAT: it would enable ELJ to market a 'blond' cigarette to compete with CAT's 'blond' brands. But ELJ's brand would be cheaper as it would be made out of local 'blond' tobacco. CAT could not afford to compete, as it had to import its 'blond' tobacco. Imported tobacco was more expensive after a law passed in 1964 made the tax on a packet of twenty cigarettes of imported tobacco twenty-six cents, and the tax on a packet of local tobacco only seven cents.[33] The strategy was attractive and the political climate seemed right. ELJ had already established that it had friends in high places when it had asked President Balaguer for a series of tax exemptions of nearly $7 million worth of imported 'blond' tobacco. The President gave ELJ half the exemptions it asked for, to the consternation of some of the local press:

> In terms of official assistance, one could well say that no private company—or even a state-run one—has received more support from the present regime and in such a generous way . . . On this occasion, maybe without thinking twice about how this would damage the state corporation (CAT), Balaguer acted in a way which could be regarded as too generous ['*demasiado afectuoso*'] for a Head of State and conceded 50 per cent of the exemption requested.[34]

Given ELJ's plans for a new local tobacco industry and a new local brand, it was with some anxiety that CAT watched Philip Morris buy its way into ELJ in 1969, bringing with it marketing skills, expertise and capital resources which the state company could not match. (Buying into existing tobacco companies was one of the most common ways in which the tobacco multinationals increased their Third World penetration.) CAT now knew it was at a double disadvantage: it had not the resources to develop its own local 'blond' tobacco which would enable it to launch its own local brand; and it knew it could not compete with Philip Morris' wealth and experience. CAT looked back on Philip Morris' arrival in the Dominican Republic with some bitterness mixed with envy:

When E L J was comprised totally of native capital, it competed on an equal footing with the state company. In those days, the majority of the Dominican people preferred our brands to theirs . . . Because E L J wasn't successful, it became associated with the multinational Philip Morris. Growing 'blond' tobacco was really a strategy to penetrate the cigarette market by developing a project which the public looked upon favourably.[35]

By 1972, E L J's production of local 'blond' tobacco had increased nearly ten-fold. That summer Philip Morris–E L J (which is how C A T refer to the company) were ready to launch Nacional, the new brand they had planned together, made entirely of local 'blond' tobacco. But on May 12th, 1972, their plans suffered a serious setback. The law of 1964, which had taxed local cigarettes at seven cents for twenty and imported ones at twenty-six cents, was changed. This had been the foundation on which the whole Nacional strategy had been built. The National Congress proposed a new law, Law 333, under which the differential was to be removed; all cigarettes made of blond tobacco were now to be taxed at the same rate of twenty-six cents.[36] (Cigarettes made of dark tobacco were still to be taxed at seven cents.) Law 333 threatened Philip Morris–E L J's plans.

Philip Morris immediately brought in the heavy guns. Two senior executives from the company, John Thompson and Walter Sterling Surrey, talked to President Balaguer to try to get the law changed. Philip Morris' intervention was understandable and perfectly legitimate in defence of their interests which were threatened by the new law. They discussed the matter with President Balaguer on May 19th, 20th and 22nd—a week after Law 333 had been published. The President immediately set up a Commission of senior officials to review the situation. Mr Thompson and Mr Surrey met the Commission and insisted that the tax on local 'blond' tobacco should be reduced from twenty-six cents to thirteen cents. The Commission stated publicly that the government could not meet the demand for such a large reduction. It pointed out that to grant such a request would create substantial problems for the state-owned company (C A T) which had to be protected as the main source of work for a large and important area of the country. In view of this, the Commission said it could only recommend a reduction of five cents to President Balaguer, not thirteen cents as Messrs Thompson and Surrey had sought.

The negotiations were protracted and complex. Philip Morris understandably argued that it had to protect its investment in ELJ and secure the Dominican company's future. The argument on the Dominican side, equally understandably, stressed the need to protect its own state industry. At one stage it was suggested that Philip Morris–ELJ should split its harvest with CAT so that the state company could also market a cigarette made out of locally grown 'blond' tobacco. After six months of detailed negotiations involving Mr Thompson and Mr Surrey, President Balaguer and the Commission, agreement was finally reached.

On December 29th, 1972, Law 333 which had caused Philip Morris and ELJ such great concern because of the twenty-six cent tax, was changed. The National Congress passed Law 451, which made the new tax on cigarettes made of local 'blond' tobacco eighteen cents—five cents more than Philip Morris had originally asked for and three cents less than the Commission had originally been prepared to concede. ELJ launched its new brand Nacional which was made entirely of locally grown 'blond' tobacco and which had been the reason for the six months of intensive lobbying. As its makers had hoped, smokers in the Dominican Republic took to the new cigarette in a big way. Nacional took off.

CAT was extremely bitter at the passing of Law 451 and subsequently did little to hide its anger. The state company claimed that the new law did not only benefit Nacional, but Philip Morris' own Marlboro brand. For years, CAT's best selling cigarette, Montecarlo, which was made of imported 'blond' tobacco, had dominated the market. Now Montecarlo had a rival made even more powerful by the advantage which CAT claimed Law 451 gave it. According to CAT's analysis, Marlboro was made of seventy per cent imported 'blond' tobacco and thirty per cent of local 'blond' tobacco, whereas Montecarlo was made entirely of imported 'blond' tobacco. This, CAT argued, gave Marlboro an advantage, because Marlboro only paid forty-five per cent in tax while Montecarlo paid fifty-three per cent.

(Nacional, made entirely of local 'blond' tobacco, only paid thirty-six per cent.)[37] To CAT, these were the economics of the law which it said Philip Morris had been instrumental in changing.

When I was in the Dominican Republic I went to visit Eduardo Leon, the President of ELJ. He lives in a beautiful villa in Santiago, with an armed guard at the gate and guard dogs in the grounds. Mr Leon was away at the beach. When I finally managed to speak to him by telephone, I asked him about the lobbying which his company and Philip Morris had carried out in the Dominican Republic. 'I don't like to discuss these matters,' he said. 'Why don't you find out from other sources. That would be better.' He then put down the telephone. While I was in Santiago, I also visited the headquarters of CAT and spoke to Nelson Garcia, the Director of Public Relations, and Juan Almanzar, the production manager. They were much more guarded with a visiting Englishman than their company had been with the people of the Dominican Republic a few years earlier when CAT was still smarting under the effects of Law 451.

In a series of newspaper advertisements in 1979, when it sought a further modification of the law, ELJ insisted that Law 451 had not been beneficial but had held back the further development of the island's local blond tobacco industry. CAT retaliated with its own advertisements in the national press in which it challenged ELJ's interpretation of events and accused Philip Morris–ELJ of trying to dominate the Dominican cigarette market against the national interest. It accused its rival of obtaining privileges and protection from the elected representatives of the people in the state legislature.[38] ('*Mediante la obtencion de privilegios y proteccionismo por parte de los representantes de ese pueblo en las Cámaras Legislativas*'.) The state company also accused Philip Morris–ELJ of using its powerful international influence ('*influencias internacionales*') to change the law. It claimed that as a result, Philip Morris–ELJ was protected by the state to the detriment of the state's own tobacco company: the protection, it said, had been amply conveyed by the nation's legislators in 1972.[39] CAT also charged John Thompson and Walter Surrey of Philip Morris International with getting the law changed—'a change which was accepted because of the existence of interests outside of the production of cigarettes' (*'La modificación fue aceptada por existir intereses extra productores de cigarillos'*.)[40]

Under Philip Morris' tutelage, ELJ went from strength to strength. Over the years, CAT watched its rival gradually erode its dominance of the market. Between 1978 and 1981, it saw Montecarlo's market share (its best selling brand) drop from thirty-eight per cent to twenty-nine per cent; Marlboro's rose from fifteen per cent to twenty-six per cent; and Nacional's rose from seven per cent to fifteen per cent.[41] Then in 1982, Marlboro finally made it to the top. In a spectacular leap it captured 31.5 per cent of the market to Montecarlo's 29.6 per cent.[42] The number one brand in the world had finally become the best selling cigarette in the Dominican Republic. True to its motto, Philip Morris came and saw and conquered again. Another corner of the world had become Marlboro Country.

There is an interesting postscript to the story. In 1983, Philip Morris's greatest rival, R. J. Reynolds (which had already been thwarted by Philip Morris in its attempt to gain a stake in Rothmans International) discussed the possibility of a joint venture with CAT. This would have enabled CAT to benefit from R. J. Reynolds' expertise as ELJ had from Philip Morris' and, perhaps more significantly, would have provided R. J. Reynolds with an entrée into the Dominican Republic enabling it to market its brands on Philip Morris' territory. But the discussions failed to bear fruit. In the words of a R. J. Reynolds spokesman, 'the government declined the arrangement'. To date, Marlboro has no American rivals in the Dominican Republic.

16

Breaking the Smoke Ring

The battle to break the Smoke Ring is a battle between wealth and health. The tobacco companies and governments want to keep people smoking because of the wealth cigarettes create: the interests of public health dictate that the smoking habit should be encouraged to die. The industry knows it will lose the battle if the Smoke Ring is broken; if both governments and consumers are weaned from cigarettes. It remains reasonably confident that governments will stay dependent because of revenue and jobs, but fears for the loyalty of its consumers who are the Smoke Ring's most vital and vulnerable link. It calculates that if this link can be held, the other political and economic links (which all depend on people buying cigarettes) will, barring government defection, probably take care of themselves.

Since the British Royal College of Physicians and the US Surgeon-General published their first Reports twenty years ago, the industry's strategy has been to reassure its consumers in two ways: by developing low tar cigarettes to alleviate health concerns (while at the same time challenging the medical evidence); and by spending billions of dollars on advertising and promotion to perpetuate the image of smoking as a socially desirable habit. These two elements are designed to serve as scientific and social reinforcement for the industry's greatest ally, the nicotine to which its consumers are addicted. (The power of the addiction is shown by one dramatic statistic: even after a lung cancer operation, forty-eight per cent of patients start smoking again [if they survive], most within a year of surgery.[1]) As long as the industry can keep most of its consumers addicted, the profits will continue to pour in. The tobacco companies are staking their long term future on low tar cigarettes.

But medical authorities do not believe that smokers are right to be 'reassured' by low tar cigarettes. In 1981, the US Surgeon-General, Dr Julius B. Richmond, devoted his entire Report, 'The Changing Cigarette', to the assumption that low tar cigarettes 'may somehow' reduce the risks of smoking. He concluded that on the basis of the existing medical evidence there was 'no such thing as a safe cigarette'.[2] He acknowledged that the decline in the incidence of lung cancer was attributed to lower tar cigarettes, but warned that the reduction in risk was 'minimal and limited'. He emphasised that no such conclusion could be reached for heart disease, emphysema, bronchitis or the effect which smoking had on pregnancy. Dr Richmond also issued an ominous, new warning:

> An additional concern is that the production of cigarettes with lower 'tar' and nicotine yields may involve the increasing use of additives for tobacco processing or flavoring. Some additives available for use are either known or suspect carcinogens or give rise to carcinogenic substances when burned. The use of these additives may negate beneficial effects of the reduction of 'tar' yield, or might pose increased or new and different disease risks.[3]

The Surgeon-General's advice to smokers who wanted to be safe was to quit altogether. He warned the industry's consumers that it was not safe to stay in the Smoke Ring. Clearly the industry remains confident that they will stay.

There are, however, obvious signs of strain. In America there are thirty million ex-smokers: in Britain there are eight million and non-smokers now outnumber smokers by two to one.[4] But the Smoke Ring shows no sign of breaking. The industry calculates that as long as a sufficient number of people carry on smoking to generate sufficient revenue and jobs, governments will not be inclined to defect. It knows that they are as hooked on tobacco as smokers: that finding alternative sources of revenue will be neither easy nor popular; that adding tobacco workers and tobacco farmers to the lengthening lines of the unemployed would be politically unacceptable; that destroying one of the world's most successful industries will be seen as a supreme act of folly. In turn, governments know they are trapped in the Smoke Ring and can only break out if they are prepared to make sacrifices at incalculable political cost. But the escape is possible if the political will exists. Revenue can be raised from other sources, although the process will be painful and unpopular (in Britain, for example, the industry claims that in order to make up the £11.5 million in tax which smokers pay *each day*, VAT would have to be increased from fifteen per cent to twenty-two per cent or the basic rate of income tax would have to be increased by nearly five pence in the pound);[5] new jobs can be created as companies are forced to diversify even more once governments make it clear that the days of the cigarette are numbered; and vast amounts of money can be saved once the health services are no longer burdened with cigarette-related diseases and industry is spared the thousands of hours of lost production. Of course the problem is immense: resources cannot be switched overnight, any more than the habits of a lifetime can, or should, be changed by administrative fiat. Social security costs will increase as people live longer. But, in the end, only a political decision can bring real change. Consumers cannot be weaned from cigarettes unless governments lead the way.

The fate of Joe Califano in America and Sir George Young in Britain are clear indications that no government in a country where the industry is powerful, however noble its professed intentions, has been prepared to give its full backing to a Health Minister determined to break the Smoke Ring. The politics of tobacco are the politics of trouble. To let matters take their course, to accept the industry's argument that low tar is the answer, to allow advertising to continue in the name of freedom and to let smokers kill themselves if they want to, is the politically comfortable course. But if government believes in its responsibility for the health of its citizens, it is a course which it cannot accept, however politically hazardous the alternative may be.

Cigarettes kill people and, on the evidence, low tar cigarettes will continue to do so, although perhaps in smaller numbers. In Britain smoking is still responsible for eight times more deaths than road accidents.[6] Despite its protestations, the industry knows the medical facts are no longer in dispute. If the tobacco companies really believed that cigarettes did not cause cancer, they would not have spent twenty years developing low tar cigarettes by trying to remove the carcinogens: nor would they be basing their long term strategy on low tar cigarettes if they really did not believe they were less dangerous.

The industry continues to woo and reassure its consumers, in particular those in developing countries, with the myth that smoking is socially desirable. Governments can break the myth by banning all cigarette advertising and promotion. Revenue would not crash overnight, factory gates would not close tomorrow, tobacco farmers would not go out of business and nations would still remain free. An advertising ban would be a sign that smoking was no longer considered socially acceptable, a belated recognition by the state that cigarettes are lethal. Despite the industry's defence, that advertising does not attract new smokers, does not appeal to young people, and only encourages brand switching, advertising gives smoking society's seal of approval. That is why it is so vitally important to the industry. Without advertising, cigarettes are naked, as the experience of three Scandinavian countries—Sweden, Finland and Norway—clearly shows.

Sweden introduced anti-smoking legislation (the Tobacco Labelling Act) in 1977: sixteen different health warnings were introduced and printed on cigarette packets in rotation; the changes were accompanied by considerable publicity and widespread educational programmes. In July 1979 regulations were introduced which restricted the size of advertisements in newspapers and magazines and only permitted the advertisements to depict the cigarette pack against a plain background.[7] In the following year, the number of men and women smoking fell by six per cent: in Britain it has taken eight years for men and women to register a similar drop. The apparent decline amongst children was even more encouraging: in 1977 (the year the Act became law) nine per cent of thirteen-year-old boys and eleven per cent of thirteen year-old girls were smokers; among sixteen-year-olds, twenty-five per cent of boys smoked and forty per cent of girls. By 1980, a clear decline was apparent: amongst thirteen-year-olds, boys were down to five per cent and girls to six per cent (a drop of nearly half); amongst sixteen-year-olds, boys were down to twenty-one per cent (a drop of four per cent) and girls down to thirty-three per cent (a drop of seven per cent).[8]

Finland, whose lung cancer death rate is second only to that of England and Scotland, banned advertising and sales promotion of tobacco in March 1978 as part of the comprehensive legislation programme to control smoking—despite the objections of the Treasury and the Ministry of Trade.[9] (In the 1920s Finland's cigarette consumption was the highest in the world: until the late 1950s, most smokers bought Russian-type cigarettes with a very high tar content, of thirty-five to forty-five milligrams.) The law permitted no loopholes (except for foreign publications).

> Advertising for tobacco, tobacco products and imitations, and also smokers' requisites, and other sales promotion activity directed at the consumer, together with their conjunction with advertising for other products or services, or other sales promoting activity, is forbidden.

The law also prevented tobacco companies from using non tobacco goods and services to promote their brand names and image (like sportswear, clothing and holidays—which Marlboro, Peter Stuyvesant, Camel and John Player Special were to use in the United States, Europe and elsewhere).

> The linking of tobacco, tobacco products and imitations, and smokers' requisites to the sale or transfer of other products or to the performance of services is prohibited.[10]

The law also mandated that 0.5 per cent of revenue from tobacco duty should be spent on smoking health education. Again, the statistics indicate a decline—especially among young people: in 1973, nineteen per cent of fourteen-year-olds were daily smokers; by 1979 (two years after the Finnish Tobacco Act became law), the number had been more than halved—falling to eight per cent.

Norway banned all advertising under its Tobacco Act of 1975.

The ban was accompanied by an extensive public education programme, energetically directed by Kjell Bjartveit of Norway's National Council on Smoking and Health. Again the statistics signify a decline (although, as in the case of all three Scandinavian countries, the decline may also be the result of other factors, such as price increases). The number of male smokers fell from forty-six per cent, to forty-two per cent between 1978 and 1980:[11] again there was also a marked drop in the number of young people smoking.

The message from Scandinavia clearly indicates that determined political action works—although it must be remembered that each country was able to legislate in the face of a relatively weak tobacco industry. However much the statistics and the effect of an advertising ban may be disputed, its real significance is that it would deprive the industry of the instrument it has used for over half a century to seduce and condition its consumers and which it will continue to use for another half century if governments do not take it away. Few so far have done so. The tobacco companies spend $2 billion a year on advertising because advertising is their lifeblood. But the lifeblood is coming under increasing attack in many parts of the world. At the time of writing a Third World country has taken the most recent political action to break the Smoke Ring when, in the summer of 1983, a law banning all cigarette advertising and smoking in all public places came into force in the Sudan (see Appendix Three). There is mounting pressure in other parts of the world to do likewise and equal determination on the part of the tobacco industry to resist it. The pressure is not always conventional.

In Australia, where there are moves to ban cigarette advertising in several states, notably Western Australia, South Australia, Tasmania and the Australian Capital Territory, more radical measures have been taken pending successful political action. Anti-smoking activists have taken to the streets and, with aerosols of spray paint in hand, have made night-time attacks on the advertising hoardings which convey to Australians the sophisticated images of cigarettes. These guerrilla attacks have been orchestrated by an organisation comprised of many doctors called BUGA UP (Billboard Utilising Graffitists Against Unhealthy Promotions). Sydney witnessed an example of its work on

Christmas Eve 1981 when a huge Marlboro advertisement atop a building above the traffic was modified overnight from Marlboro to 'it's a bore'.[12] Other examples of BUGA UP's surgery include: Dunhill becoming 'Lung Ill'; Rothmans King Size becoming 'Rot Mans Lung Size'; Claridge (an Australian brand) becoming 'Miscaridge'; and a Benson & Hedges advertisement covered with the words 'Their Gold—Your Lungs'. In court BUGA UP pleads the defence of necessity—that the act was committed to prevent a greater evil. Light fines between $50 and $200 Australian or acquittals are the usual result. A woman in New South Wales spent fourteen days in gaol rather than pay the fine for 'improving' a billboard.[13] 'We're in the business of changing public consciousness,' said BUGAUP's Fred Cole. 'The automatic reaction is that property is sacred. More so than people's lives. When you think about it and realise the harm they're doing, where does the morality lie? You have to change community attitudes and they are changing because they've been made to think about it.'[14] But it is an uphill struggle. The Smoke Ring in Australia is as tight and effective as anywhere else: the federal government receives over $800 million Australian a year in tobacco excise duty (state governments like Victoria receive over $40 million a year from tobacco)[15]; tobacco growers receive a net subsidy, equivalent to nearly $25,000 a farm;[16] nearly 100,000 jobs depend on tobacco[17]; and the industry spends around $40 million a year on advertising and nearly $10 million a year on sports sponsorship.[18] On the other hand 3,000 Australians die every year from lung cancer and a further 8,000 from heart disease.[19] The Anti-Cancer Council of Victoria has estimated that the medical and social cost to Australia of smoking is about $1000 million a year. But BUGA UP is only spraying the Smoke Ring.

If the nineteenth-century pioneers, James 'Buck' Duke, Richard Joshua Reynolds, W. D. & H. O. Wills and John Player & Sons, tried to introduce cigarettes today, it is by no means certain that they would be allowed to launch them on to the market. In the United Kingdom in 1982, the anti-arthritis drug, Opren, was withdrawn by the Committee on Safety of Medicines after it had been associated with the deaths of sixty-one people.[20] No one talked about the need to identify the causal mechanism before action was taken. It is all too easy to forget in the middle of arguments about freedom, jobs, wealth and sport, that the tobacco industry needs the Smoke Ring to protect it because its products have accounted for the deaths of tens of millions of its consumers this century. The death toll is so enormous that the problem often seems unreal. If governments had not taken political action after the cause of cholera had been identified, they would have been accused of criminal negligence. No such accusations are made against governments for not taking effective action against cigarettes. By presenting itself to the world as a creator of wealth, a source of revenue, the supplier of jobs, the bringer of development, the provider of pleasure, the patron of sport and the arts, and the defender of freedom, the tobacco industry has successfully diverted political and public attention from the real issue at stake: that the product from which all these undoubted benefits flow has wiped out more people than all the wars of this century. Although the cause of death has now been established beyond all doubt, with few exceptions governments only continue to go through the motions of dealing with the problem. As the British Royal College of Physicians recognised in its fourth report, 'Health or Smoking', published in November 1983, the problem remains political:

> Smoking still kills, and at a time when some 100,000 of our citizens are dying prematurely from its effects every year and millions more will die elsewhere, the Royal College of Physicians would be failing in its duty if it did not urge the government to reverse its present attitude of inactivity and even of encouragement towards the tobacco industry and tackle this hidden holocaust with the urgency once given to cholera, diphtheria, poliomyelitis and tuberculosis.

The clear lesson of the past twenty years is that the Smoke Ring can only be broken if governments detach themselves from it. Consumers cannot do it alone. To do so requires an act of rare political courage.

APPENDIX 1

Written Answer, from *Hansard*, February 7th, 1979:

TOBACCO AND SMOKING: GOVERNMENT GRANTS

Lord HOUGHTON of SOWERBY asked her Majesty's Government:

What amount of Government aid has been given to the tobacco industry for modernisation of plant and machinery and how this compares with the grant to the Health Education Council to discourage smoking as the principal known cause of lung cancer.

Lord LEONARD: Assistance to the United Kingdom tobacco industry for plant and machinery has been granted under Section 7 of the 1972 Industry Act. Assistance so granted or approved totals £5.3 million in the form of interest relief grants and £12 million in Regional Development grants. In addition, assistance under the Industries Development Act (Northern Ireland) 1966 and 1971 and under the Industrial Investment General Assistance Act (Northern Ireland) 1966 and 1971 amounted to £12.1 million. As a result of this assistance over 3,200 new jobs have been or will be created and a further 600 preserved.

I understand from the Department of Health and Social Security, since the end of 1972 the Health Education Council spent about £2.3 million of its budget in specific publicising of the dangers of smoking. In addition, the Council has spent about £1.8 million on the Better Health Campaign which includes warnings about the dangers of smoking to health; it is however not possible to isolate the amount spent on this element.

From *Hansard*, April 3rd, 1979:

THE TOBACCO INDUSTRY: STATE ASSISTANCE

Lord HOUGHTON OF SOWERBY asked Her Majesty's Government:

Which firms in the tobacco industry have received grants or loans from state funds, and the amounts, the purpose and the authority for this expenditure of public money.

Lord LEONARD: Assistance offered or given to individual companies is, for the most part, commercially confidential and the full information requested by the noble Lord is not therefore available. However, under the provisions of the 1972 Industry Act, some details of assistance are, in certain circumstances, disclosed and the following information has already been published in *Trade and Industry*:

(i) Offer of an interest relief grant amounting to £1.5 million to Carreras Rothmans for their cigarette factory in Darlington.

(ii) Payment of a regional development grant of £1.833 million to Carreras Rothmans for their Darlington cigarette factory.

(iii) Payment of a regional development grant amounting to £2.358 million to Imperials for their new smoking materials factory in Ayrshire.

(iv) Payment of a regional development grant of £0.567 million to Imperials for their cigarette and cigar factory in Glasgow.

(v) Payment of a regional development grant of £0.171 million to Imperials for their Liverpool pipe tobacco and cigarette factory.

(vi) Payment of a regional development grant of £0.603 million to Imperials for their Newcastle cigarette factory.

(vii) Payment of a regional development grant of £0.488 million to British-American Tobacco for their cigarette and smoking tobacco factory in Liverpool.

No information is disclosed regarding assistance given under the Industries Development Act (Northern Ireland) 1966 and 1971 and the Industrial Investment General Assistance Act (Northern Ireland) 1966 and 1971.

APPENDIX 2

Civil Service Pay and Conditions of Service Code (United Kingdom)

ACCEPTANCE OF GIFTS AND REWARDS

9882 The behaviour of officers as regards the acceptance of gifts, hospitality, etc., should be governed by the following general guidance. The conduct of a civil servant should not foster the suspicion of a conflict of interest. Officers should therefore always have in mind the need not to give the impression to any member of the public or organisation with whom they deal, or to their colleagues, that they may be influenced, or have in fact been influenced, by any gift or consideration to show favour or disfavour to any person or organisation whilst acting in an official capacity. An officer must not, either directly or indirectly, accept any gift, reward or benefit from any member of the public or organisation with whom he has been brought into contact by reason of his official duties. The only exceptions to this rule are as follows:

a. isolated gifts of a trivial character or inexpensive seasonal gifts (such as calendars);

b. conventional hospitality, provided it is normal and reasonable in the circumstances. In considering what is normal and reasonable, regard should be had:

i. to the degree of narrow personal involvement. There is of course no objection to the acceptance of, for example, an invitation to the annual dinner of a large trade asssociation or similar body with which a department is much in day to day contact; or of working lunches (provided the frequency is reasonable) in the course of official visits;

ii. to the usual conventions of returning hospitality, at least to some degree. The isolated acceptance of, for example, a meal would not offend the rule whereas acceptance of frequent or regular invitations to lunch or dinner on a wholly one-sided basis even on a small scale might give rise to a breach of the standard of conduct required.

9883 If, in the application of these exceptions, an officer has any doubts about the propriety of himself or a member of his family accepting any gift, reward or benefit he must consult his Establishment Officer. Similarly, should an officer feel that there are circumstances surrounding a particular gift or occasion which are not covered by exceptions but which merit special consideration, he should consult his Establishment Officer at the earliest opportunity.

APPENDIX 3

The Regulation of Cigarette Smoking Act, 1982 (the Sudan)

The People's Assembly, in accordance with the Constitution and with the assent of the President of the Republic, makes the following Act:

Title and Commencement
1. This Act shall be cited 'The Regulation of Cigarette Smoking Act, 1982' and shall come into force after six months from publication in the official gazette.

Definitions
2. In this Act, unless the text requires otherwise:

'Cigarettes'	mean cigar and cigarettes made of tobacco of all sorts and include pipe tobacco and all means used for smoking of tobacco.
'Closed Public Places'	include public vehicles, closed cinema houses and any other closed place frequented by members of the public

Obligatory writing of the phrase
'Smoking is harmful to the Health'
3 (1) All makers and importers of cigarettes shall write the phrase 'smoking is harmful to the Health' on every packet of cigarettes whether produced locally or imported.
(2) The competent court shall seize any packet of cigarettes which does not bear the phrase stated in sub-section (1) above, until the requirement of the section is fulfilled.

Prohibition of Advertising for Cigarettes
4. No advertisement shall be made for cigarettes in the press, the radio, the TV, any publicity board, cinema, stage, oral publicity or any other means of advertisement originating in the Sudan or prepared for publication therein.

Prohibition of Cigarette Smoking in Closed Public Places
5. No smoking shall be made in closed public places.

Power of Arrest without Warrant
6. Any policeman may arrest without a warrant from a judge, any person contravening Section 5.

Penalties

7 (1) Whoever contravenes Section (3) shall be punished with imprisonment for a term not exceeding six months or with a fine not exceeding five hundred pounds or with both.

(2) Whoever contravenes Section (4) shall be punished with imprisonment for a term not exceeding three months or a fine not exceeding three hundred pounds or with both.

(3) Whoever contravenes Section (5) shall be punished with imprisonment for a term not exceeding seven days or a fine not exceeding twenty pounds or both.

Issue of Regulations

8. The Minister of Health may issue regulations necessary for implementation of the provisions of this Act.

NOTES

INTRODUCTION: THE ORIGINS

1 'Smoking and Health', a Report of the Royal College of Physicians on smoking in relation to cancer of the lung and other diseases, 1962, p. 43, Pitman Medical Publishing Co. Ltd.

2 'Smoking and Health', Report of the Advisory Committee to the Surgeon-General of the Public Health Service, 1964, p. 31, US Department of Health, Education and Welfare, Public Health Service.

3 'Smoking and Health Now', a Report of the Royal College of Physicians, 1971, p. 9, Pitman Medical and Scientific Publishing Co. Ltd.

4 'Smoking and its Effects on Health', Report of a World Health Organisation Expert Committee, p. 50, Technical Report Series 568, World Health Organisation, Geneva, 1975.

5 'Smoking or Health', a Report of the Royal College of Physicians, 1977, pp. 72–3, Pitman Medical Publishing Co. Ltd.

6 'Smoking and Health', a Report of the Surgeon-General, 1979, pp. 1–18/22, US Department of Health, Education and Welfare, Public Health Service.

7 'The Health Consequences of Smoking for Women', a Report of the Surgeon-General, 1980, p. 7, US Department of Health, Education and Welfare.

8 'The Health Consequences of Smoking. Cancer', a report of the Surgeon-General, 1982, p. xi, US Department of Health and Human Services.

9 Lester Breslow, 'Control of Cigarette Smoking from a Public Policy Perspective', *Annual Review of Public Health*, 1982, 3; 129–51, University of California, School of Public Health, Los Angeles, California.

10 Figures based on World Health Statistics Annuals, 1977–80.

11 'Control of Cigarette Smoking from a Public Policy Perspective', *op. cit.*, p. 133.

12 Heather Ashton and Rob Stepney, *Smoking—Psychology and Pharmacology*, p. 143, Tavistock Publications, 1982.

13 'Marketing and Distribution of Tobacco', p. ix, United Nations Conference on Trade and Development (UNCTAD), June 1978.
14 'Tobacco Industry Profile', 1981, The Tobacco Institute, Washington DC.
15 *Business Week*, December 12th, 1964.
16 'Maxwell International Estimates', World Tobacco, 1982.
17 G. F. Todd, 'Statistics of Smoking in the UK', Tobacco Research Council, Research Paper 1, 1969, 5th Edition.
18 'Seventy-Second Report of the Commissioners of HM Customs and Excise', 1981, Cmnd. Paper 8521, HMSO.
19 Parliamentary Question (PQ), March 2nd, 1982 (adjusted to include Scotland).
20 *Smoking—Psychology and Pharmacology*, *op. cit.*, Ch. 2, 'The Importance of Nicotine'.
21 *Ibid*, p. 27.

CHAPTER ONE: HEALTH: EVADING THE ISSUE

1 Susan Wagner, *Cigarette Country. Tobacco in American History and Politics*, p. 44, Praeger Publishers, 1971.
2 Norman Longmate, *King Cholera. The Biography of a Disease*, p. 191, Hamish Hamilton, 1966.
3 *Ibid*.
4 *Ibid*, p. 231.
5 *Ibid*, p. 209.
6 'Smoking and Health', a Report of the Royal College of Physicians, 1962, *op. cit.*, p. 14.
7 'Smoking and Health', a Report of the Advisory Committee to the Surgeon-General, 1964, *op. cit.*, p. 25.
8 'Smoking and Health', a Report of the Royal College of Physicians, 1962, *op. cit.*, p. 3.
9 'Smoking and Health', a Report of the Advisory Committee to the Surgeon-General, 1964, *op. cit.*, p. 26.
10 'Smoking and Health', a Report of the Royal College of Physicians, 1962, *op. cit.*, p. 12.
11 *British Medical Journal*, September 30th, 1950, p. 739. Quoted in: *Trust in Tobacco*, Morris Corina, p. 239, Michael Joseph, 1975.
12 'The Health Consequences of Smoking. Cancer', a Report of the Surgeon-General, 1982, *op. cit.*, p. 49.
13 'Smoking and its Effects on Health', a Report of a World Health Organisation Expert Committee, 1975, *op. cit.*, p. 21.
14 'Smoking and Health Now', a Report of the Royal College of Physicians, 1971, *op. cit.*, p. 36.
15 'Smoking and Health', a Report of the Royal College of Physicians, 1962, *op. cit.*, p. 4.

16 *Ibid*, p. 53.
17 *Daily Mail*, December 13th, 1966. Referred to in the Royal College of Physicians' Report, 'Smoking and Health Now', 1971, p. 21.
18 Report of the Central Health Services Council for the period ending December 31st, 1949, p. 1, HMSO.
19 *Ibid*, p. 19, 1951.
20 *Ibid*, p. 28, 1953.
21 *Ibid*.
22 *Ibid*.
23 *Ibid*, 1955.
24 *Ibid*, 1955.
25 'Smoking and Health Now', a Report of the Royal College of Physicians, 1971, *op. cit.*, p. 143.
26 'Statistics of Smoking in the UK', *op. cit.*
27 Letter to Professor Charles Fletcher, August 26th, 1980.
28 Theodore C. Sorensen, *Kennedy*, p. 249, Bantam Books, 1965.
29 Maurine B. Neuberger, *Smoke Screen: Tobacco and the Public Welfare*, p. 62, Prentice-Hall, Inc., 1963.
30 *Ibid*, p. 63.
31 *Trust in Tobacco, op. cit.*, p. 233.
32 *Smoke Screen, op. cit.*, p. 65.
33 'Smoking and Health', a Report of the Advisory Committee to the Surgeon-General, 1964, *op. cit.*, p. 33.
34 *Business Week*, December 12th, 1964; December 11th, 1965.
35 BBC TV *Panorama*, 'A Dying Industry?', April 14th, 1980.
36 'The Smoking Controversy; a Perspective', a statement by the Tobacco Institute, December 1978.
37 BBC TV *Panorama, op. cit.*
38 'Smoking and Health', a Report of the Royal College of Physicians, 1962, *op. cit.*, p. 26.
39 'The Smoking Controversy; a Perspective', *op. cit.*
40 R. J. Reynolds, *Smoking and Health*, Pride in Tobacco series of booklets.
41 'Tobacco and Health', compiled by the AMA–ERF Committee for Research on Tobacco and Health, American Medical Association Education and Research Foundation, 1978.
42 *Ibid*.
43 Philip J. Hills, *Washington Post*, June 11th and 12th, 1981.
44 'Tobacco in the United States', US Department of Agriculture, February 1979.
45 *Sunday Herald-Leader* (Lexington, Kentucky), 'Up in Smoke', an Investigation by Gary Cohn, March 14th, 1982.
46 *Ibid*.
47 'A Study of the US Tobacco Industry's Economic Contribution to the

Nation, its Fifty States and the District of Columbia', pp. 29 ff., the Wharton School, Applied Research Center, University of Pennsylvania, 1979.
48 *Sunday Herald-Leader*, Special Report: 'The Tobacco Institute', Gary Cohn, November 15th, 1981.
49 'The Health Consequences of Smoking. Cancer', a Report of the Surgeon-General, 1982, *op. cit.*, p. 16.
50 BBC TV *Panorama, op. cit.*
51 *Ibid.*

CHAPTER TWO: WEALTH: THE TOBACCO GIANTS

1 *The American Tobacco Story* (published by the American Tobacco Company), 1964, p. 18.
2 William R. Finger (Editor), *The Tobacco Industry in Transition*, Ch. 15, p. 171, 'Diversification and International Expansion', James Overton, Lexington Books, D. C. Heath & Co., 1981.
3 *Trust in Tobacco, op. cit.*, p. 65.
4 *Ibid*, p. 12.
5 *The Story of the Imperial Group* (published by the Imperial Group), 1975.
6 *Trust in Tobacco, op. cit.*, pp. 129 and 103.
7 *Ibid*, p. 129.
8 *Ibid.*
9 *Ibid*, p. 265.
10 *Ibid*, p. 23.
11 *Ibid*, p. 75.
12 *Ibid*, p. 209.
13 *Ibid*, p. 209.
14 'Marketing and Distribution of Tobacco', UNCTAD, *op. cit.*, p. 50.
15 *The Tobacco Industry in Transition, op. cit.*, Ch. 18, p. 203, 'World Tobacco: a Portrait of Corporate Power', Frederick Clairmonte.
16 *Ibid.*
17 R. J. Reynolds Industries *Annual Report*, 1980, p. 9.
18 *The World of BAT Industries*, p. 6 (Published by BAT). Also: BAT Industries *Annual Report* and Accounts, 1981.
19 BAT Industries *Annual Report* and Accounts, 1981.
20 *Confectionery and Tobacco News (CTN)*, November 6th, 1981.
21 'Smoking Issues', BAT employee information, p. 15, BAT (UK) and Export Ltd.
22 BAT *House Magazine*, 'The Stories Behind the Brand Name du Maurier', undated.
23 Janet Guyon, *Wall Street Journal*, June 30th, 1982.
24 David Lascelles, *Financial Times*, undated.

25 Philip Morris Inc., *Annual Report*, 1978, pp. 5 and 6.
26 *Wall Street Journal, op. cit.*
27 Philip Morris Inc., *Annual Report*, 1978, p. 6.
28 *Ibid*, p. 11.
29 *Ibid*, p. 10.
30 *The Tobacco Industry in Transition, op. cit.*, Ch. 15, p. 180.
31 'Global Presence', R. J. Reynolds Industries Presentation to Security Analysts, November 8th–11th, 1981.
32 R. J. Reynolds, *Annual Report*, 1980, p. 23.
33 'Global Presence', *op. cit.*
34 *Ibid.*
35 *The Tobacco Industry in Transition, op. cit.*, Ch. 16, p. 197, 'R. J. Reynolds Industries: A Hundred Years of Progress in North Carolina', J. Paul Sticht.
36 'Discussions with Reynolds. A Potential Merger?', Ian McBean and Neil Gullan, Wood, Mackenzie & Co., April 8th, 1981.
37 *Business Week*, December 15th, 1980, p. 52: December 20th, 1982, p. 74.
38 'Global Presence', *op. cit.*, p. 34.
39 *Newsweek*, April 20th, 1981.
40 Derek Harris, *The Times*, April 4th, 1981.
41 'Discussions with Reynolds. A Potential Merger?', *op. cit.*
42 *Ibid.*
43 Answers to questions from Action on Smoking and Health at Rothmans International AGM, September 15th, 1982.
44 Proceedings of the European Parliament, February 12th–13th, 1980, p. 280, para. 526.
45 *The Times*, April 29th, 1981.
46 'Global Presence', *op. cit.*, p. 40.
47 *The Tobacco Industry in Transition, op. cit.*, Ch. 15, p. 186.
48 American Brands Inc., *Annual Report*, 1981.
49 *Business Week*, December 31st, 1955.
50 *Business Week*, December 26th, 1970.
51 *Business Week*, December 15th, 1980.
52 American Brands Inc., *Annual Report*, 1981.
53 *The American Tobacco Story, op. cit.*, pp. 38–9.
54 Advertisement reproduced in an article by Dr Alan Blum, 'Cigarettes are Very Kool', *Encyclopaedia Britannica*, 1982, p. 152.
55 Wood, Mackenzie & Co., 'Imperial Strategic Assessment', June 15th, 1982.
56 *Ibid.*
57 *Observer*, September 5th, 1982.
58 Wood, Mackenzie & Co., 'Imperial Strategic Assessment', *op. cit.*
59 *Ibid.*

60 'TAC, Statistics of Smoking in the UK', *op. cit.*
61 Maxwell International Estimates, 'World Tobacco', July 1982.
62 Imperial Group Ltd., *Annual Report* and Accounts, 1981, p. 8.
63 *Ibid.*

CHAPTER THREE: THE MEDIA GETS THE MESSAGE

1 'Controlling the smoking epidemic', Report of the WHO Expert Committee on Smoking Control, p. 32 (citing UNCTAD Report), Technical Report Series 6363, World Health Organisation, Geneva, 1979.
2 Federal Trade Commission, Staff Report on the Cigarette Advertising Investigation, May 1981, pp. 2:3, 2:4, 2:5.
3 *Ibid.*
4 Article quoted by Beverly Mosher and Margaret J. Sheridan, American Council on Science and Health (ACSH), *News and Views*, Vol. 1, No. 2, February 1980. See also: *Mother Jones*, 'Smoking: The Truth No One Else Will Print', January 1979; Action on Smoking and Health Newsletter (USA) Volume VIII, No. 1, January–February, 1978, p. 2.
5 American Council on Science and Health (ACSH), *News and Views*, Vol. 3, No. 3, May/June 1982.
6 *Ibid.*
7 Eve Pell, Media Alliance Newsletter, October 1982.
8 Karin Moser, *The Citizen*, June 26th, 1979.
9 Jill Margo, *Sydney Morning Herald*, December 3rd, 1981.
10 Bob Duffield, *Sydney Morning Herald*, October 29th, 1982.
11 Phil Wilkins, 'Anti-tobacco Bill threatens Test', *The Australian*, October 28th, 1982.
12 *South Perth Times*, Vol. 4, No. 32, October 26th, 1982.
13 Media Expenditure Analysis Ltd. (MEAL), Figures supplied December 1982.
14 Wood, Mackenzie & Co., 'Imperial Strategic Assessment', *op. cit.*
15 Imperial Group Ltd., *Annual Report* and Accounts, 1981.
16 Oliver Gillie, 'Transplant', *Sunday Times* Magazine, October 19th, 1980.
17 Christopher Hird, 'Taking on the tobacco men', *New Statesman*, February 27th, 1981.
18 Letter from C. R. Cory, Managing Director, W. D. & H. O. Wills, *New Statesman*, March 27th, 1981.
19 Christopher Reed, *The Guardian*, May 13th, 1982.
20 Terry Ann Knopf, 'TV Today', *The Patriot Ledger*, November 10th, 1982.
21 *Advertising Age*, November 22nd, 1976.

22 *The Guardian, op. cit.* This information is also based on the following press reports:
23 Associated Press (syndicated). Datelined Seattle, September 14th, 1982 (in Bakersfield *Californian* and several other local papers); *The Seattle Times*, September 8th, 1982 (Warren King); *The Patriot Ledger*, November 10th, 1982 (Terry Ann Knopf); *Boston Herald American*, November 12th, 1982 (Monica Collins); *Minneapolis Star & Tribune*, July 24th, 1982 (Will Jones); CBS Evening News with Bob Schieffer, November 13th, 1982 (Barry Petersen); *Peninsula Times Tribune*, May 13th, 1982 (Ruthann Richter); *The Boston Globe*, October 15th, 1982 (Jack Thomas); *The Charlotte Observer*, November 29th, 1982 (Allen Cowan); Jack Anderson syndicated column, May 6th, 1982; *Washington Post; San Francisco Examiner*, July 8th, 1982 (Michael Dougan).
24 Orna Feldman, *Columbia Journalism Review*, May/June, 1983.
25 John O'Connor, *Advertising Age*, November 15th, 1976.
26 *The Patriot Ledger, op. cit.*
27 *The Boston Globe, op. cit.*
28 Jim Dufur, *The Sacramento Bee*, June 24th, 1982.
29 *The Charlotte Observer, op. cit.*
30 *Peninsula Times Tribune, op. cit.*
31 Bard Lindeman, *Miami Herald*, February 18th, 1977.
32 Jack Anderson, *Raton Range*, May 7th, 1982 (Syndicated).
33 *The Seattle Times, op. cit.*
34 *Ibid.*
35 Barry Petersen, CBS Evening News with Bob Schieffer, *op. cit.*
36 Jack Anderson, *op. cit.*
37 CBS Evening News, *op. cit.*
38 *Peninsula Times Tribune, op. cit.*
39 Jack Anderson, *op. cit.*
40 John O'Connor, *Advertising Age, op. cit.*
41 George Gordon, *Daily Mail*, November 17th, 1976.
42 Elaine Warren, *Los Angeles Herald Examiner*, September 9th, 1982.
43 *The Patriot Ledger, op. cit.*
44 *The Boston Globe, op. cit.*
45 I re-interviewed John Holmes on June 13th, 1982, at his ranch in Miami, New Mexico.
46 *Columbia Journalism Review, op. cit.*
47 I interviewed Mrs Beatrice Farris and family at their house in Mustang, Oklahoma on June 12th, 1982.
48 *The Patriot Ledger, op. cit.*
49 I interviewed Mrs Dixie Julian on June 17th, 1982, at her mother's house in Kemmerer, Wyoming.
50 *Tobacco International*, June 15th, 1979.

51 I interviewed Mrs Freda Lee and her daughter Linda at their home in Pinedale, Wyoming on June 17th, 1982.
52 *Boston Herald American, op. cit.*
53 *Peninsula Times Tribune, op cit.*; and *The Sacramento Bee, op. cit.*
54 *Columbia Journalism Review, op. cit.*
55 *Ibid.*

CHAPTER FOUR: THE GOLDEN GOOSE

1 Proceedings of the European Parliament, *op. cit.*
2 Figures provided by Ministry of Agriculture, Fisheries and Food, London.
3 Ann Hill (Editor), *A Counter-Blast to Tobacco*, p.36, The Rodale Press, 1954.
4 72nd Report of the Commissioners of Her Majesty's Customs and Excise, 1981, Cmnd. 8521, HMSO.
5 TAC. Statistics of Smoking in the UK, *op. cit.*
6 HM Customs and Excise, *op. cit.*
7 Professor Donald I. Mackay and Ronald T. Edwards, 'The UK Tobacco Industry: Its Economic Significance', Planning and Industrial Development Advisers, 1982.
8 'Smoking and Health Now', *op. cit.*, p. 141.
9 Department of Employment, Bridgeton, Glasgow, September 6th, 1982.
10 Tobacco Workers Union, 'Smoking and Health', Comments on Trades Union Congress Social Insurance and Industrial Welfare Committee (SIIWC) document 3/3.
11 *Ibid.*
12 *Ibid.*
13 ASTMS *Journal*, August–September 1982. Letters, p. 11.

CHAPTER FIVE: REFUSING THE MEDICINE

1 *Smoking—Psychology and Pharmacology, op. cit.*, p. 181.
2 'Smoking and Health Now', a Report of the Royal College of Physicians, *op. cit.*, p. 17.
3 'TAC. Statistics of Smoking in the UK', *op. cit.*
4 Richard H. S. Crossman, *Diaries of a Cabinet Minister*, Vol. 2, p. 532, edited by Dr Janet Morgan, Hamish Hamilton and Jonathan Cape, 1976.
5 *Ibid*, p. 532.
6 *Ibid*, Vol. 3, p. 147.
7 *Ibid*, Vol. 3, pp. 202–3.
8 Letter to Professor Charles Fletcher, May 22nd, 1980.

9 *Hansard*, January 16th, 1976, Col. 817.
10 Paper by Rt Hon Dr David Owen to an S D P members' conference on Health and Social Services Policy at the Royal Commonwealth Society, March 6th, 1982.
11 Medicines Act, 1968, Sect. 105 (b).
12 'Smoking *or* Health', a Report of the Royal College of Physicians, *op. cit.*, p. 28.
13 *Hansard*, January 16th, 1976, Cols. 825 and 826.
14 *Ibid*, Cols. 825 and 826.
15 *Ibid*, Cols. 814, 816–18.
16 *Ibid*, Col. 817.
17 *Ibid*, Cols. 855–6, 858.
18 *Ibid*, Col. 819.
19 Mike Daube, 'The politics of smoking: thoughts on the Labour record', *Community Medicine*, 1979, 1, pp. 306–14.
20 'Tobacco Substitutes and Additives in Tobacco Products', first Report of the Independent Scientific Committee on Smoking and Health, p. 3, DHSS, 1975, HMSO.
21 *Retail Confectioner and Tobacconist*, June 1978.
22 *Ibid*.
23 *Community Medicine*, Vol. 3, No. 1, August 1981, p. 194.
24 *Financial Times*, June 25th, 1981.
25 *Ibid*.
26 'Controlling the Smoking Epidemic', Report of the WHO Expert Committee on Smoking Control, *op. cit.*, p. 72.

CHAPTER SIX: ALL IN THE GAME

1 Jean Simkins, 'Sponsorship 1980–81', Economist Intelligence Unit Special Report No. 86, p. 12, The Economist Intelligence Unit Ltd.
2 Marlboro British Grand Prix, official programme, July 18th, 1982, p. 7.
3 *Ibid*, p. 1.
4 *Now!* magazine, January 16th, 1981, p. 58.
5 *The Times*, June 28th, 1982. Source: Sportscan.
6 *Ibid*.
7 Statistic provided by the Independent Broadcasting Authority.
8 'Sponsorship 1980–81', Economist Intelligence Unit, *op. cit.*, p. 57.
9 Figure supplied by J. Walter Thompson, London (1982 rate).
10 J. Khosi, *Campaign*, August 22nd, 1981.
11 *The Times*, June 28th, 1982, *op. cit.*
12 DHSS press release, No. 77/55, David Ennals' speech on smoking and prevention, March 8th, 1977.
13 *British Medical Journal*, Vol. 284, February 6th, 1982, pp. 395–6.

14 BBC TV *Panorama, op. cit.*
15 *Ibid.*
16 *Ibid.*
17 Peter Taylor, *The Listener*, April 17th, 1980.
18 *Ibid.*
19 BAT Annual General Meeting, June 9th, 1982. Statement by the Chairman, Sir Peter McAdam, in response to questions from Action on Smoking and Health. Also: *Campaign*, July 16th, 1982, p. 12.
20 'Sponsorship of Sport by Tobacco Companies in the UK', May 1982, p. 5, Sect. G.
21 *Campaign*, editorial, July 16th, 1982.
22 J. Allitt, *Campaign*, October 9th, 1982.
23 Margaret Hood, *Marketing Week*, July 8th, 1983.

CHAPTER SEVEN: POLISHING THE IMAGE

1 Leslie Geddes-Brown, *The Times*, June 6th, 1982.
2 Glyndebourne Festival brochure, quoting 'The Story of Glynde-bourne', by Spike Hughes.
3 *Hansard*, May 9th, 1980, Cols. 754–6.
4 Association for Business Sponsorship of the Arts (ABSA), Leeds Castle Conference, October 19th–21st, 1980, Brochure.
5 Michael C. Jensen, *New York Times*, Business and Finance Section, February 19th, 1978.
6 *Business and the Arts*, a guide for sponsors, ABSA, 1981.
7 *Ibid.*
8 *Ibid.*
9 Leslie Geddes-Brown, *The Sunday Times*, May 10th, 1981.
10 Business Support for the Arts, April 1980–March 1981, ABSA.
11 Shyama Perera, *The Guardian*, June 3rd, 1982.
12 *The Guardian*, letters page, June 7th, 1982.

CHAPTER EIGHT: THE FREEDOM FIGHTERS

1 Statistical Section, House of Commons Library, February 3rd, 1983.
2 Mike Daube, *Community Medicine, op. cit.*
3 'World Conference on Smoking and Health', a summary of the proceedings, September 1967. Sponsored by the National Inter-agency Council on Smoking and Health.
4 *Community Medicine, op. cit.*, p. 314.
5 BBC TV *Panorama, op. cit.*
6 FOREST Newsletter No. 1, quoting Chairman's speech at press conference on June 18th, 1979.

7 FOREST Newsletter No. 5, January 1982.
8 Christopher Hird, *New Statesman*, February 27th, 1981.
9 *Hansard*, Vol. 984, No. 171, May 9th, 1980.
10 ASH Press Release, November 21st, 1980.
11 *Hansard*, November 21st, 1980, quoted from DHSS press release.
12 Fact Sheet: Private Members' Bill Procedure, Public Information Office, House of Commons, December 1982.
13 Paul Foot, *Daily Mirror*, September 30th, 1981.
14 Adam Raphael, *Observer*, November 15th, 1981.
15 Richard Woodman, Press Association, September 30th, 1981.
16 *Ibid.*
17 *Eastern Daily Press*, August 6th, 1981.
18 *The Lancet*, December 15th, 1979, p. 1310.
19 Mike Daube, *The Times* Health Supplement, October 23rd, 1981. Also: *British Medical Journal*, quoted in ASH *Bulletin*, Issue 84, November 19th, 1981.
20 *Ibid.*
21 Letter to B. Watson, February 9th, 1982.
22 *Hansard*, January 16th, 1976, paras. 857 and 860.
23 *The Times* Health Supplement, *op. cit.*
24 DHSS press release, October 27th, 1982.
25 Dr Keith Ball, ASH Press Release, October 27th, 1982.
26 *Hansard*, Vol. 27, No. 150, para. 613, July 9th, 1982.

CHAPTER NINE: THE GOLDEN LEAF

1 The Tobacco Institute, Washington DC. *Time, Newsweek,* and *US News and World Report*, Autumn 1978.
2 A Study of the US Tobacco Industry's Economic Contribution to the Nation, Its Fifty States and the District of Colombia, *op. cit.*
3 Bryan R. Luce, MBA, and Steward O. Schweitzer, PhD, 'Smoking and Alcohol Abuse, a Comparison of their Economic Consequences', *The New England Journal of Medicine*, Vol. 298, No. 10, March 9th, 1978, Massachusetts Department of Public Health.
4 'The Health Consequences of Smoking. Cancer', a Report of the Surgeon-General, 1982, *op. cit.*, p. 63.
5 *The Tobacco Industry in Transition*, *op. cit.*, Ch. 8, 'Vegetable and Fruit Crops: Viable Alternatives for Farmers', Frank Adams, p. 95.
6 *Business Week*, December 20th, 1982.
7 Congressional Record, S. 9846, Senate, September 17th, 1981.
8 *Congressional Quarterly*, September 5th, 1981, p. 1676.
9 Congressional Record, *op. cit.*, S. 9847.
10 William O. Mizelle and William D. Givan, 'History of Tobacco

Control Programs and Marketing', p. 4, Southern Extension Marketing Publication, 79–1, September 1979.

11 *Ibid.*

12 Rob Christensen, *Raleigh News and Observer*, October 25th, 1981.

13 'Tobacco Programs, Production Rights and Effects on Competition', Report by the Comptroller-General of the United States, p. 1, US General Accounting Office, April 23rd, 1982.

14 Rob Christensen, *op. cit.*

15 George Anthan, *Des Moines Register*, August 24th, 1981. Quoted in Congressional Record, *op. cit.*, S. 9851.

16 'Tobacco Programs, Production Rights and Effects on Competition', *op. cit.*

17 *Ibid*, pp. iii–iv.

18 *Ibid*, p. 25.

19 Congressional Record, *op. cit.*, S. 9859.

20 *Ibid*, S. 9846.

21 Rob Christensen, Washington correspondent, 'Coalition Saved Tobacco Program', *Raleigh News and Observer* (undated).

22 Congressional Record, *op. cit.*, S. 9847.

23 *Ibid*, S. 9860.

24 *Ibid*, S. 9874.

25 *Ibid*, S. 9859.

26 Rob Christensen, 'Coalition Saved Tobacco Program', *op. cit.*

27 *Ibid.*

28 Alan Ehrenhalt (Editor), *Politics in America. Members of Congress in Washington and at Home*, p. 597, Congressional Quarterly Press, 1982.

29 Rob Christensen, 'Coalition Saved Tobacco Program', *op. cit.*

30 *Politics in America. Members of Congress in Washington and at Home, op. cit.*, p. 473.

31 Rob Christensen, 'Coalition Saved Tobacco Program', *op. cit.*

32 *Ibid.*

33 *Ibid.*

34 *Ibid.*

35 *Ibid.*

CHAPTER TEN: UNFAIR AND DECEPTIVE PRACTICES

1 'Your Federal Trade Commission. What It Is and What It Does', US Government Printing Office, 1975.

2 *Ibid.*

3 *Ibid.*

4 *Cigarette Country. Tobacco in American History and Politics, op. cit.*, p. 139.

5 Lyndon Baines Johnson, *The Vantage Point. Perspectives of the Presidency 1963–69*, p. 91, Popular Library, 1971.
6 *Ibid*, p. 543 ff.
7 Elizabeth Drew, *New York Times* Magazine, May 4th, 1969.
8 *Cigarette Country. Tobacco in American History and Politics*, *op. cit.*, p. 164.
9 Michael Pertschuk, *Revolt Against Regulation: The Rise and Pause of the Consumer Movement*, p. 86, University of California Press, 1982.
10 *Business Week*, December 26th, 1970; December 15th, 1980.
11 Federal Trade Commission Staff Report on the Cigarette Advertising Investigation, May 1981, Ch. 2, p. 4.
12 Resolution Directing Use of Compulsory Process in Non Public Investigation. File No. 762 3065. May 11th, 1976. United States of America before Federal Trade Commission.
13 Ed Zuckerman, *Herald-Leader*, Washington Bureau, undated.
14 *Ibid*.
15 Richard L. Gordon, *Advertising Age*, January 29th, 1979.
16 *Ibid*.
17 Oversight of the Federal Trade Commission. Hearings before the Sub-committee for Consumers of the Committee on Commerce, Science and Transportation. United States Senate, 96th Congress. Serial No. 96–69.
18 *Ibid*.
19 *Ibid*.
20 *Ibid*.
21 Larry Kramer, *Washington Post*, July 4th, 1979.
22 *Ibid*.
23 Jack Anderson (with Tony Capaccio), *Washington Post*, June 22nd, 1981.
24 This and the references for the following documents were placed in the record of the Hearings before the House Commerce Committee Sub-committee on Oversight and Investigations chaired by John D. Dingell, a Michigan Congressman. The Hearings were on 'Cigarette Advertising and the HHS [US Department of Health and Human Services] Anti-Smoking Campaign', June 25th, 1981, Serial No. 97–66. This meant that the confidential documents subpoenaed by the FTC were now inserted in the public record. In effect, sections of the unexpurgated FTC Report of the Cigarette Advertising Investigations were inserted in the record.
25 'FTC Report on Tar and Nicotine Content of the Smoke of 167 Varieties of Cigarettes', May 1978.
26 'Cigarette Advertising and the HHS Anti-Smoking Campaign', *op. cit.*

27 *Ibid.*
28 *Ibid.*
29 *Ibid.*
30 *Ibid.*
31 Annabel Ferriman, *The Times*, London, March 24th, 1982.
32 Media statement issued in the USA by Brown & Williamson, following article by Gary Cohn in the *Lexington Sunday Herald*, July 5th, 1981.
33 *Washington Representatives 1979. Lobbyists, Consultants, etc.,* p. 338, Columbia Books Inc., Washington DC.
34 News release from Senator Wendell Ford, February 11th, 1980.
35 Oversight of the Federal Trade Commission. Hearings before the Sub-committee for Consumers of the Committee on Commerce, Science and Transportation, *op. cit.*
36 Bailey Morris, *Washington Star*, February 7th, 1980.
37 Oversight of the Federal Trade Commission. Hearings before the Sub-committee for Consumers of the Committee on Commerce, Science and Transportation, *op. cit.*
38 *Ibid.*
39 *Smoking—Psychology and Pharmacology, op. cit.*, p. 181.
40 Michael deCourcy Hinds, *New York Times*, June 22nd, 1982.
41 Anthony Hilton, *Marketing Week*, January 30th, 1981.
42 Anthony Hilton, *The Sunday Times*, undated.
43 Arthur M. Louis, *Fortune*, November 17th, 1980, p. 121.
44 Steve Lohr, *New York Times*, January 16th, 1981.
45 Sam Hooper, *Advertising Age*, May 4th, 1981.
46 *Ibid.*
47 Federal Trade Commission *News Notes*, Vol. 34–83, May 13th, 1982.
48 *Business Week*, December 20th, 1982.
49 *Ibid.*

CHAPTER ELEVEN: THE SIX MILLION DOLLAR MEN

1 BBC TV *Panorama, op. cit.*
2 Letter from Professor Jonathan E. Rhoads, MD, University of Pennsylvania School of Medicine to Mr Jack McDowell of Woodward & McDowell, October 27th, 1978.
3 Speech by Wilson W. Wyatt, Jnr, before Public Affairs Council State Relations Conference, July 7th, 1980. Cited in United States Court of Appeals for the District of Columbia Circuit. Petitioners Reply Brief. March 26th, 1982. Action by Paul Loveday and Californians for Smoking and No Smoking Sections against US Federal

Communications Commission. This document is referred to here-
after as Petitioners Reply Brief.

4 Petitioners Reply Brief, *ibid*.
5 'A Study of Public Attitudes toward Cigarette Smoking and the
Tobacco Industry in 1978', Vol. 1. Prepared for the Tobacco
Institute, May 1978. The Report is cited in full in the F T C's Report to
Congress for 1978.
6 Wilson W. Wyatt, Speech reported in Petitioners Reply Brief, *op. cit.*
7 *Ibid.*
8 *Ibid.*
9 Steven Lydenberg, 'Bankrolling Ballots, Update 1979. The Role of
Business in Financing Ballot Question Campaigns', Council on
Economic Priorities, New York.
10 *Ibid.*
11 Edward A. Grefe, *Fighting to Win. Business Political Power*, Law
and Business Inc., p. 11, Harcourt Brace Jovanovich Publishers,
1981.
12 *Zephyrhills News*, April 5th, 1979.
13 *Ibid.*
14 Victor F. Zonana, *Wall Street Journal*, July 2nd, 1980.
15 *Fighting to Win, op. cit.*, p. 158.
16 *Ibid*, p. 55.
17 Tobacco Institute campaign financial return through 2.10.78.
18 *Fighting to Win, op. cit.*, p. 159.
19 Tobacco Institute campaign financial return, *op. cit.*
20 Gladwin Hill, *New York Times*, March 16th, 1978.
21 Court Report, No. 275588. In the Superior Court of the State of
California, Department Number One. Campaign for Clean Indoor
Air—Paul Loveday *et al.* and Californians for Common Sense.
Testimony of Vigo G. Nielsen, Jnr, August 11th, 1978.
22 Tobacco Institute campaign financial return, *op. cit.*
23 Tony Russo, Treasurer, *The United Democrat*, Edition Three,
Published by Concerned Democrats of Alameda County.
24 Figures from campaign financial returns and computations by Dr
Stanton A. Glantz.
25 'Bankrolling Ballots', *op. cit.*
26 *Ibid.*
27 *Miami Herald*, October 17th, 1980.
28 Steven Lydenberg, 'Bankrolling Ballots, Update 1980. The Role of
Business in Financing Ballot Question Campaigns', Council on
Economic Priorities, New York.
29 Quoted in Joint Appendix (ref. J.A.55) to Petitioners Brief, US Court
of Appeals for the District of Columbia Circuit, No. 81–2061.
30 John Stanton, *Peninsula Times Tribune*, October 1st, 1980.

31 *Ibid.*
32 Paul Loveday, Attorney for Petitioners (Californians for Smoking and No Smoking Sections) in the US Court of Appeals for the District of Columbia Circuit. No. 81–2061. On Petition for Review of Order of Federal Communications Commission. Joint Appendix, March 31st, 1982. Campaign returns at end of joint Appendix.
33 *Ibid.*

CHAPTER TWELVE: TOBACCO AND THE WHITE HOUSE

1 *Time* Magazine, September 14th, 1981.
2 Taken from *When Free Men Shall Stand* by Senator Jesse Helms, p. 16. Copyright 1976 by Jesse Helms. Used by permission of Zondervan Publishing House.
3 *Ibid.*
4 Joseph A. Califano, Jnr, *Governing America: An Insider's Report from the White House and the Cabinet*, p. 13, Simon & Schuster, New York, 1981. Reprinted by permission of the Sterling Lord Agency, Inc. Copyright © 1981 by Joseph A. Califano, Jnr.
5 *Ibid*, p. 24.
6 *Ibid*, p. 183.
7 *Ibid*, p. 190.
8 *Ibid*, p. 185.
9 *Ibid*, p. 185.
10 *Ibid*, p. 186.
11 *Ibid*, p. 186.
12 *Ibid*, p. 195.
13 *Ibid*, pp. 195–6.
14 *Ibid*, p. 187.
15 *Ibid*, p. 196.
16 *Ibid*, p. 189.
17 *Ibid*, p. 190.
18 Thirty-First World Health Assembly, Part II, p. 523, Committee A, Eighteenth Meeting.
19 *Ibid.*
20 *Governing America, op cit.*, p. 191.
21 *Ibid.*
22 *Ibid*, p. 192.
23 'Smoking and Health', a Report of the Surgeon-General, 1979, pp. i-v, US Department of Health, Education and Welfare, Public Health Service.
24 *Ibid.*
25 *Governing America, op. cit.*, p. 194.

26 *Ibid*, p. 195.
27 *Ibid*, p. 196.
28 Remarks by Secretary Joseph A. Califano, Jnr, to the Fourth World Conference on Smoking and Health, Stockholm, June 19th, 1979.
29 BBC TV *Panorama, op. cit.*

CHAPTER THIRTEEN: TOBACCO IN THE WHITE HOUSE

1 *Conservative Digest*, October 1981. Article based on *The Reagan Revolution* by Rowland Evans and Robert Novak, published by E. P. Dutton Inc, New York.
2 *Ibid.*
3 *Ibid.*
4 *Politics in America. Members of Congress in Washington and at Home, op. cit.*, p. 893.
5 *Congressional Club News*, February 1981.
6 'Cigarette Advertising and the HHS Anti-Smoking Campaign', *op. cit.*
7 'The Health Consequences of Smoking. Cancer', a Report of the Surgeon-General, *op. cit.*, p. xi.
8 *Ibid*, p. vi.
9 'Cigarette Advertising and the HHS Anti-Smoking Campaign', *op. cit.*, p. 10.
10 *Ibid*, p. 46.
11 FTC Staff Report on the Cigarette Advertising Investigation, May 1981, Ch. 5, pp. 1–2.
12 Arthur L. Amolsch (Editor), *FTC: Watch*, pamphlet, Washington Regulatory Reporting Associates, January 22nd, 1982.
13 *Ibid.*
14 Steve Kelly, *Charlotte Observer*, March 16th, 1982 and February 20th, 1982.
15 Congressional Record, House of Representatives, November 12th, 1981, Vol. 127, No. 165.
16 Congressional Record, Senate, November 30th, 1981, Vol. 127, No. 185.
17 Statement of Edward A. Horrigan, Jnr, on S. 1929 before the Committee on Commerce, Science and Transportation, undated.
18 Statement by Edward N. Brandt, Jnr, MD, before the Sub-committee on Health and the Environment Committee on Energy and Commerce, March 11th, 1982.
19 Steve Kelly, *The Charlotte Observer*, March 17th, 1982.
20 *Ibid.*
21 Christine Russell, *Washington Post*, March 18th, 1982.

22 Transcript of Senate Hearing before Senator Hatch, March 16th, 1982.
23 *Washington Post*, June 23rd, 1983.

CHAPTER FOURTEEN: THE THIRD WORLD — A GROWING PROBLEM

1 'The Economic Significance of Tobacco', Prepared by the FAO Commodities and Trade Division, October 1982. ESC: 83/1. Food and Agriculture Organisation of the United Nations, Rome.
2 Malcolm D. Bale and Danuta Nowicki, 'Tobacco: The World Situation, Prospects, and Market Structure', p. 1, Division Working Paper No. 1980–4, May 1980, the World Bank.
3 *Ibid*, p. 16.
4 *Ibid*, p. 37.
5 *Newsweek*, October 25th, 1982.
6 'Controlling the smoking epidemic', *op. cit.*
7 BBC TV *Panorama, op. cit.*
8 *The Economist*, November 17th, 1979.
9 *Ibid*.
10 'Global Presence', *op. cit.*
11 Presentation to the Los Angeles Society of Financial Analysts, March 13th, 1980, Philip Morris Inc.
12 Maxwell International Estimates, *op. cit.*, July 1982.
13 Letter to Baroness White, June 12th, 1981.
14 *Trust in Tobacco, op. cit.*, p. 265 (the actual advertisement appeared in 1979).
15 BBC TV *Panorama, op. cit.*
16 Bernardo Kucinski, *The Guardian*, September 21st, 1982.
17 BBC TV *Panorama, op. cit.*
18 Maxwell International Estimates, *op. cit.*, July 1981, October 1982.
19 BAT Industries *Annual Report and Accounts*, 1981.
20 'Leaf Tobacco: Its Contribution to the Economic and Social Development of the Third World', p. 65, the Economist Intelligence Unit Ltd. (Referred to as EIU Report.)
21 *Ibid*, p. 91 (actual figure from other source).
22 BBC TV *Panorama, op. cit.*
23 Mike Muller, *Tobacco and the Third World: Tomorrow's Epidemic*, p. 61, War on Want, 1978.
24 John Madeley, *Spur*, the Newspaper of the World Development Movement, May 1982. A further and less conservative estimate is of 300 trees per acre, quoted by Muliwa Kyendo in *The Daily Nation* (Kenya), August 14th, 1981. I have based my calculations on the more conservative estimate.
25 *Tobacco and the Third World: Tomorrow's Epidemic, op. cit.*, p. 61.

26 Statistic quoted in 'Tobacco in Kenya—Monitoring the Activities of BAT' by Kate Currie and Larry Ray, University of Lancaster, December 1981. They base the statistic on 'The Success Story of Peasant Tobacco Production in Tanzania' by J. Boesen and A. T. Hohele, Scandinavian Institute of African Studies, Uppsala, 1979.

27 EIU Report, *op. cit.*, p. 64.

28 *Ibid*, p. 71.

29 'Growing with British-American Tobacco', BAT, 1974.

30 BBC TV *Panorama, op. cit.*

31 *Ibid.*

32 Report of a World Health Organisation Workshop on Smoking and Health Issues in Developing Countries, Colombo, Sri Lanka, November 18th-20th, 1981.

33 *Ibid.*

34 *Ibid.*

35 *Ibid.*

36 *Ibid.*

37 International Conference on Tobacco and Health, organised by the Swaziland Government and the World Health Organisation, Mbabane, Swaziland, April 26th-29th, 1982.

38 *Ibid.*

39 *Ibid.*

40 *Ibid.*

41 'Controlling the smoking epidemic', *op. cit.*, p. 84.

42 Frederick Clairmonte, 'Marketing and Distribution of Tobacco', a study prepared by the UNCTAD Secretariat, June 16th, 1978, *op. cit.*

43 BBC TV *Panorama, op. cit.*

44 *Ibid.*

CHAPTER FIFTEEN: THE NATIVES PREFER BLOND

1 'Tobacco Outlook and Situation', USDA (US Department of Agriculture), March 1982, p. 9 ff.

2 *Ibid.*

3 *Ibid.*

4 Jasper Womach, 'Tobacco Programs of the US Department of Agriculture: Their Operation and Cost', Update 26, February 1981, p. 11. Congressional Research Service, Report No. 81-85 ENR.

5 *Ibid*, p. 12.

6 *Ibid*, p. 13.

7 *Congressional Quarterly*, June 18th, 1977, p. 1206.

8 Margaret Sheridan, American Council on Science and Health, *News and Views*, April 1980, Vol. 1, No. 3, p. 11.

9 *Congressional Quarterly, op. cit.*

10 Ferrel Guillory, 'The Politics of Tobacco in North Carolina', *North Carolina Insight*, Vol. 4, No. 2, p. 35.
11 *Congressional Quarterly, op. cit.*
12 *The Tobacco Industry in Transition, op. cit.*, p. 126.
13 *Ibid.*
14 UNCTAD, 'Marketing and Distribution of Tobacco', *op. cit.*, p. 24.
15 Securities and Exchange Commission, Washington, Form 8K, Current Report, R. J. Reynolds Industries Inc, September 1976.
16 UNCTAD, 'Marketing and Distribution of Tobacco', *op. cit.*, p. 24. Also: *Wall Street Journal*, December 28th, 1976.
17 Securities and Exchange Commission, Washington, Form 8K, Current Report, Philip Morris Inc, December 1976.
18 Deborah Sue Yaeger and Raymond Joseph, *Wall Street Journal*, December 28th, 1976. See also: *Wall Street Journal*, December 30th, 1976.
19 *Ibid.*
20 *Ibid.*
21 *Ibid.*
22 *Ibid.*
23 *Ibid.*
24 Arthur Schlesinger, Jnr, *A Thousand Days*, quoted by Philip Geylin in an article, 'Dominican Stress Test' (unsourced).
25 *The Vantage Point, op. cit.*, pp. 187–205.
26 *Album de la Muerte de los 12 años Balaguerista*, Frente Nacional Antirregresionista Dominicano, May 1982.
27 Lindsey Hilsum, *New Internationalist*, September 1982, p. 32.
28 *Ibid.*
29 *Ibid.*
30 *Ultima Hora*, January 11th, 1971.
31 *Listin Diario*, December 28th, 1979.
32 Jose Israel Cuello H., *Renovacion*, undated, p. 7.
33 Comunicado, *Listin Diario*, May 24th, 1972.
34 Rene Bermudez, 'Balaguer, Tobaco Rubio y Merengue', *El Nacional*, May 12th, 1972.
35 'La Verdad sobre el tobaco rubio dominicano' (CAT), *Ultima Hora*, November 1st, 1979.
36 Comunicado, *Listin Diario, op cit.*
37 'La Verdad . . .', *Ultima Hora, op. cit.*
38 *Ibid.*
39 *Ibid.*
40 'La ley 451 si ha beneficiado a la Philip Morris: E Leon Jimenes', *El Sol*, November 2nd, 1979.
41 Maxwell International Estimates, *op. cit.*, July 1982.
42 *Ibid.*

CHAPTER SIXTEEN: BREAKING THE SMOKE RING

1 *British Medical Journal*, January 15th, 1983, Vol. 286, No. 6360, p. 163.
2 Statement by Julius B. Richmond, MD, Surgeon-General, January 12th, 1981.
3 'The Health Consequences of Smoking. The Changing Cigarette', a report of the Surgeon-General, 1981, p. 8, US Department of Health and Human Services. Public Health Service.
4 *The Guardian*, July 6th, 1983. The Health Education Council Advertisement.
5 Series of advertisements in the national press run by the Tobacco Advisory Council, 'Speaking up for smokers', in February 1983 before the March Budget.
6 *The Guardian*, July 6th, 1983, *op. cit.*
7 Oliver Gillie, *The Sunday Times*, February 8th, 1981.
8 Testimony of Michael Daube on the Comprehensive Smoking Education Act (S.1929), May 5th, 1982, Washington DC.
9 Legislative and Administrative Action for Control of Tobacco-smoking in Finland, p. 5, The National Board of Health, Helsinki, June 1979.
10 *Ibid*, p. 14.
11 *The Sunday Times*, February 8th, 1981, *op. cit.*
12 Renee Bittoun, *The Medical Journal of Australia*, July 24th, 1982.
13 *Billbored*, BUGA UP Newsletter, No. 2, September 1982.
14 Interview with Berwyn Lewis in the magazine *Adguage*, January 1982, referred to in *The Medical Journal of Australia, op. cit.*
15 Ross Warneke, 'Smoking Fights Back', *The Age*, Saturday Extra, February 12th, 1982.
16 New South Wales Cancer Council, Submission by Dr Gordon Sarfaty to the Industries Assistance Commission Inquiry into the Tobacco Growing and Manufacturing Industry.
17 *The Age, op. cit.*
18 Jill Margo, *Sydney Morning Herald*, December 3rd, 1981.
19 New South Wales Cancer Council, *op. cit.*
20 *British Medical Journal*, August 11th, 1982, Vol. 285, No. 6340, p. 459.

BIBLIOGRAPHY

GENERAL

Ashton, Heather and Stepney, Rob, *Smoking: Psychology and Pharma-cology*,Tavistock Publications, London and New York, 1982. Cambridge.

Califano, Joseph A. Jnr., *Governing America. An Insider's Report from the White House and the Cabinet*, Simon & Schuster, New York, 1981.

Corina, Maurice, *Trust in Tobacco*, Michael Joseph, London, 1975.

Crossman, Richard H. S., *Diaries of a Cabinet Minister*, Edited by Dr Janet Morgan, Hamish Hamilton and Jonathan Cape, London, Vol. I, 1975; Vol. II, 1976; Vol. III, 1977.

Ehrenhalt, A., *Politics in America. Members of Congress in Washington and at Home*, Congressional Quarterly Press, Congressional Quarterly Inc., Washington DC, 1982.

Finger, William R., *The Tobacco Industry in Transition: Policies for the 1980s* (a North Carolina Center for Public Policy Research book), Lexington Books, D. C. Heath & Co., Lexington, Mass., 1981. Copyright © 1981

Friedman, Kenneth Michael, *Public Policy and the Smoking-Health Controversy*, Lexington Books, D. C. Heath & Co., Lexington, Mass., 1975. Copyright © 1975.

Grefe, Edward A., *Fighting to Win. Business Political Power*, Law and Business Inc., Harcourt Brace Jovanovich, New York, 1981

Head, Victor, *Sponsorship. The Newest Marketing Skill*, Woodhead-Falconer in association with The Institute of Marketing, Cambridge, 1981.

Helms, Jesse, *'When Free Men Shall Stand'. A Sobering Look at the Super Taxing, Super Spending, Super Bureaucracy in Washington*, Zonder-van Publishing House, Grand Rapids, Michigan, 1976.

Jacobson, B., *The Ladykillers: Why Smoking is a Feminist Issue*, Pluto Press, London, 1981.

Johnson, Lyndon Baines, *The Vantage Point. Perspectives of the Presidency 1963–69*, Popular Library, 1971.

Muller, Mike, *Tobacco and the Third World: Tomorrow's Epidemic?* War on Want and Mike Muller, 1978.
Neuberger, M., *Smoke Screen: Tobacco and the Public Welfare*, Prentice-Hall, Inc., Englewood Cliffs, New Jersey. Copyright © 1963.
Sobel, Robert, *They Satisfy. The Cigarette in American Life*, Anchor Books, Anchor Press/Doubleday, Garden City, New York, 1978.
Sorensen, Theodore C., *Kennedy*, Bantam Books, New York, 1966.
Tucker, David, *Tobacco: an International Perspective*, Euromonitor Publications Ltd., London, 1983.
Wagner, Susan, *Cigarette Country. Tobacco In American History and Politics*, Praeger Publishers, New York, Washington, 1971.
Whiteside, Thomas, *Selling Death: Cigarette Advertising and Public Health*, Liveright, New York, 1971.

MEDICAL

Roemer, R., 'Legislative Action to Combat the World Smoking Epidemic', World Health Organisation, Geneva, 1982.
The Royal College of Physicians, 'Smoking and Health', a Report of the Royal College of Physicians on Smoking in relation to cancer of the lung and other diseases, Pitman Medical Publishing Co. Ltd., London, 1962.
The Royal College of Physicians, 'Smoking and Health Now', a Report of the Royal College of Physicians, Pitman Medical and Scientific Publishing Co. Ltd., London, 1971.
The Royal College of Physicians, 'Smoking or Health', a Report of the Royal College of Physicians, Pitman Medical Publishing Co. Ltd., London, 1977.
The Royal College of Physicians, 'Health or Smoking?', Follow-up Report of the Royal College of Physicians, Pitman Publishing Ltd., London, 1983.
The US Surgeon-General, 'Smoking and Health' a Report of the Advisory Committee to the Surgeon-General of the Public Health Service, US Department of Health, Education and Welfare, Public Health Service, 1964.
The US Surgeon-General, 'Smoking and Health', a Report of the Surgeon-General, US Department of Health, Education and Welfare, 1979.
The US Surgeon-General, 'The Health Consequences of Smoking for Women', a Report of the Surgeon-General, US Department of Health, Education and Welfare, 1980.
The US Surgeon-General, 'The Health Consequences of Smoking. The Changing Cigarette', US Department of Health and Human Services, Public Health Service, Office on Smoking and Health, 1981.

[312]

The US Surgeon-General, 'The Health Consequences of Smoking. Cancer', a Report of the Surgeon-General, US Department of Health and Human Services, Public Health Service, Office on Smoking and Health, Rockville, Maryland 20857, 1972.

World Health Organisation, 'Smoking and its Effects on Health', a Report of a WHO Expert Committee, Technical Report Series 568, World Health Organisation, Geneva, 1975.

World Health Organisation, 'Controlling the Smoking Epidemic', a Report of the WHO Expert Committee on smoking control, Technical Report Series 636, World Health Organisation, Geneva, 1979.

INDEX

public relations 135
purchased by American Tobacco
  Co. 37
sponsorship 101, 103
start in Northern Ireland 25, 70
success 37–9, 41
tobacco substitutes 95
See also Benson and Hedges
Galloway, James Clarence 153–6,
  227–9, 245–6
Garrett, Tony, 119, 121
General and Municipal Workers Union
  73
Gibson, Paul 57
gift coupons 82, 84–5
Gill, Barrie 101–2, 106, 111
Gillie, Oliver 49–53
Glantz, Dr Stanton 62–4, 201–3
Godber, Sir George 2, 6, 9, 21
Godfrey, P. 249
Good Housekeeping 45
Good Relations 135–6
government
  approached by medical colleges
    106–7
  general attitude to smoking 274–7,
    280–1
  grant to ASH (UK) 43
  grants to tobacco industry 167
  inaction xvii, xix, 1, 107
  inquiry into reduction in smoking 71
  reaction to Royal College Report
    (1962) 7–9
  See also departments, economics,
    employment, legislation, minis-
    ters, revenue
Government Actuary 6
Grayden, Bill 48
Grefe, Ed 194–6, 198–202, 205
Group Against Smokers' Pollution (G
  ASP) 42, 197, 201
growing (tobacco) *See* farmers
Guardian, The 71
Guerin, Dr Michael 186–7

HEW (Health, Education and Welfare), Secretary for 208, 211, 213,
  215–16, 223
Hamburg research laboratories 18–19
Hammond, Dr Cuyler 3
hamsters 18–19
Hanauer, Peter 205

Harper's Bazaar 46
Harris, Tom 17
Harrogate laboratories (of British
  tobacco industry) 13, 18
Hatch, Senator 236–7, 240
Hatfield, Senator Mark 158, 160, 162,
  262
health 5, 170, 185
  See also anti-smoking, death, illness,
    legislation, medical evidence, *spe-
    cified diseases and* warnings
'Health Consequences of Smoking' 229
Health Education Council 42, 96
'Health or Smoking' 281
health warnings. *See* warnings
heart disease
  American deaths 214
  Australia 280
  controversy 15–16
  low tar cigarettes 275
  research by Hamburg Institute 19
  Royal College of Physicians (1977)
    xiv
  Senator Packwood on 235
  Sunday Times article 49–53
  Surgeon-General's Report (1964) xii
  Surgeon-General's Report (1979) xv
  Third World 254
Heath, Edward, M.P. 86
Helms, Senator Jesse 159–62, 166,
  208–38 *passim*, 262
Hermans R 100
Hill, George Washington 38
Hill, Nick 50–1, 53
Hill, Professor Austin Bradford 3–5
Hobbs, William 214
Holmes, John 55, 57–9
Hopp, Mark 47
Horn, Dr Daniel 3
Horrigan, Edward A. 237
House Appropriations Sub-committee
  on Health Education and Welfare
  215
Howell, Denis, M.P. 70, 89, 106, 143
Huddleston, Senator Walter 162
Humphrey, Senator Hubert 262
Hunter Committee (Independent
  Scientific Committee on Smoking
  and Health) 90, 95, 97–8
Hunter, Dr Robert (later Lord Hunter)
  90, 96
  See also Hunter Committee

INDEX

Lovelock, Sir Douglas 68
Lovesey, John 52
'low tar' cigarettes
advertising xvi, 88, 129–30, 185–8
competition (USA) 185–6
DHSS on 90
government revenue preserved by 97
industry's stance xvi, 12, 274
kill people 277
lung cancer reduced by 275
market share 80, 186–7
measurement by machine (USA)
185–8
new form (1977) 95
number of brands 97
research into effects 139
Surgeon-General's Report(1981)275
lung cancer
AMA reports (1968 ? 1978) 16–17
advertisement showing celebrities
who died from 206
Australia 280
Brazil 255
Cancer Committee's report 6
death by xii-xiii, 3, 212, 230, 255,
278
'Death in the West' 55–59
effect of low tar 275
evidence of causation xiii-xiv
Finland 278
forty-eight per cent smoke after
operation for 275
incubation period 2–3
industry's defence against charge of
causing 14–15
Kentucky views on 18
other causes of 4
President Carter's father's death
from 212
rarity early this century 2–3
rate xv, 5
reduction with 'low tar' cigarettes
275
risk increased by smoking 3–4
Royal College of Physicians Report
(1962) xii
spread similar to cholera 2
Surgeon-General's Report (1964)
xii, 10
Surgeon-General's Report (1979)
xiv-xv
television documentaries xiii

Third World 254
women, among 230
See also cancer

McAdam, Sir Peter 68
Mackay, Professor Donald 69
MacFarlane, Neil, M.P. 106, 112, 149
Macleod, Iain, M.P. 5, 81
Maccabee, Paul Fishman 46–7
Mademoiselle 45
Magnuson, Senator Warren 172–3
Marketing and Research Counselors,
Inc 178
Martin, Michael, M.P. 70, 75
Masironi, Dr Roberto 260
Masius 51
maternity complications xv
See also pregnancy
May, Tony 38–9
medical evidence
accepted by Enoch Powell 7
believed by majority (USA) 191
case alleged not to be proven 12
confirmed by tobacco industry's research 14–15
Congress's reaction 21
children affected by smoking 189
government attitude 108
Imperial's views 40
Kilroy-Silk on 91
'low-tar' cigarettes 277
Morris's attitude 31, 56–8
no longer in dispute 277
'no such thing as a safe cigarette' 275
non-smokers affected by smoking
189
Patrick Jenkin persuaded by 130
press reports 44–53
reaction of tobacco companies xvi,
11–12, 21
rejected by Alan Long 249
Reynolds attitude 33
Rothman's reaction 35–6
'second-hand' dangers of smoking
189
smoking established as cause of
death 281
US magazine coverage 45–7
verdict of leading authorities ix
See also illness, names of diseases,
doctors and organisations, reports
and research.

[323]

Medicines Act (1968) 88–90, 92–4,
140
Medicines Commission 90
Merritt, John 159, 162–3
Michael, Prince of Kent 100
Miller, James C. 232–4
Minister/Ministry of Arts 114
Minister/Ministry of Health
advisers to 5
attempts to legislate 80–2, 85–6,
128–9, 140–1, 146–7
campaign to warn recommended 6,
13
cancer sub-committee 5–6
medical evidence accepted 7, 92
opposed to restraint on advertising
etc. 7, 137, 147
smog banished 6
sponsorship 99–100, 105–6, 119,
128, 144–5, 149
thinking affected by revenue from
tobacco 5, 92
tobacco substitutes 96–7
voluntary agreement with companies 82–3, 87–9, 91–4, 140, 149
see also anti-smoking, Central
Health Services Council, Health
Education Council *and* Sir George
Young
Minister/Ministry of Sport 89, 101,
105–6, 112, 143–4, 149
Mitchell family 74
Mitchell, Senator George 161
Mitchell, Stephen and Son 24
Mitchell, Warren 125
Molyneaux, James, M.P. 70
Mondale, Vice-President 213, 222
Monro, Sir Hector, M.P. 101, 143–4
Mop-Up (Movement Opposing the
Promotion of Unhealthy Products)
63
Philip Morris
AMA pension fund holding 17
advertising 29, 44–5, 53–8
Brazilian interests 247, 249
buys into ELJ 269
Club Marlboro 138–9
contributions to California cam-
paigns 203, 205
critical of medical evidence 31, 57–8
diversification 30
Dominican interests 69–73

failure to acquire Gallaher 37
giant multinational xvi, 27
image 30–1
'low tar' cigarettes 186–7
markets 26
President Carter's stock-holding 212
profits 32
'public affairs' unit 194–5, 203
'questionable payments' 264–6
Rothmans acquisition 36
sales 26, 29–30, 37
sponsorship 100–1, 109, 121
success 28–30
young smokers 214
See also companies *and* Grefe
Moyle, Roland, M.P. 94, 96–7
Ms 45
Mulligan, Raymond J. 215
Murdoch, Rupert 52–3

NBC (National Broadcasting Cor-
poration) 62
NHS (National Health Service) xvii,
73, 78, 81, 86
NSM (New Smoking Material) 95–6
Natcher, Congressman William 215
National Assocation for the Advance-
ment of Coloured Peoples 166–7
National Broadcasting Corporation
(NBC) 62
National Cancer Institute 9
National Council on Smoking and
Health (Norway) 279
National Health Service (NHS) xvii,
73, 78, 81, 86
Nelmes, Dr Andy 98
New Smoking Material (NSM) 95–6
New York Times 174
New Yorker 45
Newsweek 102
Nicolson, Sir David 35, 64
nicotine xvii-xviii, 88, 274–5
Nightingale, Florence 1
non-smokers 189–90, 192, 198, 204–
6, 218, 275
See also anti-smoking campaign
Nonsmokers' Rights Foundation 62
North Carolina. *See* Southern States

OMB (Office of Management and
Budget) 237–9
Ochsner, Dr Alton 3